iOS Forensics for Investigators

Take mobile forensics to the next level by analyzing, extracting, and reporting sensitive evidence

Gianluca Tiepolo

BIRMINGHAM—MUMBAI

iOS Forensics for Investigators

Group Product Manager: Vijin Boricha
Publishing Product Manager: Vijin Boricha
Senior Editor: Athikho Sapuni Rishana
Content Development Editor: Sayali Pingale
Technical Editor: Arjun Varma
Copy Editor: Safis Editing
Associate Project Manager: Neil Dmello
Proofreader: Safis Editing
Indexer: Manju Arasan
Production Designer: Roshan Kawale
Marketing Coordinator: Sanjana Gupta

First published: April 2022
Production reference: 1110422

Published by Packt Publishing Ltd.
Livery Place
35 Livery Street
Birmingham
B3 2PB, UK.

978-1-80323-408-3

www.packt.com

Dedicated to those who try, whether they fail or succeed.

Contributors

About the author

Gianluca Tiepolo is a cybersecurity researcher who specializes in mobile forensics and incident response. He holds a BSc degree in computer science and an MSc in information security, as well as several security-related certifications.

Over the past 12 years, he has performed security monitoring, threat hunting, incident response, and intelligence analysis as a consultant for dozens of organizations, including several Fortune 100 companies. Gianluca is also the co-founder of the start-up *Sixth Sense Solutions*, which developed AI-based anti-fraud solutions. Today, Gianluca works as a Security Delivery Team Lead for consulting firm *Accenture Security*.

In 2016, he authored the book *Getting Started with RethinkDB*, published by Packt Publishing.

Mobile forensics is a field that is exploding with potential and opportunities. I am fortunate to work with some of the most talented analysts, examiners, and investigators who have supported me throughout the writing of this book and contributed much to the book's contents.

Writing a book is no easy task, and no work is truly the result of one mind.

I want to thank Vijin Boricha, who was the first person to believe in this project and set the conditions that led to the publishing of this book. I want to particularly thank Neil Dmello — my project coordinator — who supported me through the many iterations and rewrites, yet always remained encouraging. Thank you to my editors — Sayali Pingale and Athikho Sapuni Rishana — for their feedback and guidance. Thanks also to my technical reviewer, Domenica Lee Crognale. This book is so much better thanks to her tremendously insightful suggestions.

To the entire Packt Publishing team who pulled this all together, my sincere thanks to you all.

This book has been an amazing journey into the world of iOS forensics, the outcome of which would never have been possible without the contributions of the entire community. I would like to thank all the people who work in the DFIR industry who are driven by their passion and dedication.

About the reviewer

Domenica Lee Crognale has worked in digital forensics for more than 16 years, with 13 years specifically dedicated to mobile devices. She has performed mobile forensic investigations for both law enforcement and the intelligence community in support of the US federal government. She received a BSc in business administration from Old Dominion University, and her master's in cybersecurity management from Purdue Global University. She is currently employed by the SANS Institute full time, where she co-authors and instructs a six-day course, FOR585, focusing on smartphone forensic analysis. She also serves as a faculty advisor for candidates enrolled in the SANS Technology Institute's masters in cybersecurity degree program.

I'd like to thank my family and friends who understand the time and commitment it takes to research and test data that is constantly changing. Working in this field would not be possible without the supportive mobile forensics community that has developed over the last several years. Thank you to all of the trailblazers who make this field an exciting place to work each and every day. We are grateful for everything you do!

Table of Contents

Section 2 – iOS Data Analysis

3

Using Forensic Tools

4

Working with Common iOS Artifacts

5

Pattern-of-Life Forensics

6

Dissecting Location Data

7

Analyzing Connectivity Data

8
Email and Messaging Forensics

9
Photo, Video, and Audio Forensics

10
Analyzing Third-Party Apps

11

Locked Devices, iTunes Backups, and iCloud Forensics

Section 3 – Reporting

12

Writing a Forensic Report and Building a Timeline

Index

Other Books You May Enjoy

Preface

Over the past few years, digital forensic examiners have seen a remarkable increase in requests to extract and analyze data from iOS and Android mobile devices. Smartphones and the rich data associated with them have become the single most important source of evidence in virtually every type of investigation. The examination and extraction of data from these devices present numerous unique challenges: modern devices contain so much data that it takes someone with training and experience to add context to the data and understand where that data comes from, how it was generated, and what it means for the investigation.

Finding artifacts on a mobile device is the easy part but recognizing whether those artifacts are evidence can be much harder. Too often, mobile examiners rely on automated tools to extract and process the data, simply allowing the software to identify it without completely comprehending how the actual file that contains this data was created, what it means, and what is going on behind the scenes. Forensic tools and commercial software definitely have their place, but they're not enough. The modern investigator needs to take an in-depth look at the artifacts and learn how to recognize which artifacts are potentially evidence and which are just noise.

Most technical books tend to be tool-focused and often take on a cookbook approach to mobile forensics. This book takes a completely different approach, by guiding you through logical steps that explain what's going on behind the scenes and how to interpret the data. By the end of this book, the examiner will be able to collect the data from an iOS device using multiple techniques and demonstrate unequivocally where the data came from and what it entails for the investigation.

Who this book is for

This book is intended specifically for forensic analysts or digital investigators who need to acquire and analyze information from mobile devices running iOS. This book may also be useful for cybersecurity experts and researchers, as it provides an in-depth look at how iOS devices work behind the scenes.

What this book covers

The way this book is organized is to start with an overview of mobile forensics and what you should know about it. The first section goes over the forensic process and discusses different options to acquire data from iOS devices. The second section describes approaches and best practices to analyze the data, such as manually parsing through the artifacts. This section also covers the most popular forensic tools that are used in an examination. The final section of the book discusses how to build a timeline and best practices for the creation of a forensic report.

Chapter 1, Introducing iOS Forensics, introduces the topic of mobile forensics by describing the forensic process and the iOS operating system.

Chapter 2, Data Acquisition from iOS Devices, describes all available options to successfully acquire the data from an iOS device. We'll discuss logical, physical, and filesystem acquisitions, and much more, such as agent-based extractions.

Chapter 3, Using Forensic Tools, describes why forensic tools are important and how an investigator can benefit by using them. The chapter takes an in-depth look at some of the most popular tools, such as Cellebrite Physical Analyzer and Magnet AXIOM.

Chapter 4, Working with Common iOS Artifacts, introduces common artifacts that can be found on iOS devices, such as SQLite databases and Property lists. We'll learn how to identify these artifacts, where to find them, and how to analyze them.

Chapter 5, Pattern-of-Life Forensics, focuses on artifacts that can help an investigator understand a user's day-to-day activities, such as what apps were used and for how long.

Chapter 6, Dissecting Location Data, is all about extracting, analyzing, and understanding location-related artifacts.

Chapter 7, Analyzing Connectivity Data, discusses cellular forensics, networking data, Bluetooth and Wi-Fi artifacts, and browsing history.

Chapter 8, Email and Messaging Forensics, describes different email clients and messaging applications and how to analyze their data.

Chapter 9, Photo, Video, and Audio Forensics, dives deep into multimedia forensics.

Chapter 10, Analyzing Third-Party Apps, introduces third-party applications. You will learn how to analyze any kind of application and how to quickly locate artifacts from the most popular iOS apps.

Chapter 11, Locked Devices, iTunes Backups, and Cloud Forensics, discusses more advanced topics, such as working with locked devices and extracting forensic data from iCloud.

Chapter 12, Writing a Forensic Report and Building a Timeline, puts together all the knowledge acquired in the previous chapters by teaching you how to produce a comprehensive timeline report.

To get the most out of this book

This book is designed to allow you to use any kind of operating system, so most of the examples can be replicated by using Windows, macOS, or Linux; however, it should be noted that some commercial forensic tools are only available on Windows.

Software covered in the book	OS requirements
Cellebrite UFED	Windows
Cellebrite Physical Analyzer	Windows (minimum 16 GB of RAM is highly recommended)
Magnet AXIOM	Windows
Elcomsoft iOS Forensic Toolkit	Windows, macOS
DB Browser for SQLite	Windows, macOS, Linux

Download the color images

We also provide a PDF file that has color images of the screenshots/diagrams used in this book. You can download it here: `https://static.packt-cdn.com/downloads/9781803234083_ColorImages.pdf`

Conventions used

There are a number of text conventions used throughout this book.

`Code in text`: Indicates code words in text, database table names, folder names, filenames, file extensions, pathnames, dummy URLs, user input, and Twitter handles. Here is an example: "We're providing a ZIP archive as the input file and we're exporting the report to the `output` folder."

A block of code is set as follows:

```
SELECT ROWID, text FROM message
ORDER BY ROWID DESC
LIMIT 5;
```

Any command-line input or output is written as follows:

```
python3 ileapp.py -t zip -i ../iphone_dump.zip -o output
```

Bold: Indicates a new term, an important word, or words that you see onscreen. For example, words in menus or dialog boxes appear in the text like this. Here is an example: "Once you've added all evidence sources to the case, click on **GO TO PROCESSING DETAILS** to continue."

> **Tips or Important Notes**
> Appear like this.

Disclaimer

The information within this book is intended to be used only in an ethical manner. Do not use any information from the book if you do not have written permission from the owner of the equipment. If you perform illegal actions, you are likely to be arrested and prosecuted to the full extent of the law. Neither Packt Publishing nor the author of this book takes any responsibility if you misuse any of the information contained within the book. The information herein must only be used while testing environments with proper written authorization from the appropriate persons responsible.

Get in touch

Feedback from our readers is always welcome.

General feedback: If you have questions about any aspect of this book, mention the book title in the subject of your message and email us at customercare@packtpub.com.

Errata: Although we have taken every care to ensure the accuracy of our content, mistakes do happen. If you have found a mistake in this book, we would be grateful if you would report this to us. Please visit www.packtpub.com/support/errata, selecting your book, clicking on the Errata Submission Form link, and entering the details.

Piracy: If you come across any illegal copies of our works in any form on the Internet, we would be grateful if you would provide us with the location address or website name. Please contact us at copyright@packt.com with a link to the material.

If you are interested in becoming an author: If there is a topic that you have expertise in and you are interested in either writing or contributing to a book, please visit authors.packtpub.com.

Share Your Thoughts

Once you've read *iOS Forensics for Investigators*, we'd love to hear your thoughts! Scan the QR code below to go straight to the Amazon review page for this book and share your feedback.

https://packt.link/r/1803234083

Your review is important to us and the tech community and will help us make sure we're delivering excellent quality content.

Section 1 – Data Acquisition from iOS Devices

You will learn the correct iOS device workflow and understand the basics of how the iOS operating system works. At the end of part one, you will be able to successfully extract a full filesystem image from an iOS device.

This part of the book comprises the following chapters:

- *Chapter 1, Introducing iOS Forensics*
- *Chapter 2, Data Acquisition from iOS Devices*

1
Introducing iOS Forensics

Over the past decade, smartphones have undergone a profound revolution, impacting our lives in all possible ways: our devices are no longer just smart *phones* – they have become data hubs that store all kinds of information from our digital (and not so digital) life.

Today, from the palm of our hand, we can surf the web, buy theater tickets, get food delivered to our door, or call an Uber. We're using our devices to read eBooks, take notes, engage in creative tasks, and share our lives with our followers through social media. We have progressively replaced our digital cameras with our iPhone camera roll. Smartphones can keep track of physical activity, interact with external devices, give us directions, and remind us of that important meeting that we might forget. We use productivity apps to get stuff done and we make payments using Apple Pay. And – of course – we use our iPhones to get in touch with people on the other side of the world. With the massive spread of iPads and tablets in general, our devices are no longer just communication devices. They have become an almost unlimited content platform where we can enjoy movies, TV series, or simply listen to our favorite music.

To be able to provide these amazing features, mobile devices collect huge amounts of data that is processed by iOS and sometimes synced to iCloud. This information documents and reveals the thoughts and activity of a user substantially more than any data stored in any desktop computer.

Mobile forensics is all about collecting this data, preserving it, assessing it, validating it, and extracting meaningful insights that can be presented as evidence.

In this chapter, we will cover the following topics:

- Understanding mobile forensics
- Dissecting the iOS operating system
- Understanding iOS security
- Establishing a workflow

Understanding mobile forensics

Apple devices are popular all over the world due to the user experience they provide, their magnificent design, and their revolutionary features, so it shouldn't come as a surprise that in 2016, Apple announced that over one billion iPhones had been sold. Over the past 5 years, mobile device usage has grown particularly fast, with data from 2021 indicating that there were one billion *active* iOS devices.

The information that's stored on a smartphone can help address crucial questions in an investigation, revealing whom an individual has been in contact with, where they have been, and what they've been doing with the device. As new features are added to the device and more apps are made available through the App Store, the amount of information that's stored on iOS devices is continuously growing.

Mobile forensics can be defined as the process of recovering digital evidence from a mobile device under forensically sound conditions using validated means.

The kind of evidence we can recover from a device depends on the device itself and what techniques are used for data extraction, but generally, smartphones contain personal information such as call history, messages, emails, photos, videos, memos, passwords, location data, and sensor data. No other computing device is as personal as a mobile phone.

Typically, the examination process should reveal all digital evidence, including artifacts that may have been hidden, obscured, or deleted. Evidence is gained by applying established scientifically based methods and should describe the content and state of the data fully, including where it is located, the potential significance, and how different data sources relate to each other. The forensic process begins by extracting a copy of the evidence from the mobile device. Once a copy is available, the next step involves analyzing the data, identifying evidence, and developing the contents of a final report.

The new golden age for iOS forensics

Over the past 3 years, the digital forensics industry has undergone a major revolution.

In 2019, the discovery of the **checkm8** exploit for iOS devices was a complete game-changer as it opened new doors for digital forensics investigators, allowing full filesystem extractions of hundreds of millions of Apple devices. If you've never seen a full filesystem extraction before, you'll probably be surprised by the extent and variety of data that the device stores!

Checkm8 is based on an un-patchable hardware flaw that lives directly on the chips of iOS devices, ranging from devices running Apple's A11 chip down to the A5 generation. This includes devices from the iPhone 4S to iPhone X and several iPads.

This vulnerability is specifically a BootROM exploit, which means it takes advantage of a security flaw in the initial code that iOS devices load during the boot process, and it can't be overwritten or patched by Apple through a software update.

At the end of 2019, **checkra1n** was released, the first public, closed source jailbreak based on the checkm8 exploit. Digital investigators and forensics analysts have quickly adopted checkra1n to get access to the device's filesystem and keychain; however, as with all jailbreaks, this solution has several drawbacks as using a jailbreak inevitably modifies some data on the device's filesystem and is not considered forensically sound.

For these reasons, vendors such as Cellebrite, Elcomsoft, and Oxygen Forensic have developed proprietary solutions based on the original checkm8 exploit that work by patching the device's RAM. These tools allow investigators to perform full filesystem extractions without touching system and user partitions and without making any changes to the device as the exploit runs in memory.

In other words, on selected devices, the checkm8 vulnerability can be exploited to extract the full filesystem *without* actually jailbreaking the device. The following table shows the list of devices that are vulnerable to the checkm8 exploit:

iPhone 4S	iPhone 5/5c/5s	iPhone 6/6s	iPhone SE
iPhone 7	iPhone 8	iPhone X	iPad 2nd – 7th gen
iPad Mini 2nd and 3rd	iPad Air 1st and 2nd	iPad Pro	Apple Watch 1st – 3rd

To exploit checkm8 for a filesystem extraction, your device must be compatible, and it must be running a supported iOS version. This is a major drawback as newer devices, such as the latest iPhone 13, are not supported. There are, however, other options.

In 2020, vendors such as Elcomsoft and Belkasoft introduced agent-based extraction, a new acquisition method that allows full filesystem extractions without jailbreaking the device. Once installed on the device, the agent escapes the sandbox through software exploits, gaining unrestricted access to the device and establishing a connection between the device and the computer. Agent-based extraction is forensically safe, and it is usually a lot faster and safer than most jailbreaks. At the time of writing, supported devices include all iPhones from the 5s up to the iPhone 12, running iOS versions 9.0 to 14.3.

In May 2020, a major update for the **unc0ver** jailbreak was released, adding support for devices based on A12-A13 chips. At the time of writing, unc0ver supports jailbreaking all devices from the iPhone 5s up to the iPhone 12. Supported iOS versions range from iOS 11 to iOS 14.3.

Although jailbreaking a device allows full filesystem extraction, it's not considered a forensically sound process. An investigator should consider safer options such as checkm8 or agent-based extractions first if they're supported.

> **Tip**
>
> It's important to note the difference between checkm8-based extractions and jailbreaking the device through checkra1n or unc0ver. Tools such as **Cellebrite UFED** and **Elcomsoft iOS Forensics Toolkit** leverage the checkm8 exploit to temporarily provide access to the entire filesystem by running the exploit in the device's RAM. When the extraction is complete, the device will reboot as normal. No permanent changes will be made to the device.
>
> On the other hand, jailbreaking the device will leave permanent traces and will also require installing third-party packages such as `Cydia` or `AFC2`, making additional changes to the device.

Challenges in iOS forensics

Smartphones are considered live, dynamic systems, and for this reason, they pose several challenges from a forensic perspective because data and files are constantly changing.

One of the main complications that a digital investigator may face is dealing with a locked device: recent iOS updates make passcode cracking almost impossible and other options will have to be considered to extract as much data as possible.

The growing number of devices and the variety of the software they run makes it extremely difficult to develop a single tool and a consistent workflow to address all eventualities. This is usually because a particular method that's used to extract data from one device will stop working when a new version of iOS is released; in fact, forensic extraction tools usually rely on security vulnerabilities to gain access to the device's filesystem and extract a lot more data than what you would normally find in an iTunes backup, or even to unlock a device when the passcode is unknown. When a new iOS update is released, these vulnerabilities could potentially be patched, thus rendering the tools useless.

The modern investigator will have to take these issues into account when approaching an Apple device and decide, on a case-by-case basis, what the best technique will be to obtain the broadest amount of valuable evidence.

Dissecting the iOS operating system

Performing a forensic examination of digital evidence from a mobile device requires not only a full understanding of the data but also basic knowledge of *how* the device itself works and *how* that data was generated. This is particularly challenging on iOS devices due to the closed source nature of the platform, which makes it difficult to understand how exactly iOS interfaces with all this data and what's going on behind the scenes on the device.

Apple invests heavily in restricting the operating system and application software that can run on their hardware through several security features: applications running on Apple devices don't interact directly with the underlying hardware – they do so through a system interface. The iOS can be defined as an intermediary between the device's hardware components and the applications on the device.

> **Tip**
>
> Many publications provide information regarding iOS hardware. For a full list of iPhone components and devices, you can refer to the Apple Support page: `https://support.apple.com/specs/iphone`.

Understanding the iOS filesystem

Since iOS 10, **Apple File System (APFS)** has replaced HFS+ as the default filesystem. APFS is a proprietary filesystem that has been designed with mobile devices in mind: it's optimized for SSD storage and supports strong encryption. On iOS devices, the filesystem is configured into two logical disk partitions – the system partition and the user partition:

- The system partition contains the iOS operating system and all the preloaded applications that come with the device but contain little evidentiary information. The system partition is only updated when a firmware upgrade is performed on the device.

- The user partition, which is mounted to the `/private/var` directory, contains all user-created data and provides most of the evidentiary information that's pertinent to investigators.

Where is data stored on the iOS filesystem?

One of the examples of how iOS manages communication between applications and hardware is sandboxing, which enables users to interact with an application without accessing the filesystem directly, ensuring that each app is *contained* within one or more specified containers that are automatically created when a new app is installed on the device. This organization makes things a lot easier for investigators as all the files related to a specific app are grouped in specific locations.

Each container has a specific role:

- The bundle container contains the application itself, including all the assets that come with the application when it is downloaded from the App Store.

- The data container holds data for both the application and the user and is further divided into several directories that the application can use to organize its data.

- The group container is where applications can store data that can be shared with other apps of the same group.

The following diagram shows the containers for each application:

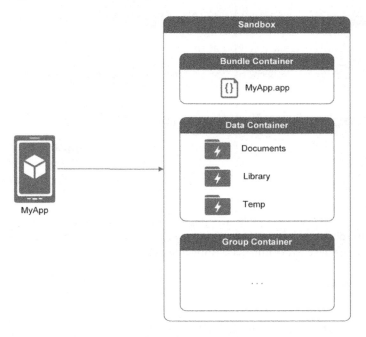

Figure 1.1 – A representation of application containers

The data container contains several different folders:

- Documents/: This folder contains user-created files and is automatically included in iTunes backups and iCloud backups.

- Library/: This folder is used by the application to store app-related data and is not created by the user. This folder is included in iTunes and iCloud backups.

- Temp/: Contains application-related temporary files and is not included in backups.

As you can see, all application files are perfectly organized into their respective data containers. However, you may be wondering where exactly these containers are stored on the device's filesystem. Each application on a device is identified through a **globally unique identifier (GUID)**, also known as a BundleID identifier. This identifier is uniquely generated when an application is first installed and can change if the app is updated or reinstalled.

Application bundle containers are stored at the following path on the iOS filesystem:

```
/private/var/containers/Bundle/Application/<app-GUID>/
```

Application data containers are stored at the following path:

```
/private/var/mobile/Containers/Data/Application/<app-
GUID>/
```

Group containers are stored at the following path:

```
/private/var/mobile/Containers/Shared/AppGroup/<app-
GUID>/
```

> **Tip**
>
> In this section, we've seen where applications store data on the iOS filesystem. But what about system artifacts? System-related data is stored all over the filesystem, so we won't find everything all in one place! We'll dive deep into system artifacts and where to find them in *Chapter 4, Working with Common iOS Artifacts*.

How is data stored on the iOS filesystem?

So far, we've learned how iOS organizes application data into containers and where these containers are stored on the filesystem. Now, let's discuss the types of files that commonly contain useful evidence within the iOS filesystem.

Other than user-generated content (such as documents, photos, videos, or text files), data stored on an iOS device usually consists of the following items:

- **SQLite databases**: SQLite is a standalone, self-contained database that can store just about any kind of data, including binary BLOBs, all in one file. SQLite databases are the primary source of storage for applications and system data, so parsing these databases will be one of the focus points of most digital investigations. Databases can also be extremely useful if you wish to attempt to recover deleted data, as deleted records usually leave a digital trace in the database itself or its temporary files. Essential artifacts such as SMS messages, WhatsApp conversations, contacts, call logs, notes, and browser history are all stored in SQLite databases.

- **Property List Files (Plists)**: Plists are structured files that are used by iOS and applications to store, organize, and access data on the device. These can be stored in XML format or binary format. Typically, plists are used to store application settings or user preferences.

- **Other file types**: This includes log files, XML files, Protocol Buffers, and Realm databases. These file types will be covered in depth later in this book.

This is what a property list looks like in XML format:

```xml
<?xml version="1.0" encoding="UTF-8" standalone="yes"?>
<!DOCTYPE plist PUBLIC "-//Apple//DTD PLIST 1.0//EN"
"http://www.apple.com/DTDs/PropertyList-1.0.dtd">
<plist version="1.0">
    <dict>
        <key>UUID</key>
        <string>3bdd52c7-ee36-4689-8517-c5fed2c98s5</string>
        <key>ClientID</key>
        <string>3bdd52c7-ee36-4689-8517-c5fed2c98s5</string>
        <key>ClientEnabled</key>
        <false/>
    </dict>
</plist>
```

In the following chapters, we will do a deep dive into the details to understand what the best practices are for parsing plists and querying SQLite databases, how to handle SQLite temporary files in a forensically sound way, and where to locate core iOS artifacts.

Understanding iOS security

Apple devices are widely known for their ability to secure user data. With every release of a new iOS device or update to the iOS operating system, Apple works hard to improve security by introducing new features and by patching known vulnerabilities. In the following sections, we'll go over the key elements of Apple's security model.

User authentication

To secure physical access to the device, some form of user authentication is required. iOS devices implement authentication through two mechanisms:

- Passcode authentication
- Biometric authentication

By default, Apple devices suggest a six-digit numeric passcode, although the user can choose a four-digit passcode too or a custom alphanumeric code. Once a passcode has been set, the user will have to enter it every time the device is turned on and when it wakes up.

To improve the user experience while maintaining high-security standards, with the iPhone 5s, Apple introduced biometric authentication through Touch ID, which uses fingerprints as a passcode. With the release of the iPhone X, Apple introduced Face ID, which employs face recognition to unlock the device.

Unlocking passcode-protected iOS devices is one of the main challenges in mobile forensics.

Because there are a relatively small number of numeric passcodes, brute-force guessing attacks could theoretically be used to exploit authentication. However, this is extremely risky as iOS is designed to rate-limit passcode entry attempts, and data can be permanently deleted from the device if too many failed attempts occur.

This passcode is not just used to unlock the device itself – it's one of the key features of the iOS data protection model: the passcode, combined with the hardware encryption key, is used to generate a unique and extremely strong encryption key that is used by an algorithm to encrypt user data.

Encryption and Data Protection

While user authentication provides a degree of security in preventing unauthorized access to the physical device, these mechanisms could still be bypassed by exploiting vulnerabilities in software or hardware. A compromised device could potentially allow unauthorized access to the device's filesystem. For this reason, starting with the iPhone 4, the entire filesystem is encrypted using strong cryptography algorithms. However, with the release of the iPhone 5s, Apple set a new precedent in mobile security by introducing a technology called **Data Protection**, which relies on multiple dedicated components to support encryption and biometrics.

Secure Enclave

At the heart of iOS's security is Secure Enclave, a dedicated **system on a chip (SoC)** isolated from the main processor and operating system that provides cryptographic operations for data protection and key management.

Secure Enclave's main components are as follows:

- **Secure Enclave Processor (SEP)**, which runs an Apple-modified version of the L4 microkernel and provides computing power exclusively to Secure Enclave.

- A memory protection engine.

- A **True Random Number Generator (TRNG)**, which is used to generate random cryptographic keys.

- Dedicated **Advanced Encryption Standard (AES)** hardware engines, which communicate directly with the SEP through a secure channel and perform in-line encryption and decryption as files are written or read.

- A **unique ID (UID)**, a cryptographic key that uniquely identifies the device. The UID is randomly generated and fused directly into Secure Enclave's hardware during device manufacturing, so it isn't visible outside the device.

- A dedicated, secure, nonvolatile storage system that can only be accessed by Secure Enclave. This is where data encryption keys are stored, ensuring that these are never exposed to iOS systems or applications.

The following diagram shows the different components of Secure Enclave:

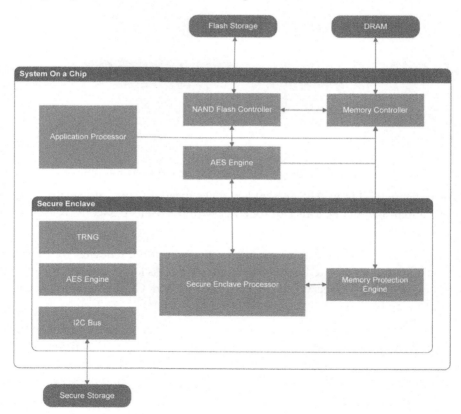

Figure 1.2 – Secure Enclave components

Secure Enclave is responsible for several different security-related operations, including generating and storing keys necessary for encrypting data on the device and evaluating biometric data from Touch ID and Face ID.

SEP uses the UID to generate cryptographic keys that are tied to the specific device. This adds another layer of security: if the device's SSD storage is physically moved to a different device, files can't be decrypted and thus will be inaccessible, since every device has a unique UID and the original UID is required to decrypt files.

iOS Data Protection keys

Data protection on iOS is implemented by generating and managing a hierarchy of cryptographic keys.

To make things easier, before we delve into the details, let's take a look at what keys are used during the encryption and decryption processes and what their purpose is:

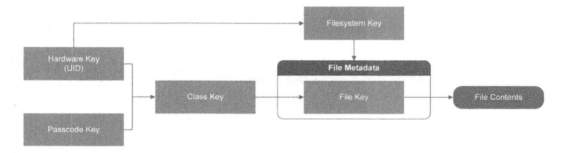

Figure 1.3 – Cryptographic keys used for iOS data protection

- The device's UID is an AES 256-bit key that's fused directly into Secure Enclave during manufacturing. This key, together with the user's passcode, is used to unlock *class keys*.

- Class keys are generated when specific events occur on the device; for instance, when a device is unlocked, a *complete protection* class key is created. Shortly after the device locks, the decrypted class key is discarded. Class keys are used to wrap and unwrap file keys.

- File keys are 256-bit keys that are used to encrypt the content of each file; these keys are per-file keys and, as such, are randomly generated every time a new file is created on the user partition. File keys are encrypted using a class key and are then stored in the file's metadata. The metadata of all the files is encrypted with the filesystem key.

- The filesystem key is a random key that is generated when iOS is first installed or when the device is wiped. The filesystem key is stored on the device, and it's been designed to be quickly erased if the user requests it. Deleting the filesystem key makes all the files on the filesystem inaccessible.

iOS Data Protection classes

Let's take a closer look at the class keys.

Apple allows developers to specify security settings for each file by selecting a protection class that is assigned to a file when it is created. There are four different protection classes, depending on how the file is meant to be accessed:

- **Complete Protection**: Class keys for this protection are decrypted when a device is unlocked and are automatically evicted shortly after device lock, so a file associated with this protection class will only be accessible when the device is unlocked.

- **Protection Unless Open**: This protection class allows files to be created and encrypted when the device is locked, but only decrypted when the device is unlocked. This is used, for example, when an email attachment is downloading in the background.

- **Protected Until First User Authentication**: Class keys for this protection are decrypted when the device transitions from a **before first unlock** (**BFU**) state to an **after first unlock** (**AFU**) state and remain in memory, even if the device is locked.

- **No Protection**: The class keys for this protection class are always available in memory when the device is on.

Encrypting content while performing normal operations on a device can be challenging. Protection classes allow files to be encrypted safely, modulating the degree of protection based on *how* and *when* each file needs to be accessed.

For example, data that is useful to applications running in the background, such as messages or contacts, can be assigned to the *Protected Until First User Authentication* class; this allows data to be accessible to the device while keeping it encrypted.

iOS data encryption and decryption

When a file is written to the filesystem, the content of the file is encrypted with a per-file key, which is wrapped with a class key and stored in a file's metadata. The metadata is then encrypted using the filesystem key.

We've already seen how class keys are generated using a combination of the hardware's UID and the user's passcode while the filesystem key is generated upon iOS installation and stored on the device. Now, let's analyze the individual file encryption process step by step:

1. Every time a file is created on the filesystem, Secure Enclave creates a 256-bit file key and passes this key to the hardware AES engine.

2. The AES engine encrypts file content while it is written to flash memory using the provided file key.

3. The file key is then wrapped with one of the four class keys, depending on the assigned protection class, and is stored in the file's metadata.

4. Metadata for all the files is encrypted with the filesystem key.

All key handling happens in Secure Enclave, thus never exposing the operations to the system and its applications.

The decryption process works the other way round:

1. When a file is opened, its metadata is decrypted using the filesystem key, revealing the wrapped file key and the assigned protection class.

2. The file key is unwrapped using the class key and is then passed to the AES engine.

3. The hardware AES engine decrypts file content while it reads the file from memory, using the provided file key.

> **Tip**
> Key wrapping is the process of encrypting one key using another key to securely store or transmit it.

Although the data protection architecture may seem complex, it provides both flexibility and good performance.

By now, you should have a basic understanding of where iOS stores application data, how data is structured, and how iOS leverages authentication and data protection to guarantee a high level of security on all devices.

In the next section, we will learn about the guidelines for a forensically sound examination process.

Establishing a workflow

Although there is no well-established standard process for mobile forensics, there are some common guidelines that can be followed to ensure that the examination will be carried out through a proper methodology. This will make the process forensically sound and the results reliable.

Generally, a mobile forensics examination can be broken down into the following six steps:

1. Seizure and identification
2. Preservation
3. Acquisition
4. Analysis
5. Validation
6. Reporting

> **Tip**
> The key point to understand here is that the process you use to examine the mobile device and extract data from it is what makes the examination forensic. It is neither the software nor the hardware you use, but solely the process that you use during the examination that makes it truly forensic.

These guidelines and processes should be periodically reviewed as technology continues to evolve and different mobile devices are marketed.

Seizure and identification

The first step pertains to the physical seizure of the device. This involves gathering information on the type of incident that the device was involved in and at least some basic information on the device's owner.

The way the seizure occurs depends on your jurisdiction, so you should be familiar with laws regarding seizing and analyzing smart devices and what the requirements are (that is, a search warrant is usually required). At this stage, you should also have a general understanding of what data you are expected to find, as this will help you define specific objectives and plan the next steps according to your requirements.

First and foremost, you need to document everything you do and consider how to preserve evidence. *How* you handle the device matters and it can have a huge impact on the outcome of the investigation.

You should also note the state that the device was found in. The following are some examples:

- Is the device powered on or off?
- Is the device protected by a passcode?
- Is the passcode known?
- Is the SIM card present?
- Is there any visible damage?
- What's the date and time on the device?
- If the device is on, what apps are running?
- Basic ownership information.

One of the fundamental aspects of a forensically sound process is that operations should be carried out without altering or changing the contents of data that resides on the device in any way. Note that iOS devices are live, dynamic computer systems, so any kind of interaction with the device would result in changes to system files and databases, not to mention the possibility of inadvertently deleting temporary files that could contain useful evidence. Care should be taken to limit all interaction with the device, except for the preservation operations, which will be indicated in the next section.

Once the device has been seized, an investigator could be tempted to manually access data from the device, such as by running messaging apps and viewing conversations directly from the device's screen; however, this should be strongly discouraged as this would result in system logs and other system-related files being altered, which is not forensically sound behavior.

At this stage, the investigator will also have to identify the device, its hardware model, and the iOS version. This information will be useful if you wish to start assessing what options the investigator has for extracting evidence from the device.

For each examination, the investigator should also identify the following:

- The legal authority for examining the device
- The goals of the examination
- Other sources of potential evidence (including cloud storage)

Preservation

Smartphones are, by design, meant to communicate through cellular networks, Bluetooth connections, and wireless Wi-Fi networks. To prevent the device from communicating, it is important to isolate the device as soon as possible. Isolating the device prevents new data (incoming calls, incoming messages, and so on) from modifying existing evidence and thus enforces data preservation. Additionally, if the device were allowed network access, data destruction could occur as Apple products can be remotely wiped via a *kill signal*.

The easiest way to isolate an Apple device is by enabling **Airplane** mode; this deactivates the device's wireless and cellular connections. You can enable **Airplane** mode from the device's **Settings** or, if the device is locked, directly from the control center by swiping up from the bottom. If the device is an iPhone X or newer, you can access the control center by swiping down from the top-right corner. However, it's worth noting that isolating the device can also be accomplished by putting the device in a Faraday bag, a container made of metallic shielding that blocks the radio frequencies used by cellular networks, GPS, and Wi-Fi networks.

Don't forget to keep the device charged to ensure it doesn't power off. Generally speaking, you want the device to remain in the state in which you found it:

- If the device was off, leave it off.
- If it was on, make sure you leave it on so that it doesn't lock!

This is particularly important if the device is passcode protected and the investigator doesn't have the code: if the device powers off, it would transition from an AFU state to a BFU state, rendering data recovery much more challenging and, in some cases, impossible. We will learn more about device states later in this chapter.

> Tip
>
> One of the most common mistakes is removing the SIM card from an unlocked device to isolate it from a cellular network. This may make sense when you're working with different devices, but you want to avoid removing the SIM card from iPhones or iPads because doing so will result in iOS automatically locking the device, biometric unlock will be disabled, and USB restricted mode will be activated.

After successfully seizing and isolating the device, care should be taken to maintain the device's chain of custody. NIST defines the chain of custody as follows:

> *"A process that tracks the movement of evidence through its collection, safeguarding, and analysis life cycle by documenting each person who handled the evidence, the date/time it was collected or transferred, and the purpose for the transfer."*

You can learn more about this topic by visiting the following website: `csrc.nist.gov`.

Acquisition

Acquisition is the process of obtaining information and evidence from a device.

Before the actual acquisition process begins, you should have a clear understanding of what kind of evidence you're looking for as this will have a great influence on the tools you choose to use.

Generally speaking, there are three different kinds of data acquisition, and the method the investigator chooses affects how much data can be extracted from the device:

- Logical acquisition
- Full filesystem acquisition
- Physical acquisition

In the following table, you can see what kind of data can be extracted with each method:

	Logical	Filesystem	Physical
Calls, calendars, contacts, and messages	✓	✓	✓
User content (photos, videos, notes, and so on)	✓	✓	P
Keychain	Limited	✓	✓
Third-party app data	Limited	✓	✓
Apple Pay	-	✓	✓
Location data (radio cells, GPS fixes, and so on)	-	✓	✓
Mail	-	✓	✓
User activity logs	-	✓	✓
System logs	-	✓	✓
Deleted data (unallocated space)	-	-	✓
Deleted data (SQLite databases)	Limited	✓	✓

Table 1.2 – Comparison of data that can be extracted with different acquisition methods

Logical and filesystem extractions

As you can see, a logical acquisition will extract some user-generated data from the device such as photos, messages, and notes. A logical extraction will usually be the easiest and quickest type of extraction and most forensic tools support it. However, considering the number of files available on an iOS device, only acquiring the *full filesystem* will give access to precious evidence such as third-party app data, precise location data, and pattern-of-life information.

A filesystem extraction is a representation of the files and folders from the user partition of the device; it is possible to partially recover deleted data by analyzing databases and temporary files, such as WAL files.

Physical extraction

Devices up to and including the iPhone 4 can undergo a full, forensically sound physical extraction of the entire raw disk. This kind of extraction delivers the most data as, much like a standard hard drive, both the system and the user partitions are extracted, as well as unallocated areas of the disk. This is incredibly useful as it allows investigators to recover deleted data, including messages, photos, and videos. However, with the introduction of iOS 5, Apple changed the way data was encrypted on disk and enabled other security features, such as data protection class keys. At the time of writing, extracting a physical image of modern iOS devices is simply not possible.

Choosing the best acquisition method

Investigators should always perform a logical acquisition first and then, if possible, attempt a filesystem or physical acquisition.

Jailbreaking the device is generally required to enable unrestricted access to the device's filesystem; however, more and more vendors are adding the possibility to run forensically sound checkm8-based extractions (all operations are performed in the device's volatile RAM) or agent-based extractions. Both options allow you to obtain the full filesystem without jailbreaking the device.

At the end of the day, the method you choose will usually depend on four variables:

- The state in which you find the device (locked or unlocked)
- The device model and iOS version
- The tools you have access to
- The possibility of jailbreaking the device

If the device is locked and you don't have the passcode, there is not a simple solution that can consistently bypass iOS security. However, depending on the device model, several options can provide a limited amount of data. We will examine these in detail in the next chapter.

If the device is unlocked, depending on the available tools, you can attempt a filesystem extraction. You should start with the less intrusive option, such as an in-memory checkm8 exploit, if your tools support it. If the device doesn't allow checkm8 exploiting, you can attempt an agent-based extraction if the iOS version is compatible. Although this entails installing an agent on the device and some minor changes can occur, this is considered forensically safe. If neither of these options is available, you can consider jailbreaking the device through checkra1n or unc0ver. Make sure you understand how the jailbreak works, how it affects the device, and what the risks are. Finally, if none of these options are available, you will have to go for a logical acquisition.

We will learn all about extracting data from iOS devices in the next chapter, but for now, it's important to note that the phone should be acquired using a tested method that is repeatable and is as forensically sound as possible. It is highly recommended to experiment with various tools on test devices to determine which acquisition method and tool work best with different devices.

If you don't have direct access to the device, there are other sources of evidence you can consider, such as iTunes backups and iCloud extractions.

Analysis

The main point of doing a forensic examination is to find, extract, and process evidence related to a particular case or investigation.

Although there is no standard process to analyze what you extracted from a device, here are some guidelines that should help you get started:

- Go through all the available data to become familiar with the main sources of evidence found on the device.

- Use your tools and forensic software to quickly parse common data sources, such as SMS databases, installed apps, call logs, photos, and so on.

- Attempt to recover any deleted data both with software and by manually carving binary files, logs, plists, and SQLite databases.

- Identify key artifacts by searching for keywords and details that are specific to your investigation.

- Harvest metadata from files and look for hidden evidence (timestamps, geolocation data, binary BLOBs, and so on).

- Find relationships between different artifacts.

- Perform temporal analysis on all acquired evidence, building a timeline of relevant artifacts and events.

When you're dealing with a limited amount of data, it may be possible to assess evidence by manually browsing through all the folders and viewing the contents of the files on your workstation. However, when you're looking at gigabytes of data sources, including SQLite databases, caches, and plists, you'll probably have to resort to using forensics tools. In such cases, investigators must develop a strategy to use the best tools, depending on the type of digital evidence and the goals of your investigation.

We'll cover commercial tools in detail in *Chapter 2, Data Acquisition from iOS Devices and Chapter 3, Using Forensic Tools*, but before that, it must be noted that all mobile forensics tools are just application software. These tools are not magical things that conduct autonomous processing and reporting simply by clicking a button! Digital investigators must understand the *features* and *limits* of each tool.

Mobile forensic tools typically differ in the kind of extraction that can be done, but different tools are also compatible with different devices and different versions of the iOS operating system. With the variety of different types of mobile devices, no single software supports all mobile devices.

Automated tools can speed up the time it takes to process huge datasets and I strongly believe that the modern investigator should have more than one tool available. However, this process is not a substitute for a methodical, manual forensic examination and validation.

In the end, it all comes down to the target device model, the iOS version, the type of extraction, the goal of the examination, and how the produced evidence might be used later.

Validation

After processing evidence from the device, the investigator must verify the accuracy of all the steps that have been carried out. This process should not focus exclusively on verifying the data extracted from the device. It should also entail validating the tools that were used for the examination and validating the entire process to ensure it has been carried out in a forensically sound way.

Unfortunately, validation is one of the most overlooked aspects.

Before starting an examination, it is highly recommended to experiment with various tools on test devices and known datasets to determine which acquisition and analysis tools work best with specific iOS device models and versions.

Established procedures should lead to the process of acquisition and analyzing a device. This is especially true when an investigator is working on data from third-party apps or **Unidentified Forensic Objects (UFOs)**. Practices must be tested to ensure that the results that have been obtained are *valid* and independently *reproducible*.

An examiner who is called to testify on their findings should be able to explain not only *what* evidence was found, but also *where* that data was found and *how* the iOS operating system generated those artifacts. This could entail manually decoding binary data and file carving. Analyzing actual binary files that user data was parsed from, along with SQLite databases and plists, offers the investigator the opportunity to perform deep analysis of the iOS device's filesystem, extracting evidence that could be missed by relying only on automatic tools.

The following list resembles some of the best practices regarding verification and validation:

- **Hash values**: All the files that are extracted from the device should be hashed during the acquisition process to ensure that no changes occur. If you're doing a filesystem extraction, you can calculate the hashes for each file at the end of the process. Data integrity can be verified by calculating the hash for a single file and checking it against the original value.

- **Deterministic tools**: All the tools that are used for an examination should be deterministic: a given tool should produce the same output when given the same input data, under the same circumstances.

- **Data verification**: Check if known data stored on the device is reported accurately, without any modifications. Generally, data that's extracted from the device should match the data that's viewed on the device's screen.

- **Tool accuracy**: The quality of the output of a tool should be checked by using multiple tools to extract/process the same data and compare results.

- **Process testing**: When working on UFOs or artifacts where there is not an established examination process yet, validate your findings by testing each solution on different devices and under known control conditions and evaluate the results of each test.

Reporting

The last step in the mobile forensics process is reporting. Reporting can be defined as the process of preparing a detailed summary of what was done to acquire and analyze digital evidence from a mobile device. A forensic report should also include all the relevant evidence, presented in a clear, concise manner, and the conclusions that were reached in the investigation.

Many forensic tools provide a built-in reporting feature that allows you to automatically generate a digital report that includes items from the investigation, such as the following:

- Key artifacts
- Device identification (model, s/n, phone number, and so on)
- Case number and the analyst's name
- Date and time of when the examination took place
- Tools that were used for extraction and analysis

Depending on your jurisdiction, a forensic report should also describe how the data was extracted (logical, physical, or filesystem extraction) and explain what measures were taken to ensure the entire process was repeatable and forensically sound.

Timeline analysis

One of the most common forms of forensic reporting includes temporal analysis, which is defined as the process of creating a timeline of events that occurred on the device at a specified date and time.

A timeline generally includes data from a variety of sources; for example, location data, system logs, and messaging evidence can be combined and can lead to the discovery of what happened, where it happened, and when it happened.

Determining when events occurred on the device and associating device usage with an individual by reporting logs, files, and timestamps can be extremely useful.

Summary

In this chapter, we learned what the goal of a forensic examination is and how the discovery of the checkm8 vulnerability provides new opportunities for data acquisition from iOS devices.

First, we introduced the iOS operating system and discussed some key elements of its security architecture, such as Secure Enclave and Data Protection. Then, we went through the steps of an iOS forensic examination.

The first step is seizing the device and adopting techniques to preserve evidence, such as placing the device in a Faraday bag or enabling Airplane mode. There are different ways to acquire data from an iOS device, depending on the model, iOS version, and what tools are available. This chapter covered logical and filesystem acquisition techniques, as well as jailbreaking and agent-based extractions.

Analyzing artifacts should be done by following a thorough validation process that ensures that commercial tools produce consistent results and that evidence has been processed in a forensically sound way.

Finally, we learned what key elements should be included in a forensic report.

The next chapter will discuss iOS data acquisition in detail and provide a hands-on approach to the tools that are used to conduct a forensic examination.

2

Data Acquisition from iOS Devices

Mobile devices present a unique set of challenges compared to desktop computers when approaching the data acquisition phase. While in the world of desktop computers there is a consolidated workflow that allows an investigator to carry out a so-called *forensically sound* acquisition, when we're dealing with mobile devices there is no single, one-size-fits-all procedure that can be adapted to each and every device. This becomes even more evident when we are dealing with iOS devices, as the variety of models and different versions of iOS implies that the procedure to be carried out to achieve a satisfactory acquisition will be different, depending on the device itself. Often, a particular tool, exploit, or vendor solution will stop working if the device is updated to a new iOS release. This is the case for most jailbreaks that rely on publicly disclosed vulnerabilities that are subsequently patched by Apple. A further challenge is represented by the possibility of dealing with locked devices; in this case, the chances of extracting useful information from the device are much more limited.

For these reasons, data acquisition is arguably the most challenging aspect of the iOS forensic workflow. In this chapter, therefore, we will discuss various solutions, starting by distinguishing the different types of acquisition methods and their limits. We will then move on to the practical phase, in which we will learn how to perform a logical, a filesystem, and a physical acquisition of an iOS device.

In this chapter, we will cover the following topics:

- Understanding acquisition methods
- Jailbreaking the device
- Triaging the device
- Performing a logical acquisition
- Performing a full filesystem acquisition

Understanding acquisition methods

In the first chapter, we briefly discussed acquisition methods and the difference between a logical, filesystem, and physical extraction. We will now be building on that foundation and diving deep into more advanced topics to gain a full understanding of how they work and what kind of data we can expect from each of these acquisition methods.

Logical acquisitions

A logical acquisition is usually the easiest and fastest way to extract the most common types of evidence from an iOS device. If the device is unlocked or if you have the passcode, you will certainly be able to perform a logical acquisition, as all iOS devices support it; based on the **Apple File Connection (AFC) protocol**, this acquisition is essentially equivalent to running a local (iTunes) backup, and some forensic tools will actually rely on Apple's libraries and iTunes capabilities to extract data from the device.

A logical acquisition can be performed using free software like **iTunes**, third-party libraries such as `libimobiledevice`, or by using forensic software. In the following sections of this chapter, we will use three of the most popular digital forensics tools to perform a logical acquisition: *Cellebrite UFED*, *Elcomsoft iOS Forensic Toolkit*, and *Magnet ACQUIRE*.

As we've learned from the previous chapter, the main limitation in a logical acquisition is the depth and quality of the data that is extracted; although it will include *most* user-generated content, such as text messages, call logs, photos, and notes, it will *not* include other precious artifacts, such as emails, location data, third-party apps, and precise system logs. The key point to understand here is that both Apple and iOS developers can restrict logical extractions by deciding which files will be included in a backup and which files will not be backed up. For instance, many popular applications, such as **Twitter**, **Facebook**, **Instagram**, **Telegram**, or **Signal**, do not include their files in a local backup, so these artifacts will not be available through a logical acquisition.

To make things even more complicated, with the release of iOS 4, Apple introduced a feature that enables the user to **encrypt** local backups using a password. This setting can be activated by using iTunes and, once enabled, all subsequent backups will be automatically encrypted using the provided password. In other words, if I decide to enable backup encryption, the next time I attempt a local backup on any computer, the password will be required to read the backup files. Clearly, this poses a problem for the forensic investigator on several fronts; if backup encryption is enabled and the password is unknown, data extracted from a logical acquisition will be useless, as it won't be possible to decrypt it. Some forensic tools, such as Elcomsoft Phone Breaker, allow investigators to attack the encrypted backup by brute-forcing the password; however, this does not guarantee that the password will be effectively recovered, and brute-force attacks usually take quite a long time.

There is, however, another option. Since iOS 11, Apple introduced the possibility of removing the password used to encrypt local backups *directly* from the device.

Here's the caveat: although this solution works perfectly, it does not only remove the encryption password but also resets *all* the device's settings. Clearly, this will have an effect on some of the files stored in the device, but it may be your only option if you don't have access to the backup password.

Here's how to reset the local backup encryption password:

1. From the iOS device, go to **Settings | General | Reset**.
2. Select the **Reset All Settings** option and enter the device passcode.
3. Follow the steps to reset the device.

By following this procedure, you will not lose any user data or other passwords, but it will reset general device settings, such as wallpaper, display settings, and so on. This will, of course, cause some changes to system files and databases; for this reason, if you're dealing with a device in a criminal case, be sure you understand the consequences of making changes to the original device and make sure you have the legal authority to perform this kind of operation.

> **Tip**
>
> It's important to note that, since iOS 13, if the user decides to encrypt a local backup, a lot more data will be included, including some data from Keychain, calls, health data, Safari history, and so on. When performing a logical acquisition, most forensic tools check whether backup encryption is enabled, and if it's not, it is temporarily enabled to acquire the biggest amount of data and then disabled again when the acquisition process finishes. Keep this in mind – if you don't encrypt backups before performing a logical acquisition, you will miss crucial evidence!

To have a better understanding of what artifacts you can expect to find in a logical extraction, take a look at the following screenshot taken from *Cellebrite Physical Analyzer*, which shows what data was acquired from an iOS device through a logical acquisition:

Figure 2.1 – Data acquired through a logical acquisition

The main reason why you would want to perform a logical acquisition is when working with newer devices, because they are generally supported following the release of an iOS update, so you won't have to wait too long to start collecting evidence; however, as we've already discussed, many items will not be included in a logical acquisition.

In comparison with a standard logical extraction, a full filesystem extraction or a physical extraction gives investigators access to a lot more user data on iOS devices, including full access to Keychain, which will also include encryption keys that can be used to decrypt data from secure apps, such as **Signal**, **Wickr**, **Snapchat**, or **Facebook**.

By acquiring the full filesystem, investigators will also gain access to many of the system artifacts, such as the complete history of events that occurred on the device (locked/unlocked states, user interaction, installed applications, AirDrop, Bluetooth, camera, and airplane mode history). Also, a lot more geodata will be available from a full filesystem acquisition, including artifacts from cell towers, Wi-Fi connections, and GPS locations with the corresponding geo-coordinates and timestamps.

The following screenshots show the differences between a logical acquisition and a full filesystem acquisition from the same device; the full filesystem extraction, on the right, contains a lot more data:

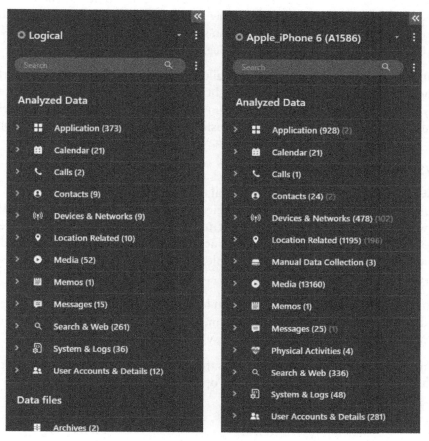

Figure 2.2 – Comparison of data extracted from a logical and a filesystem acquisition

By now, you should have a clear understanding of the benefits and limits of a logical acquisition and why it may not be sufficient to gather the required evidence. We will learn how to perform a logical acquisition later on, but before that, let's take a look at how we can extract the device filesystem by performing a physical or full filesystem acquisition.

Physical acquisitions

In the first chapter, we briefly introduced physical acquisitions and learned how a physical extraction will contain the biggest amount of evidence from a device, including data present in unallocated space on the disk that can be used to recover deleted artifacts.

A physical acquisition can be defined as a bit-per-bit copy of the device's flash memory. Clearly, this is the best of all worlds for a forensic examiner, but it isn't always possible; since data on an iOS device is encrypted, using traditional techniques such as imaging the physical volume would result in the acquisition of encrypted data, which would be completely useless. We've already seen how Apple manages security by protecting encryption keys within the Secure Enclave, so starting with the iPhone 5s, there is no way of obtaining a physical extraction of the device.

At the time of writing, the latest device that allows a physical acquisition to be performed is the iPhone 5c, a device released almost eight years ago. It's safe to say that, at present, it's highly unlikely that an investigator will run into one of these devices; nevertheless, a physical acquisition can be carried out by using the Elcomsoft iOS Forensic Toolkit.

Filesystem acquisitions

A full filesystem acquisition provides a logical representation of all files on an iOS device, and this is a great compromise between a logical acquisition and a physical one. All the data we previously saw in a logical extraction is still obtained during a filesystem acquisition, but the examiner is also granted access to raw files stored within the device. This allows investigators to access, for example, databases of all third-party applications without restrictions, and recovery of deleted artifacts can also be attempted.

Although there are many tools that allow you to perform this kind of acquisition, Apple restricts direct access to the device's filesystem, so you will have to find a workaround to gain full access to the device before a full filesystem acquisition can be performed.

So, you may be wondering – how do I access the device filesystem? Is a **jailbreak** required? Although jailbreaking is one of the available options, it is not the only one.

At the time of writing, there are three different solutions to gain access to the device's filesystem:

- Using tools that leverage Checkm8, a BootROM exploit
- Using an extraction agent
- Jailbreaking the device

Checkm8

The publication of the Checkm8 vulnerability in 2019 by the hacker *@axi0mX*, which is based on an unpatchable vulnerability present in the BootROM of millions of iOS devices, is arguably the biggest game changer ever in the forensics industry.

Checkm8 is compatible with A5 to A11-based devices; this includes all devices starting from the iPhone 5s up to the iPhone X, as there is no working implementation for 4S hardware.

Before we get into the details, it's useful to understand how the iOS boot procedure works and why the Checkm8 vulnerability cannot be patched.

iOS boot process

The first layer of security in the iOS platform is the **secure boot chain**, which refers to the sequence of steps carried out by the application processor, starting with the loading of the BootROM and ending with the loading of the iOS. This ensures that attackers cannot run a modified operating system or malicious applications on the device. The boot process relies on a **chain of trusts**, which begins from the key that is embedded into hardware during manufacturing.

The boot process of an iOS device can be broken down into five steps: the **BootROM**, the **Low-Level Bootloader (LLB)**, **iBoot**, the **kernel** bootloader, and the main operating system. iOS has a very strict process of booting the operating system, where each stage checks the authenticity of the following stage. This is achieved by digitally *signing* each step of the process. The steps are as follows:

1. When the device is powered on, the processor executes the code in the BootROM, which is a read-only block of memory that's created during the manufacturing process. The BootROM contains the **Apple Root CA** public key, which is used to decrypt the LLB.

2. The LLB is the lowest level of code that can be updated via a software update. It initializes and executes the second-level bootloader called iBoot, after verifying its authenticity. If the verification fails, the device enters recovery mode, or **Device Firmware Upgrade (DFU)** mode, which requires a factory reset to resolve.

3. The iBoot bootloader verifies, loads, and executes the iOS kernel.

4. The kernel loads the system core services and iOS components.

5. The iOS operating system is launched.

The following diagram illustrates the entire process:

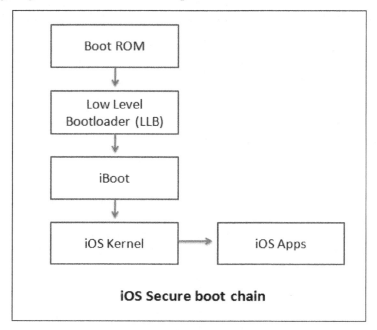

Figure 2.3 – iOS secure boot chain

As you can see, the first step in the boot process is the execution of the code from the device's BootROM. This stage of the process is implicitly trusted because, as its name implies, the BootROM is a read-only memory component that cannot be modified after manufacturing by anyone, not even by Apple.

The Checkm8 exploit is based on a vulnerability that resides within this portion of read-only memory, so this means that Apple has no way of patching it, leaving hundreds of millions of iOS devices vulnerable. To have a better understanding of what a breakthrough this is, keep in mind that the previous BootROM exploit was discovered in 2010!

> **Tip**
>
> If you're interested in the technical details, you can find a full report on the Checkm8 vulnerability at the following link: `https://habr.com/ru/company/dsec/blog/472762/`.

Although Checkm8 allows developers to get around Apple's security and run low-level code on the device's BootROM, Checkm8 is not a jailbreak by itself, as it requires additional software that leverages the exploit to perform a fully fledged jailbreak.

checkra1n

checkra1n is the first publicly available jailbreak based on the Checkm8 vulnerability, and it's the result of the hard work carried out by hackers and security researchers from all over the world. Jailbreaking the device via checkra1n allows users to gain root permissions and install unofficial applications and repositories, such as **Cydia**.

Investigators that are dealing with a device that is vulnerable to Checkm8 have the possibility of jailbreaking the device through checkra1n, thus gaining access to the entire filesystem and successfully performing a full filesystem acquisition.

However, from a forensics perspective, checkra1n definitely has its drawbacks:

- checkra1n requires a Mac or Linux system to apply the jailbreak to an iOS device. Support for Windows is under development, although it is actually possible to run checkra1n from a Windows PC by running a live CD, such as bootra1n.

- Any kind of jailbreak will leave permanent traces on the device due to the modifications that are being made to the filesystem.

- Often additional packages will need to be installed on the device, such as Cydia, **AFC2**, or **SSH**, which make more changes to the filesystem.

Checkm8 acquisitions

In light of these limitations, some vendors have come up with a built-in solution that allows investigators to perform a full filesystem acquisition, exploiting the Checkm8 vulnerability but *without* actually jailbreaking the device.

Currently, this feature is available in some of the most popular forensic tools, including *Cellebrite UFED*, *Elcomsoft iOS Forensic Toolkit*, and *Oxygen Forensic Detective*.

The difference between these solutions and performing a traditional jailbreak through checkra1n is that these tools do not modify the device in any way; the exploit is performed in the device's RAM. Once the acquisition process ends, the device will reboot normally, leaving no traces.

Whenever possible, this should be the preferred method to acquire the full filesystem from an iOS device, as this is definitely the most forensically sound solution.

Agent-based acquisitions

The main drawback in Checkm8 acquisitions is that they're not supported by newer devices like the **iPhone 12** or the **iPhone 13**, as these devices are not vulnerable to the Checkm8 exploit.

In 2020, vendors responded to these limitations by providing an alternative method to extract the full filesystem from any iOS device, including the latest iPhone 12; this solution relies on installing an extraction agent that will exploit software vulnerabilities, gain access to the entire filesystem, and establish a secure connection between the device and the computer.

Although this method requires installing an application (**the agent**) on the device, this is considered forensically safe, as the agent leaves a drastically smaller footprint compared to other solutions, like jailbreaking the device. The only traces left on the device are some minor changes in system log files; however, because of this, depending on your jurisdiction, you may need authorization or legal authority to use this method.

The following is a list of requirements to use this method:

- Supported iOS devices: all devices starting from the iPhone 5s up to iPhone 12.
- Supported iOS versions: iOS 9.0 through to iOS 14.3.
- Using an **Apple ID** registered in Apple's Developer Program is strongly recommended for installing the agent on the device, as this relieves the need to open internet access on the device.

Currently, *Elcomsoft iOS Forensic Toolkit* and *Belkasoft Evidence Center X* are the only tools that provide agent-based extraction capabilities.

Jailbreaking the device

Finally, let's talk about jailbreaks! We've seen how it's possible to extract a full filesystem from an iOS device by exploiting the Checkm8 vulnerability or by performing an agent-based acquisition. However, as we've learned, both these methods have their limitations, and there could be some cases where jailbreaking the device is your only option to perform a filesystem acquisition.

Applying a jailbreak will leave some permanent traces on the device, so this option should only be considered as a last resort and only if you have the legal authority to do so.

At the moment, the most popular jailbreaks are **checkra1n** and **unc0ver**. Both these jailbreaks allow investigators to install third-party tools such as SSH, which will give unrestricted access to the device's filesystem.

In the following table, you can check the compatibility for both these jailbreaks:

	checkra1n	**unc0ver**
iPhone 6/6 Plus/6s/6s Plus	iOS 8–12.5 ✓	iOS 11–12.5 ✓
iPhone SE	iOS 9–14.8 ✓	iOS 11–14.3 ✓
iPhone 7/7 Plus	iOS 10–14.8 ✓	iOS 11–14.3 ✓
iPhone 8/8 Plus	iOS 11–14.8 ✓	iOS 11–14.3 ✓
iPhone X	iOS 11–14.8 ✓	iOS 11–14.3 ✓
iPhone XR	✗	iOS 12–14.3 ✓
iPhone XS/XS Max	✗	iOS 12–14.3 ✓
iPhone 11/11 Pro/11 Pro Max	✗	iOS 13–14.3 ✓
iPhone 12/12 Pro/12 Pro Max	✗	iOS 14–14.3 ✓
iPhone 13	✗	✗

Jailbreaking with checkra1n

Previously in this chapter, we introduced checkra1n and we learned about its features and limitations. We'll now take a deep dive and learn how to actually perform the jailbreak:

1. The first step is to head to checkra1n's official webpage and download the required tool. You can download the latest version from `https://checkra.in`.

2. Once you have downloaded the file, run it and plug in the device. Make sure you use a USB-A cable, as currently there is no support for USB-C cables.

3. When the main window loads, check that the device is recognized. If your device is running an A11 processor, you will need to head into **Options** and then enable the **Skip A11 BPR Check** option.

    If your device runs iOS 14.6 or later, you will need to head into **Options** and then enable **Allow Untested Versions**:

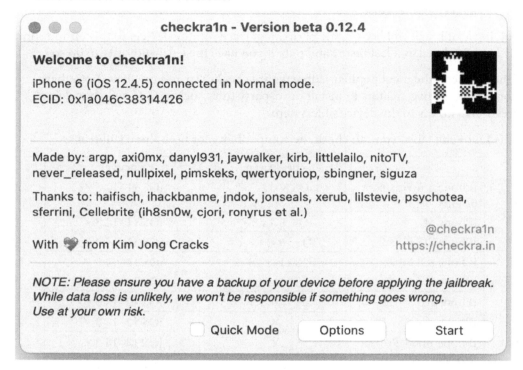

Figure 2.4 – The main checkra1n screen

4. When you're ready, click **Start**. The device will reboot into recovery mode automatically.

5. You will now be presented with instructions on how to reboot the device into DFU mode. Follow the instructions until your device shows a black screen:

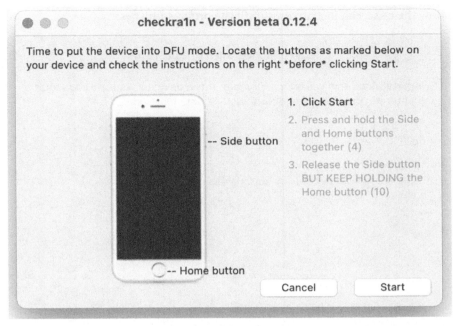

Figure 2.5 – Follow the instructions to put the device in DFU mode

6. At this point, checkra1n will begin the jailbreak process. The device will boot PongoOS and should look like this:

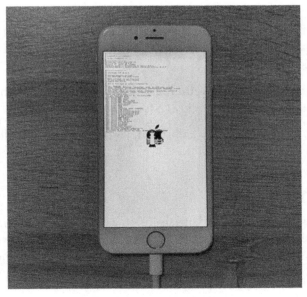

Figure 2.6 – The device booting PongoOS

7.   Follow the onscreen instructions until the process finishes:

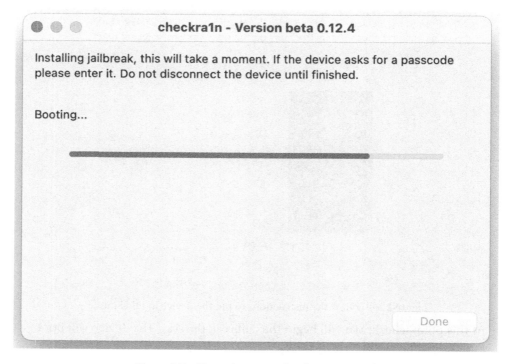

Figure 2.7 – Enter the passcode when requested

When the device reboots, you will find the checkra1n icon. Launching that application will allow you to install Cydia. Once Cydia is installed, you can proceed to install any third-party packages, such as SSH.

Remember that checkra1n is a **semi-tethered jailbreak**; if you reboot the device, you will have to jailbreak it again using the checkra1n tool.

Once the device has been successfully jailbroken, you can perform a full filesystem acquisition using the tool of your choice.

Triaging the device

When you're dealing with iOS devices, it's useful to gather some information directly from the device prior to starting the acquisition process. Knowing what iOS version is running on the device, for instance, can be useful to determine what the best acquisition method is. For this purpose, we're going to use `libimobiledevice`.

The `libimobiledevice` library is a cross-platform library that allows users to communicate with an iOS device using their native protocol to provide access to the device's filesystem, including information about the device and its internals. It works with all devices, including the most recent ones.

The first step is to head to `http://libimobiledevice.org`, where the library can be downloaded for free. If you're running Windows, instead of downloading the source files and compiling them, you can download precompiled binaries from the project's GitHub repository.

If you're running macOS, you can install the library simply by running the following command from the terminal:

```
brew install libimobiledevice
```

If you're running a Linux distribution that supports the `apt` packet manager, you can install the library by running the following command:

```
sudo apt-get install usbmuxd libimobiledevice6
libimobiledevice-utils
```

Once you have installed the library, connect the device to your forensic workstation and run the following command from the terminal:

```
ideviceinfo
```

This command will connect to the device, parse data relevant to the hardware and software, and display it on screen. Keep in mind that the device will have to be paired with the host system by entering the passcode. If you're running Linux or macOS, you can combine the previous command with the `grep` command to view some key data:

- **Identifying the device model**:

  You can read the device model by running the following command:

  ```
  ideviceinfo | grep ModelNumber
  ```

- **Identifying the iOS version**:

  To identify what version of iOS the device is running, you can run the following command:

  ```
  ideviceinfo | grep ProductVersion
  ```

- **Identifying the device serial number**:

  The device's serial number can be parsed by running the following command:

  ```
  ideviceinfo | grep SerialNumber
  ```

- **Identifying the phone number**:

  Finally, to identify the phone number related to the SIM card in the device, run the following command:

  ```
  ideviceinfo | grep PhoneNumber
  ```

Deciding the best acquisition method

Once the device has been seized, it has been correctly isolated, and you have identified the hardware model and iOS version, the next step in the examination process is assessing what the best acquisition method is to extract the richest dataset from the device while preserving **data integrity**.

Generally speaking, you'll want to keep these two concepts in mind before performing any actions on the device:

- Acquire evidence by order of **volatility**.
- Acquire evidence, starting with the less intrusive method.

The first step in any acquisition process is determining the volatility of the data of interest; for example, if the scope of the investigation is to extract photos from a device or parse text messages, clearly this doesn't pose any kind of concern because this data is written on the flash memory, it isn't volatile, and any acquisition method will extract these artifacts. However, if the investigation seeks to understand how the device was used, or if there was any human interaction on a particular date and time, or where the device was located a few days ago, these artifacts are much more volatile, as log files and databases on iOS devices are constantly overwritten. For instance, location data is generally maintained on the device for several weeks; however, *precise* location data, including cell tower data, is only maintained for a few days. In this case, we'll want to extract this kind of data as soon as possible before it gets overwritten. This means performing a full filesystem acquisition (if possible) before anything else, as logical acquisitions do not contain this data.

The investigator should have a clear understanding of how forensic tools work and what impact they have on data and on the device itself:

- Anything you decide to do (including nothing!) will have an impact on the device.
- What impact will your actions have on the data?

- Does the chosen acquisition method require a device reboot?

- Will artifacts of interest survive a device reboot?

- How long are artifacts stored on the device before being overwritten?

- What files or folders will be affected by a jailbreak?

- What changes will occur by running a Checkm8 acquisition?

- What changes will occur by performing an agent-based acquisition?

A logical acquisition will have virtually no impact on the device, so most often, this will be your first choice. If the device is vulnerable to Checkm8 and if you have tools that can perform this kind of acquisition, a Checkm8 acquisition will be the best option to gain access to the entire filesystem without making any changes to the device. If this is not an option, the next step would be considering an agent-based acquisition. Finally, as a last resort, jailbreaking the device will give the investigator access to the entire filesystem, but make sure you understand how this will affect the device and its data.

Performing a logical acquisition

Now that we've learned the theory, it's time to put it into practice by performing our first logical acquisition.

Almost all forensic tools can perform a logical acquisition; we'll concentrate on two of the most popular ones, Cellebrite UFED and Elcomsoft iOS Forensic Toolkit.

Cellebrite UFED is considered the industry standard, as it allows investigators to perform a variety of different acquisitions, including a traditional logical acquisition, a partial filesystem, a full filesystem acquisition through Checkm8, and a full filesystem acquisition from devices that have been jailbroken.

Elcomsoft iOS Forensic Toolkit, on the other hand, can perform logical acquisitions, a full filesystem acquisition from jailbroken devices, full filesystem acquisitions through agent-based extractions, and it also supports physical acquisitions from older devices.

Logical acquisition with Cellebrite UFED

In this example, we'll acquire an iPhone 6 running iOS 12:

1. The first step is to launch Cellebrite UFED and choose **Mobile device** from the main screen:

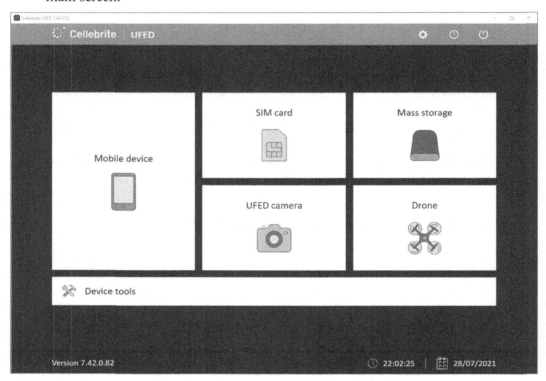

Figure 2.8 – The home screen of Cellebrite UFED

2. Next, select the **AUTO DETECT** option or choose the device model using the search function in the upper-left part of the screen:

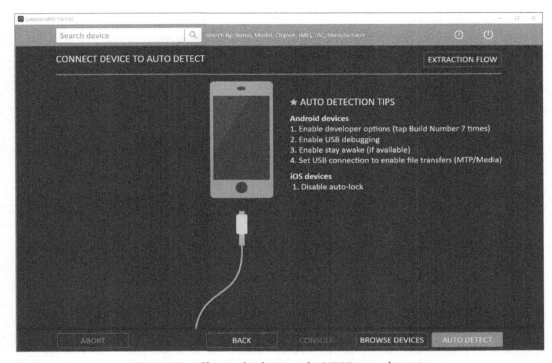

Figure 2.9 – Choose the device or let UFED auto-detect it

3. Once the device is recognized, UFED will show the available acquisition methods depending on the iPhone model. Choose the **Logical (Partial)** acquisition to continue:

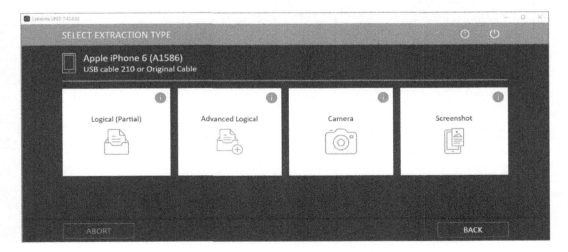

Figure 2.10 – Choose the type of acquisition

4. One of the best features of Cellebrite UFED is that it will allow you to select what data you want to extract. This will greatly speed up the extraction process, allowing you to access useful evidence within minutes. Select the artifacts that should be extracted and click **Next** to start the acquisition process:

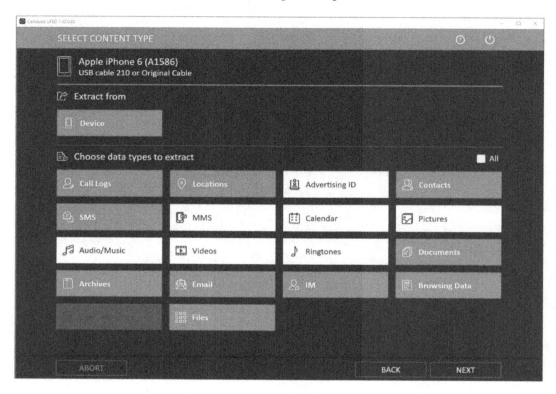

Figure 2.11 – Choose what artifacts should be extracted

5. To perform a logical acquisition, the device must be unlocked. Consider disabling **Auto-lock** from the device's settings. You should also **Trust** the computer when the device prompts you for the pairing request:

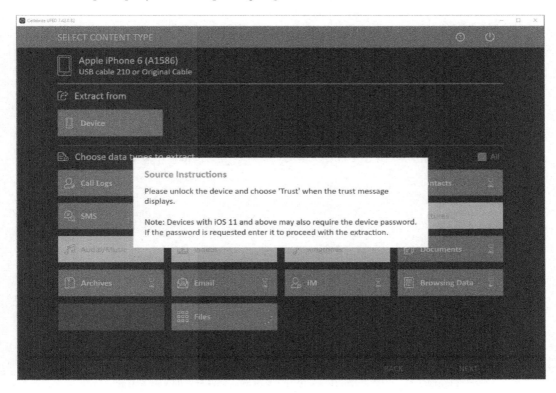

Figure 2.12 – Establish pairing between the workstation and the device

6. Wait for the task to finish successfully. The extraction summary will give you an idea of what data was extracted and how many artifacts were found:

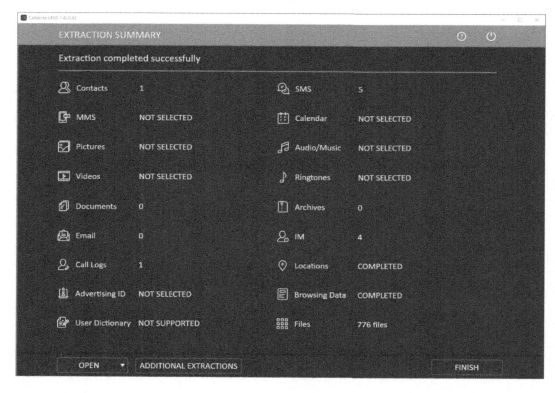

Figure 2.13 – The extraction summary displays what data was extracted

You can view the extracted data by loading the logical acquisition into a forensic tool, such as Belkasoft Evidence Center X, Elcomsoft Phone Viewer, or Cellebrite Physical Analyzer.

Logical acquisition with Elcomsoft iOS Forensic Toolkit

Another great tool to perform acquisitions from iOS devices is the forensic toolkit by Elcomsoft. This toolkit has been specially designed for iOS devices and offers some unique features, such as agent-based extractions. The steps for this are as follows:

1. Launch Elcomsoft iOS Forensic Toolkit and check whether the device is correctly recognized. As you can see from the following screenshot, the tool is divided into four sections, which each deal with different acquisition processes. In our example, we want to acquire a logical image and the device is not jailbroken, so we're going to choose the **Backup** option, which will perform a logical acquisition:

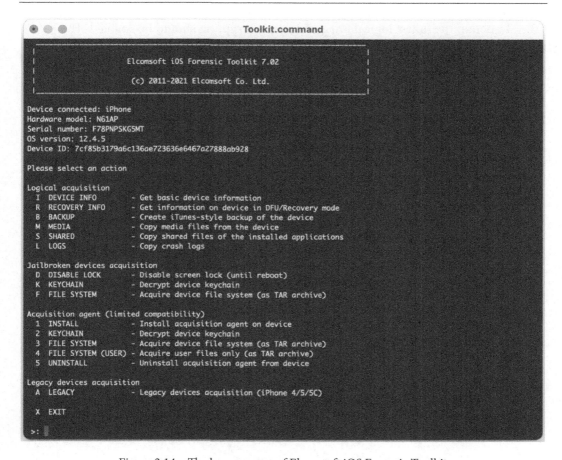

Figure 2.14 – The home screen of Elcomsoft iOS Forensic Toolkit

2. Choose the folder where the backup should be stored:

Figure 2.15 – Choose where the backup should be stored

3. To obtain the fullest logical image, backup encryption should be enabled. The toolkit will automatically detect whether encryption is enabled and, if it's not, it will enable it by setting the password to `123`. Backup encryption will be disabled at the end of the acquisition process:

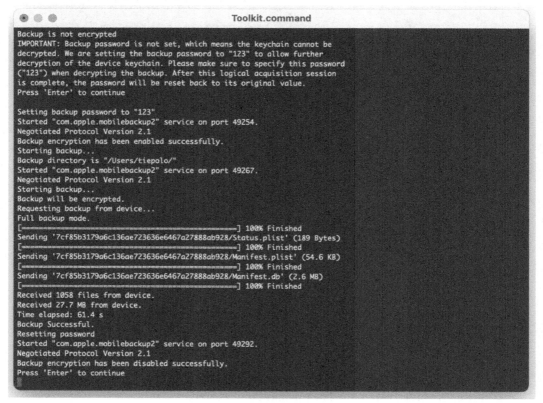

Figure 2.16 – The toolkit will show progress and debug information on screen

At the end, the toolkit will give you a summary of the acquisition process. The extracted files can now be examined using the forensic tool of your choice.

We've seen how to perform logical acquisitions using two different tools. Keep in mind that there are a variety of different tools that can perform this kind of acquisition, including free tools. In the next section, we'll learn how to perform a full filesystem acquisition.

Performing a filesystem acquisition

In the first part of this chapter, we learned that a full filesystem acquisition is generally the best way to extract the largest number of artifacts from an iOS device and that this acquisition can be carried out by jailbreaking the device, exploiting the Checkm8 vulnerability, or by performing an agent-based acquisition.

We'll now put this into practice by performing a Checkm8 full filesystem acquisition using Cellebrite UFED, which has a built-in Checkm8 solution. Then, we'll perform an agent-based acquisition using Elcomsoft iOS Forensic Toolkit.

Both acquisitions provide the same result: an image of the entire filesystem. Checkm8 acquisitions can be considered forensically sound and represent the best option, although newer devices are not compatible with this method. On the other hand, agent-based acquisitions require you to install an application on the device, which will make some minor changes to system log files, but this solution is compatible with newer devices, such as the iPhone 12.

Checkm8 full filesystem acquisition using Cellebrite UFED

Cellebrite UFED features a built-in solution to perform Checkm8 acquisitions, so the entire process is made extremely easy by simply following the onscreen instructions:

1. The first step is to launch Cellebrite UFED and select **Mobile device** from the main menu. Then, choose the device model from the search option or use **AUTO DETECT** to detect it automatically. Keep in mind that you will need to use a USB-A cable to perform the full filesystem acquisition.

2. Select **Advanced Logical** and then choose the **Full File System (checkm8)** option. The other options can be used to obtain a partial filesystem or a full filesystem extraction from jailbroken devices:

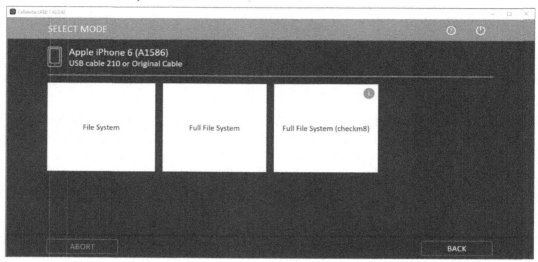

Figure 2.17 – Choose the Full File System (checkm8) option

3. Next, the device must be powered off. Once it's off, you'll want to enter **Recovery mode** and from there put the device in **DFU mode**. The onscreen instructions are pretty accurate, but, basically, once the device is off, you should press and hold the **Home** button while connecting the device. This will put the device in **Recovery mode**. From there, press both the **Power** button and the **Home** button for 10 seconds and then release the **Power** button, while keeping the **Home** button pressed for a few more seconds. This procedure may vary depending on the device model. Once the device enters DFU mode, the **Continue** button will light up:

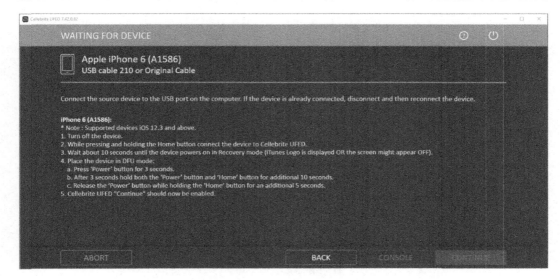

Figure 2.18 – UFED will display instructions on how to enter Recovery and DFU modes

4. At this point, UFED will exploit the device by leveraging the Checkm8 vulnerability. This could take a few minutes. The entire procedure is performed in the device's volatile memory, so no changes will occur on the device itself, and it will boot back to normal at the end of the acquisition process:

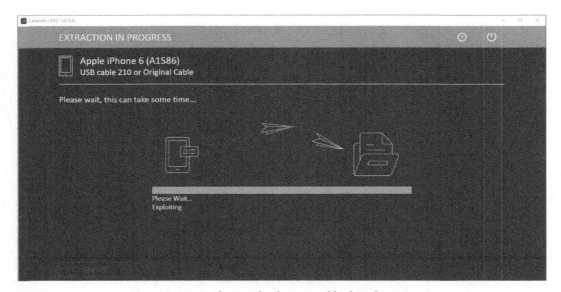

Figure 2.19 – Exploiting the device could take a few minutes

5. Once the device has been successfully exploited, the acquisition stage will start, and the device will display a progress indicator:

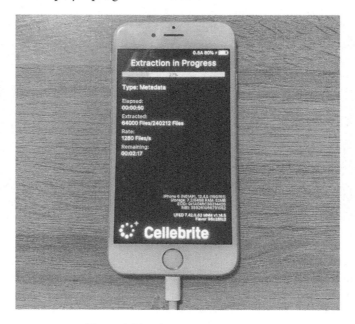

Figure 2.20 – Acquisition in process

6. The full filesystem will be imaged and archived in a DAR file, which is similar to a TAR archive:

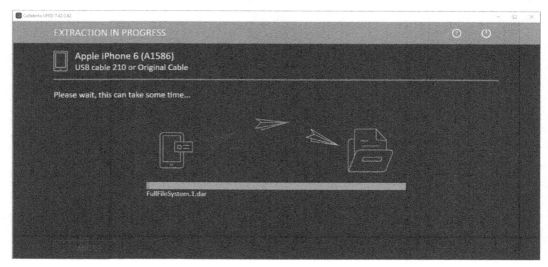

Figure 2.21 – The extraction will be archived in a DAR file

When the acquisition process ends, the device will automatically reboot normally. The resulting DAR archive can be analyzed by importing it into Cellebrite Physical Analyzer or the tool of your choice.

Agent-based full filesystem acquisition

Elcomsoft iOS Forensic Toolkit is one of the few tools that supports agent-based acquisitions. As this method requires sideloading an application (the agent) onto the device, you'll need an Apple ID. On the Windows version, you'll need an Apple Developer ID, while on macOS, you can use a traditional account:

1. To start, launch the toolkit and check that the device is correctly recognized:

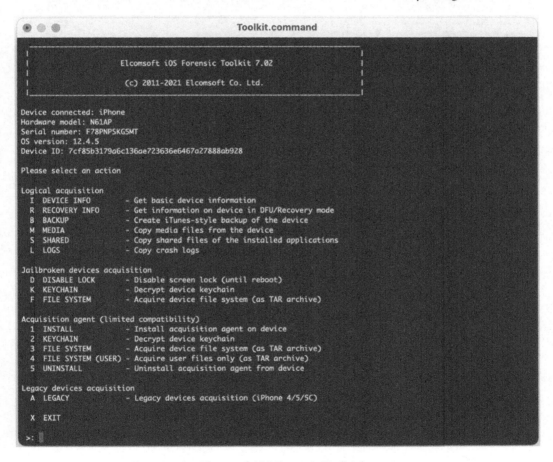

Figure 2.22 – Elcomsoft iOS Forensic Toolkit home screen

2. From the menu, choose option **1**, which will install the agent on the device. You will be asked to provide Apple ID credentials and you will have to pass two-factor authentication. Then, the agent will be signed in with your Apple ID and installed on the device:

Figure 2.23 – Installing the agent onto the device

3. Once the agent has been successfully installed, launch the application on the device. Now, to extract the keychain, choose option **2** from the toolkit.

4. When the keychain extraction process finishes, you can proceed to extract the full filesystem. Generally, you will want to choose option **4**, which will extract the user partition:

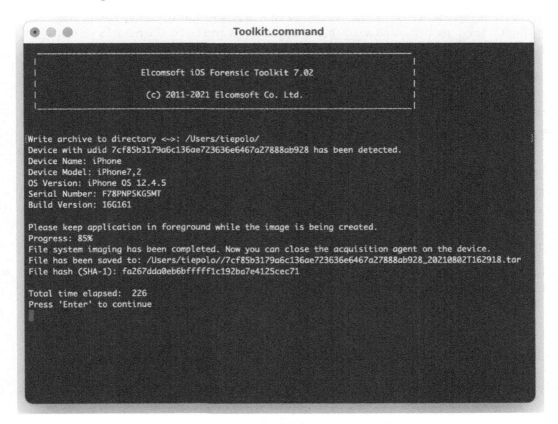

```
                    Elcomsoft iOS Forensic Toolkit 7.02

                        (c) 2011-2021 Elcomsoft Co. Ltd.


Write archive to directory <~>: /Users/tiepolo/
Device with udid 7cf85b3179a6c136ae723636e6467a27888ab928 has been detected.
Device Name: iPhone
Device Model: iPhone7,2
OS Version: iPhone OS 12.4.5
Serial Number: F78PNPSKG5MT
Build Version: 16G161

Please keep application in foreground while the image is being created.
Progress: 85%
File system imaging has been completed. Now you can close the acquisition agent on the device.
File has been saved to: /Users/tiepolo//7cf85b3179a6c136ae723636e6467a27888ab928_20210802T162918.tar
File hash (SHA-1): fa267dda0eb6bfffff1c192ba7e4125cec71

Total time elapsed:  226
Press 'Enter' to continue
```

Figure 2.24 – Acquiring the full filesystem using the agent

5. The filesystem image will be archived in a TAR file. When the process finishes, choose option **5** to uninstall the agent.

That concludes our filesystem acquisition!

Both Checkm8-based acquisitions and agent-based acquisitions are a complete breakthrough, as they allow forensically sound extractions of the entire filesystem, including all files related to third-party apps. As you've learned, a full filesystem will contain so much more data compared to a logical extraction. In the following chapters, we'll delve into these files and learn how to analyze them to gain meaningful evidence.

Summary

In this chapter, we learned the differences between acquisition methods and what kind of data we can expect to find in an iOS extraction. We learned how the Checkm8 exploit works, how this vulnerability can be used to gain access to a device's filesystem, and its limits. Then, we discussed agent-based acquisitions and learned what iOS versions support this acquisition.

Jailbreaks are a fascinating topic in the iOS world; we discussed two of the most popular ones, checkra1n and unc0ver, and their compatibility. Then, we learned how to jailbreak a device using checkra1n.

Finally, we learned how to perform a logical acquisition using Cellebrite UFED and Elcomsoft iOS Forensic Toolkit, and we approached two different options to perform a full filesystem acquisition.

Keep in mind that in this chapter, we focused on **After First Unlock (AFU)** acquisition methods, so it's imperative that the examiner has full access to the device. Over the course of the next chapters, we will look into **Before First Unlock (BFU)** acquisition methods to understand what kind of artifacts we can find in locked devices.

In the next chapter, we will discuss forensic tools, which ones are most popular, and how to use these to analyze extracted data.

Section 2 – iOS Data Analysis

In part two, you will learn where to find key artifacts and how to examine them to find meaningful information. By the end of this part, you will know how to analyze user and system data from a device.

This part of the book comprises the following chapters:

- *Chapter 3, Using Forensic Tools*
- *Chapter 4, Working with Common iOS Artifacts*
- *Chapter 5, Pattern-of-Life Forensics*
- *Chapter 6, Dissecting Location Data*
- *Chapter 7, Analyzing Connectivity Data*
- *Chapter 8, Email and Messaging Forensics*
- *Chapter 9, Photo, Video, and Audio Forensics*
- *Chapter 10, Analyzing Third-Party Apps*
- *Chapter 11, Locked Devices, iTunes Backups, and Cloud Forensics*

3
Using Forensic Tools

In the previous chapter, we learned all about the different acquisition techniques and how to use forensic tools to extract data from iOS devices. In this chapter, we will learn which are the most popular tools for data analysis, and their features and limitations.

Although using forensic tools for data analysis is not strictly required since theoretically it is possible to examine files manually, using these tools has many advantages. The most evident benefit of using forensic tools compared to manually parsing artifacts is time: if used correctly, these tools are huge time savers as they're programmed to automatically search for relevant files, look for patterns, analyze known data structures, and extract meaningful insights from common artifacts. Using the appropriate tools ensures that precious artifacts are not missed, although the investigator should always validate the output of such tools and know their limitations. There are no perfect forensic tools – every tool has its flaws! Most tools allow investigators to examine third-party applications as well as system apps, and can also be configured to automatically perform custom data carving on such applications.

In this chapter, we will cover the following topics:

- Understanding forensic tools
- Working with Cellebrite Physical Analyzer
- Working with Magnet AXIOM
- Using open source tools

Understanding forensic tools

Once the iOS device and the evidence stored within it have been successfully seized, preserved, and extracted through a forensically sound acquisition process, the next steps involve processing and analyzing the extracted data.

Currently, there are a number of commercial tools available on the market that perform data analysis, such as *Cellebrite Physical Analyzer, Oxygen Forensic Detective, Magnet AXIOM, Belkasoft Evidence Center, MSAB XRY, EnCase Forensic*, and many others. In this chapter, we'll work with two of these tools, **Cellebrite Physical Analyzer** and **Magnet AXIOM**.

We've already seen how mobile forensics presents several additional challenges compared to digital forensics, and one significant difference has to do with how data extracted from iOS devices is analyzed; with mobile device forensics, using a single tool to process and analyze the evidence is extremely risky, as one solution will not provide all the tools that support all devices and all iOS versions. Generally speaking, forensic tools work by parsing files of interest (such as SQLite databases, plists, and log files) and running a series of **plugins** on these files that look for key evidence in predefined locations. What this means is that more recent applications may not be supported because if there isn't a plugin for a given app, forensic tools will not automatically display data for that application! No one tool can process and analyze all artifacts from every mobile device.

To choose the best tools for your purpose, you need to know the following:

- Where the tool will search for data
- What a tool is doing to the extracted data
- How the tool will represent the data

For instance, iOS devices sometimes compress log files into archives to save space on disk. If your tool does not automatically extract files from archives that are found in an iOS extraction, you could be missing some key evidence. Make sure you understand exactly what files your tool parses and what files it doesn't.

Tool validation

Once the investigator has assessed which tool is the best fit for a particular scenario, the tool and its output should be **validated** before starting the examination process. Validating a tool is the process of determining through testing that it performs in a certain way and that the results are consistent.

In particular, the investigator should verify the following:

- The tool does not alter the data in any way.

- The data provided by the tool is consistent with what is displayed on the device.

- The data represented by the tool is consistent with what you find in the source file of that particular piece of data.

- The results are consistent among different forensic tools.

Validation is increasingly important when dealing with unsupported third-party applications or **Unidentified Forensic Objects (UFOs)**, as some tools have some built-in features that use heuristics to attempt data extraction from these artifacts, but sometimes the results can be incomplete or inconsistent.

> **Tip**
> One of the most common ways to get to know your tools and validate their output is by using them to analyze a known device, such as your personal iPhone. Use your device to perform normal day-to-day activity and take notes. Then, extract and analyze data from the device using several tools and check that it gets reported correctly.

Although forensic tools will greatly aid the investigator by speeding up the entire process, this software should not substitute the process of manually viewing and assessing the files that were extracted in the acquisition process.

Working with Cellebrite Physical Analyzer

Cellebrite software is generally regarded as the golden standard for mobile forensics among law enforcement and security organizations due to its powerful features, wide device compatibility, frequent updates, and easy-to-use user interface. Their most popular tools are **Cellebrite Universal Forensic Extraction Device (Cellebrite UFED)**, which we used in the previous chapter to acquire the device's filesystem, and **Cellebrite Physical Analyzer**, which is used for data analysis and reporting.

We will now learn how to import the extracted data into Physical Analyzer and then we'll go over some of the main features of this powerful tool.

Loading evidence and selective decoding

The first step in a Physical Analyzer examination is loading the evidence into the tool. You can accomplish this by using the **case wizard**, which is a step-by-step procedure that will guide you through the process and also show you some optional features that can be enabled. One of these is **selective decoding**, which allows investigators to perform faster parsing and analysis by selecting specific applications or specific categories that should be parsed in addition to common system artifacts. This is especially useful when you're dealing with devices that have dozens of installed applications, but you only need to parse very specific artifacts that pertain to a few of these apps.

Let's see how this works:

1. From Physical Analyzer's menu, choose **File | Open case** to bring up the case wizard.

2. The next step involves choosing which files to load depending on the type of acquisition that was performed. If you acquired the device using Cellebrite UFED, choose **Add | Load extraction** and select the *UFDX* or *UFD* file that was created by Cellebrite UFED. If you used a different forensic tool and performed a filesystem acquisition, choose **Add | GreyKey** and point it to the folder or archive where the extracted data is stored. Finally, if you performed a logical acquisition, choose **Add | Common source | Backup** and select the folder that contains your **iTunes** backup. Then, click **Next** to continue:

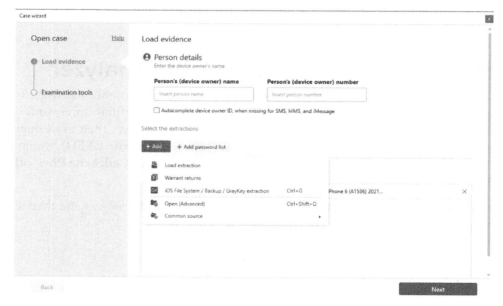

Figure 3.1 – Open the case wizard and add the folder or file that contains your data

3. In the next screen, the case wizard will display a set of examination tools that can be enabled by selecting their checkbox. Enabling parsing of **archives** can be useful to recover data from log files that have been compressed and archived by iOS; however, keep in mind that this will increase decoding time. In this example, we're going to use selective decoding to speed up the decoding process, so enable this tool and click on **Examine data** to start the process:

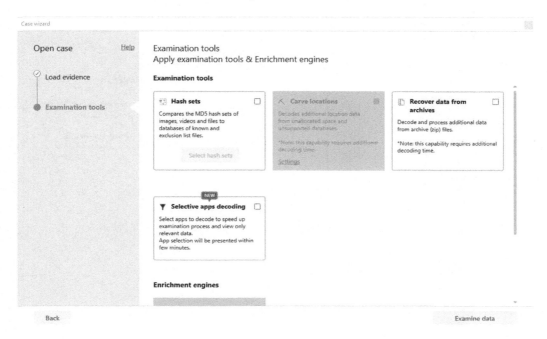

Figure 3.2 – The case wizard also allows you to enable specific examination tools

4. At this point, Physical Analyzer will scan for applications available on the device, and when it's done scanning, a list will appear with several filtration options – for example, from the **Social networking** category, we can choose to only parse **Telegram Messenger** and **WhatsApp Messenger** by checking the boxes. When you've finished, click **Continue** to start the decoding process:

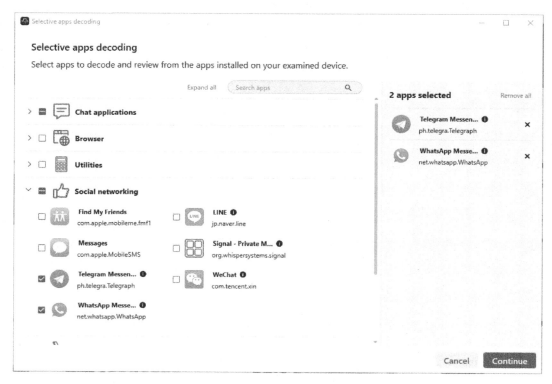

Figure 3.3 – Choose which applications should be decoded

5. When the process finishes, the **Extraction Summary** pane will be displayed, which shows some key data on the device and a list of all the artifacts divided into categories:

Figure 3.4 – Extraction Summary

Now that we have loaded and decoded the data, we will see how to view the decoded data.

Viewing decoded data

Once the extraction has been loaded and Physical Analyzer has successfully decoded the data, it's time to start digging into the artifacts to look for evidence.

One of the most useful features of this tool is that for every artifact, it will display a source link that will give the investigator an immediate understanding of *where* that data was found. For example, from **Extraction Summary**, take a look at the **Device Info** section:

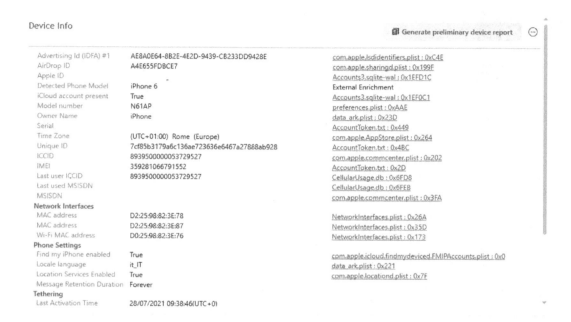

Figure 3.5 – The Device Info section gives the investigator some key data on the device

On the left side, you will find several useful artifacts, such as **Apple ID**, the device **Serial** number, and **Time Zone**. For each of these, on the right side of the screen, you will see the source, represented as the name of the file where that data was found. You can validate the output provided by the tool simply by clicking on the source file, which will open the relevant file, allowing you to double-check whether the result is consistent with the file contents.

When you're working on an examination and you want to quickly locate any artifact, you can start by looking at the **project tree**; you can find it from the menu on the left side of the screen by clicking on **Analyzed Data**. Within the project tree, you will find all the categories of data that were decoded by Physical Analyzer, allowing you to quickly get down to specific data without having to scroll through thousands of artifacts to find what you need.

For example, if we're interested in data from **Wi-Fi**, we can select the **Devices & Networks** category and then get more granular data by clicking on **Wireless Networks**:

Figure 3.6 – The project tree displays all decoded data grouped into categories

We have now successfully learned how to view the decoded data.

Using the AppGenie

Although Physical Analyzer does a pretty good job of decoding all sorts of artifacts from extraction, it may happen that there are some applications that are not parsed at all, or maybe data is only partially recovered. In such cases, using a built-in tool called the **AppGenie** can help recover more data.

The AppGenie is a research tool that parses through third-party applications, extracting additional data based on **sophisticated heuristics**. By running the AppGenie on unparsed applications, the investigator can gain access to a lot more data, such as **chats**, **contacts**, **user accounts**, **logs**, and **locations**.

Even though the AppGenie can be a great solution to quickly triage an app, it's important to understand its limits; the results provided by this tool should not be trusted blindly! The investigator should use the output provided by the AppGenie as a starting point to conduct further manual carving by examining the source files.

Let's see how we can get more data using this tool:

1. From the extraction summary, click on the **View all** button from the application's insights section:

Figure 3.7 – Physical Analyzer extraction summary

2. You will see a list of installed applications. Select the apps for which you require more data and click on the **Run AppGenie** button at the bottom of the pane:

Figure 3.8 – A list of applications installed on the device

3.   The following screen reminds you that the AppGenie is a research tool and that you *must* validate the results by manually digging into the source files:

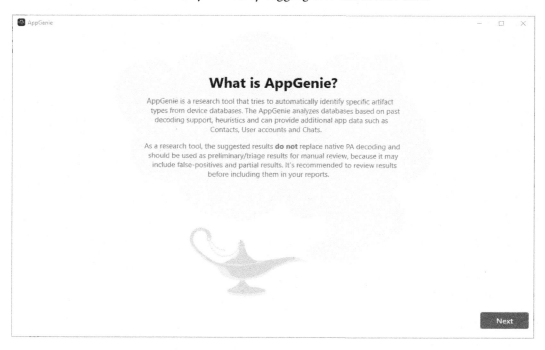

Figure 3.9 – A reminder that validation is required

4.   The final screen gives you a summary of which apps were selected for additional parsing. Click the **Start** button to make the App Genie do its magic:

Figure 3.10 – A summary of applications that should be parsed by the AppGenie

5. Once the AppGenie is done, any extracted data will be added to the project tree in the category called **AppGenie Analyzed Data**.

As you've seen in this brief introduction, Cellebrite Physical Analyzer makes browsing through thousands of artifacts a straightforward task; all data is categorized and easily accessible directly from the examination summary, and the AppGenie can help uncover unparsed evidence.

An in-depth look at all Physical Analyzer's features is beyond the scope of this chapter, so make sure you take the time to fully explore this tool and get familiar with all the rest of its useful features, such as **keyword searching**, **evidence tagging, Python scripts, and built-in reporting capabilities**.

Working with Magnet AXIOM

Magnet AXIOM is one of the most popular tools for digital forensics. It supports both computer forensics and mobile forensics, with complete support for almost all Android and iOS devices. The software has two modules, **AXIOM Process** and **AXIOM Examine**. The first module is responsible for acquiring evidence from a device or loading an existing extraction, and performs data parsing and decoding. When the decoding process is done, you can use AXIOM Examine to review all recovered artifacts and analyze the data.

Loading evidence and on-the-fly processing

One of the key features of Magnet AXIOM is that it allows investigators to start analyzing artifacts while the data is being processed. This is a life-saving feature in all those circumstances where time is a critical factor and evidence needs to be reviewed as soon as possible.

In the following example, we'll learn how to load an existing filesystem extraction from an iOS device into AXIOM Process and how to use AXIOM Examine to locate key artifacts:

1. The first step in the examination is creating a new case within AXIOM Process. Launch the application and fill in the case details. Then, click **GO TO EVIDENCE SOURCES**:

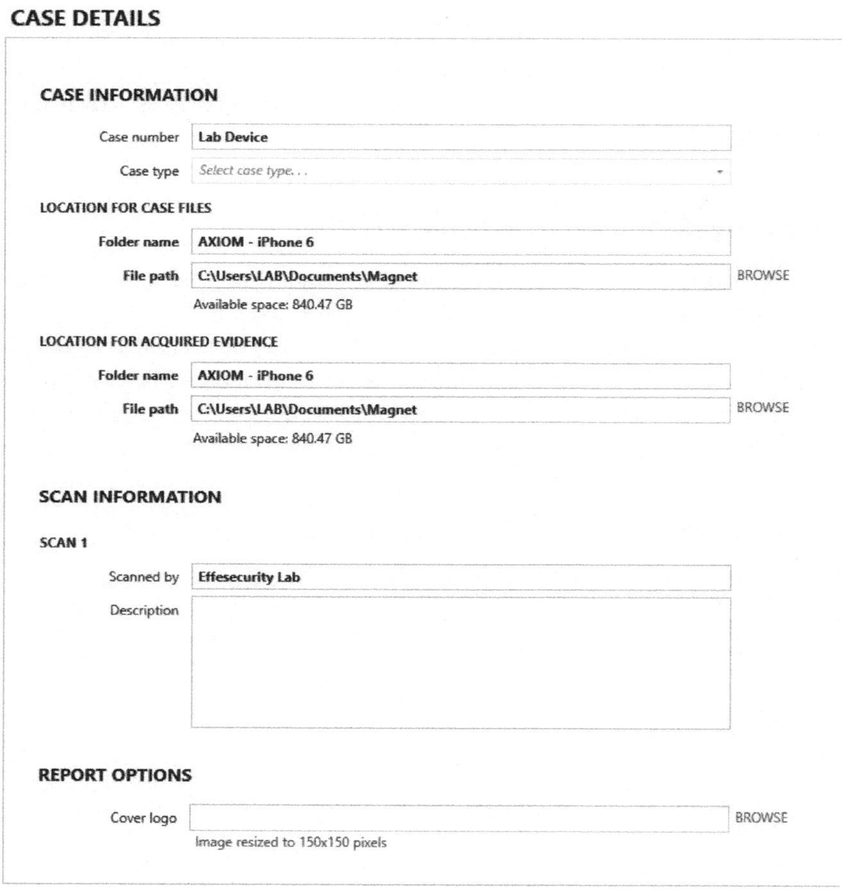

CASE DETAILS

CASE INFORMATION

Case number	Lab Device
Case type	Select case type...

LOCATION FOR CASE FILES

Folder name	AXIOM - iPhone 6	
File path	C:\Users\LAB\Documents\Magnet	BROWSE
	Available space: 840.47 GB	

LOCATION FOR ACQUIRED EVIDENCE

Folder name	AXIOM - iPhone 6	
File path	C:\Users\LAB\Documents\Magnet	BROWSE
	Available space: 840.47 GB	

SCAN INFORMATION

SCAN 1

Scanned by	Effesecurity Lab
Description	

REPORT OPTIONS

Cover logo		BROWSE
	Image resized to 150x150 pixels	

Figure 3.11 – Fill in the case details

2. The next step is selecting the evidence source. In this case, we're analyzing an iOS device, so choose **MOBILE** and then **IOS**:

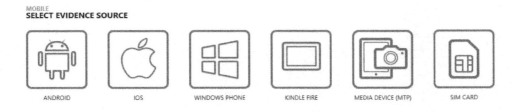

Figure 3.12 – Select the evidence source

3. Since we've already acquired the device in the previous chapter, select **LOAD EVIDENCE** and then **IMAGE**, and locate the file that contains the extracted data:

Figure 3.13 – Choose the file or folder that contains the extraction

4. Once you've added all evidence sources to the case, click on **GO TO PROCESSING DETAILS** to continue:

Figure 3.14 – The EVIDENCE SOURCES screen displays all data sources for the case

The **PROCESSING DETAILS** view allows the investigator to enable additional decoding tools, such as any **keywords** that should be searched or **archive parsing**. To make sure you get the richest possible dataset, you may want to enable the **SEARCH ARCHIVES AND MOBILE BACKUPS** option, although this will require additional decoding time. If the device contains third-party apps that aren't supported by Magnet AXIOM, you can enable the **Dynamic App Finder** (**DAF**) and configure custom artifacts to parse unsupported apps. Once you've configured the tools according to your preference, click on **GO TO ARTIFACT DETAILS** to continue:

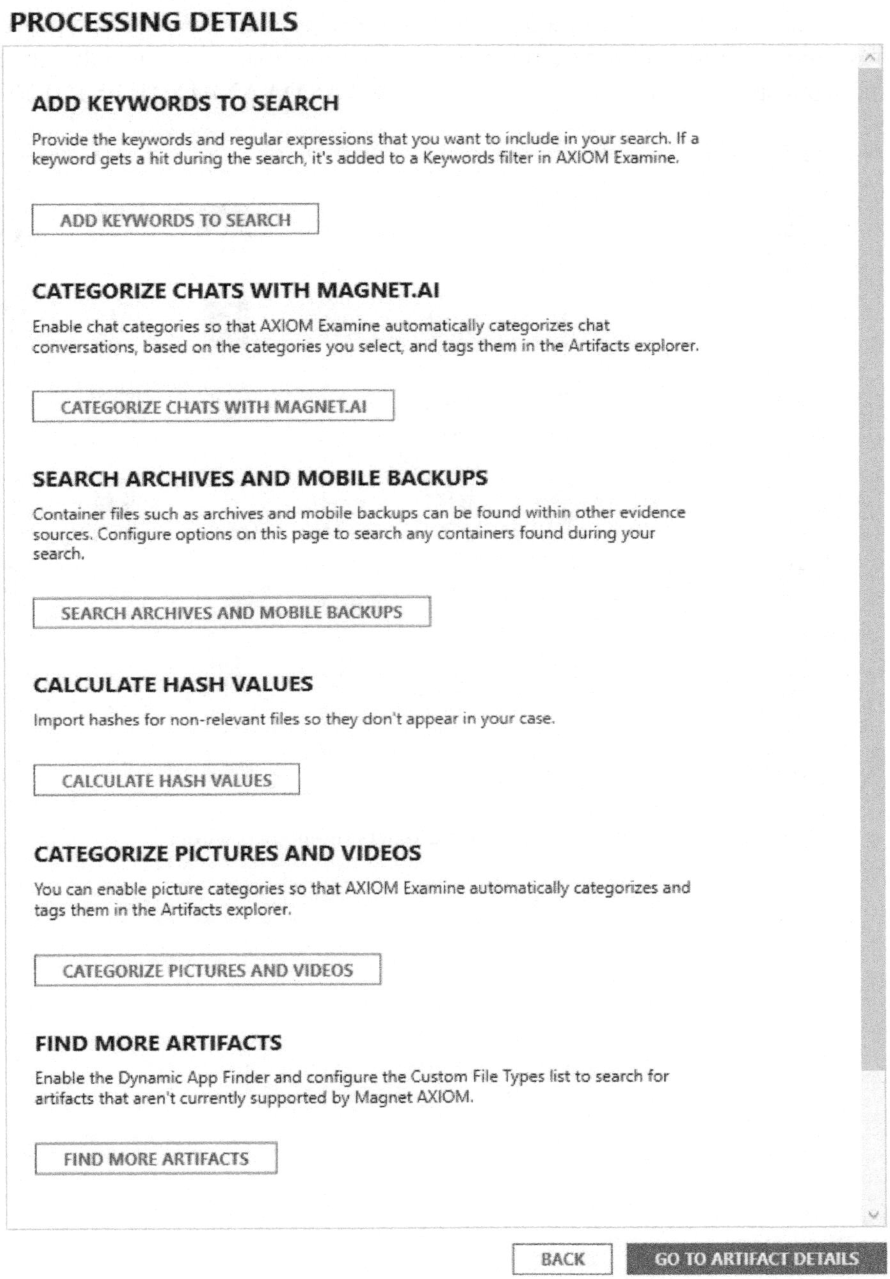

PROCESSING DETAILS

ADD KEYWORDS TO SEARCH

Provide the keywords and regular expressions that you want to include in your search. If a keyword gets a hit during the search, it's added to a Keywords filter in AXIOM Examine.

ADD KEYWORDS TO SEARCH

CATEGORIZE CHATS WITH MAGNET.AI

Enable chat categories so that AXIOM Examine automatically categorizes chat conversations, based on the categories you select, and tags them in the Artifacts explorer.

CATEGORIZE CHATS WITH MAGNET.AI

SEARCH ARCHIVES AND MOBILE BACKUPS

Container files such as archives and mobile backups can be found within other evidence sources. Configure options on this page to search any containers found during your search.

SEARCH ARCHIVES AND MOBILE BACKUPS

CALCULATE HASH VALUES

Import hashes for non-relevant files so they don't appear in your case.

CALCULATE HASH VALUES

CATEGORIZE PICTURES AND VIDEOS

You can enable picture categories so that AXIOM Examine automatically categorizes and tags them in the Artifacts explorer.

CATEGORIZE PICTURES AND VIDEOS

FIND MORE ARTIFACTS

Enable the Dynamic App Finder and configure the Custom File Types list to search for artifacts that aren't currently supported by Magnet AXIOM.

FIND MORE ARTIFACTS

BACK   GO TO ARTIFACT DETAILS

Figure 3.15 – Enable additional parsing tools and utilities

5. Select the artifacts that should be included or excluded in the decoding process. This can be useful to speed up the process when the investigator is only interested in data from specific applications. Then, click on **GO TO ANALYZE EVIDENCE:**

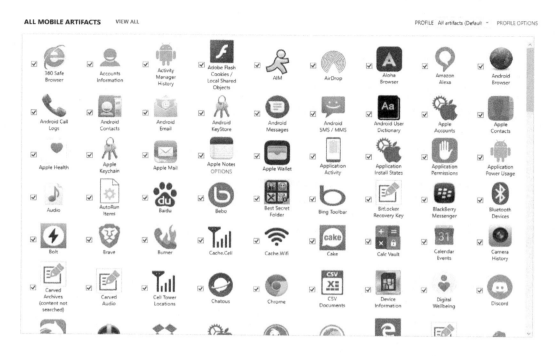

Figure 3.16 – Choose which artifacts should be decoded

6. Click on **ANALYZE EVIDENCE** to start decoding the data. AXIOM Examine opens automatically and displays any evidence that is recovered:

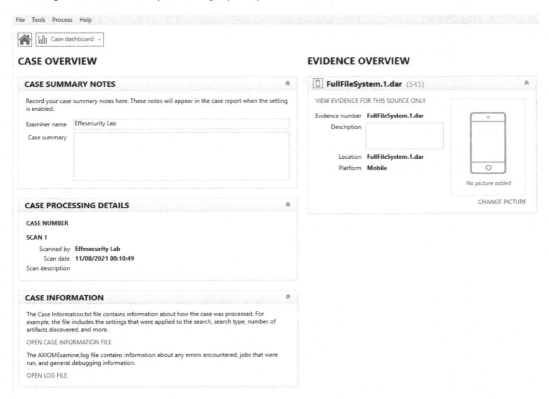

Figure 3.17 – The Case dashboard screen

7. You can check the progress from the bottom-left part of the screen and, as new data is recovered, clicking on **LOAD NEW RESULTS** will load the artifacts into AXIOM Examine so that you can start analyzing the data right away.

8. When AXIOM Process is done, the scan summary will display the results of the decoding process, including any exceptions that may have occurred.

Analyzing evidence with AXIOM Examine

The starting point for data analysis using AXIOM Examine is the **case dashboard**; from this view, you can see information about your case and relevant tags and keywords, and you can have a general idea of what artifacts were recovered by looking at the categories in the **Artifact Categories** section.

In AXIOM Examine, you can analyze evidence in several different ways.

The following is a list of useful tasks that can help you make the most of this tool:

- Browse through all the evidence using the **Artifacts** explorer, which will display the data grouped into categories. When you select an artifact, the **DETAILS** pane will show you the source file where that data was found:

EVIDENCE (26)   Column view

Potential Activity	Artifact	Artif...	Source
At Facebook home page	WebKit Browser Web History (Carved)	108	FullFileSystem.1.dar\Applications\MobileSafari.app\BuiltInBookmarkItems.plist
At Facebook home page	Safari History	149	FullFileSystem.1.dar\Applications\MobileSafari.app\BuiltInBookmarkItems.plist
At Facebook home page	Safari History	149	FullFileSystem.1.dar\Applications\MobileSafari.app\BuiltInBookmarkItems.plist
Unknown	Potential Browser Activity	11617	FullFileSystem.1.dar\private\var\db\uuidtext\9F\E12E68290D344DA2002AECB9...
Looking at Facebook legal information	Potential Browser Activity	11623	FullFileSystem.1.dar\private\var\db\uuidtext\9F\E12E68290D344DA2002AECB9...
Looking at Facebook legal information	Potential Browser Activity	11621	FullFileSystem.1.dar\private\var\db\uuidtext\9F\E12E68290D344DA2002AECB9...
Looking at Facebook legal information	Potential Browser Activity	11631	FullFileSystem.1.dar\private\var\db\uuidtext\49\D116B807F93F48AD657DE2768...
At Facebook home page	KnowledgeC Application Web Usage	14397	FullFileSystem.1.dar\private\var\mobile\Library\CoreDuet\Knowledge\knowledg...
At Facebook login page	KnowledgeC Application Web Usage	14397	FullFileSystem.1.dar\private\var\mobile\Library\CoreDuet\Knowledge\knowledg...
At Facebook home page	KnowledgeC Application Web Usage	14404	FullFileSystem.1.dar\private\var\mobile\Library\CoreDuet\Knowledge\knowledg...
At Facebook login page	KnowledgeC Application Web Usage	14404	FullFileSystem.1.dar\private\var\mobile\Library\CoreDuet\Knowledge\knowledg...
At Facebook home page	KnowledgeC Application Web Usage	14407	FullFileSystem.1.dar\private\var\mobile\Library\CoreDuet\Knowledge\knowledg...
At Facebook login page	KnowledgeC Application Web Usage	14407	FullFileSystem.1.dar\private\var\mobile\Library\CoreDuet\Knowledge\knowledg...
At Facebook home page	KnowledgeC Application Web Usage	14410	FullFileSystem.1.dar\private\var\mobile\Library\CoreDuet\Knowledge\knowledg...
Unknown	KnowledgeC Application Web Usage	14410	FullFileSystem.1.dar\private\var\mobile\Library\CoreDuet\Knowledge\knowledg...
Unknown	KnowledgeC Safari History	15102	FullFileSystem.1.dar\private\var\mobile\Library\CoreDuet\Knowledge\knowledg...
At Facebook login page	KnowledgeC Safari History	15119	FullFileSystem.1.dar\private\var\mobile\Library\CoreDuet\Knowledge\knowledg...
At Facebook login page	KnowledgeC Safari History	15161	FullFileSystem.1.dar\private\var\mobile\Library\CoreDuet\Knowledge\knowledg...
Unknown	Safari History	22789	FullFileSystem.1.dar\private\var\mobile\Containers\Data\Application\45D7E9EB...
At Facebook login page	Safari History	22789	FullFileSystem.1.dar\private\var\mobile\Containers\Data\Application\45D7E9EB...
At Facebook login page	Safari History	22791	FullFileSystem.1.dar\private\var\mobile\Containers\Data\Application\45D7E9EB...
Unknown	Safari History	22950	FullFileSystem.1.dar\private\var\mobile\Containers\Data\Application\45D7E9EB...
At Facebook login page	Safari History	22952	FullFileSystem.1.dar\private\var\mobile\Containers\Data\Application\45D7E9EB...
Unknown	Potential Browser Activity	23110	FullFileSystem.1.dar\private\var\mobile\Containers\Data\Application\45D7E9EB...
Unknown	Safari History	23191	FullFileSystem.1.dar\private\var\mobile\Containers\Data\Application\45D7E9EB...
At Facebook login page	Safari History	23193	FullFileSystem.1.dar\private\var\mobile\Containers\Data\Application\45D7E9EB...

Figure 3.18 – The Artifacts explorer

- Use the **File System** explorer to manually browse through files – for example, you can use this feature to display the contents of plists and SQLite databases. You can mark important evidence by adding tags and comments to an artifact.

- View and analyze connections between artifacts using the **Connections** explorer; by default, AXIOM Process does not automatically build connections, so you'll have to manually enable this feature from the menu within AXIOM Examine, choosing **Tools | Build connections**. After connections are built, from the **Artifacts** explorer, select the artifact that you want to view connections for and click the **Connections** icon from the **Details** pane. The tool will automatically switch to the **Connections** explorer view and display a visual map of any connection based on the artifact:

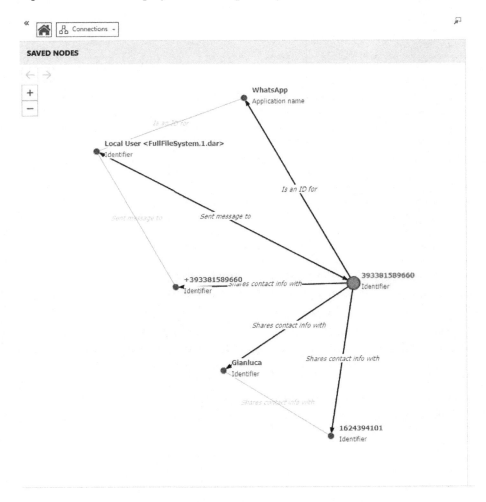

Figure 3.19 – The Connections explorer

- Review all artifacts generated in a specified timespan by building a timeline from the **Timeline** explorer. This is useful if an investigator knows when a certain event occurred and wants to see all the activity on the device at that moment:

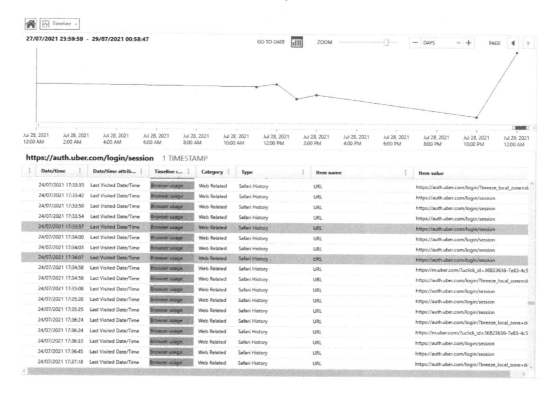

Figure 3.20 – The Timeline explorer

When the examination is complete, Magnet AXIOM's built-in **exporting wizard** allows the investigator to automatically generate a report; the exporting wizard will ask what artifacts should be included in the report and what should be excluded, and data can be exported in a number of different formats, including **Excel**, **HTML**, and **PDF**.

This completes our brief introduction to Magnet AXIOM!

Both Cellebrite Physical Analyzer and Magnet AXIOM have a lot more interesting features, such as working with **cloud** forensics. We'll be looking into this topic later on in the book.

Using open source tools

This chapter would not be complete without mentioning some of the best open source iOS forensic tools! The **DFIR (Digital Forensics and Incident Response)** community is one of the most active and helpful communities out there, and these tools are the result of the hard work and passion of security researchers, forensic examiners, and developers that have shared their knowledge with the community.

Apollo

The **Apple Pattern of Life Lazy Output'er (APOLLO)** is a Python script written by Sarah Edwards (you can find her on Twitter – `@iamevltwin`) that processes iOS and macOS artifacts to extract pattern-of-life data and combines the result into a single SQLite database or CSV file for viewing.

The script is based on a number of different modules (some of these have been written by the DFIR community), and each of these runs one or more queries to extract specific data from an iOS extraction. We'll be using this powerful tool extensively in *Chapter 5, Pattern-of-Life Forensics*.

You can download APOLLO from the project's GitHub repository: `https://github.com/mac4n6/APOLLO`.

iLEAPP

The **iOS Logs, Events, And Plists Parser (iLEAPP)** is a script written in Python 3 by Alexis Brignoni (Twitter – `@AlexisBrignoni`), which is a free alternative to commercial forensic tools. This tool can parse full filesystem iOS extractions, parsing and decoding almost every kind of artifact that you can find on an iOS device.

Personally, I find this is a great tool to be used in addition to commercial software, as it can help validate your findings.

iLEAPP can be downloaded from `https://github.com/abrignoni/iLEAPP`.

iOS Triage

This tool is a Unix **shell script** written by Mattia Epifani (Twitter – `@mattiaep`) that can be used to extract data from a jailbroken iOS device. This is a quick solution if you need to triage a device, including devices that are in **BFU** state. We'll be using iOS Triage later on in the book.

You can download this tool from GitHub: `https://github.com/RealityNet/ios_triage`.

Sysdiagnose

This is the result of research carried out by Mattia Epifani (@mattiaep), Adrian Leong, and Heather Mahalik (@HeatherMahalik) on **log files** generated by iOS devices.

These Python scripts will parse log files and provide useful evidence that could be missed by commercial forensic tools.

You can download the scripts from https://github.com/cheeky4n6monkey/iOS_sysdiagnose_forensic_scripts.

Analyzing data with iLEAPP

Let's take a look at how iLEAPP works and what kind of evidence can be extracted by using this tool.

Before installing iLEAPP, make sure that you have Python 3 installed on your system. The first step is downloading the code from GitHub by cloning the repository. You can do this by running the following command:

```
git clone https://github.com/abrignoni/iLEAPP.git
```

Then, we need to install the required packages:

```
cd iLEAPP
```
```
pip install -r requirements.txt
```

Now that everything is set, we can run iLEAPP. In this example, we're providing a ZIP archive as the input file and we're exporting the report to the output folder:

```
python3 ileapp.py -t zip -i ../iphone_dump.zip -o output
```

As you can see, we're using the -t option to specify what kind of input is provided, the -i option to specify the path to the input file, and the -o option to specify the path to the output folder.

Once iLEAPP is done processing, the results will be combined into an HTML report:

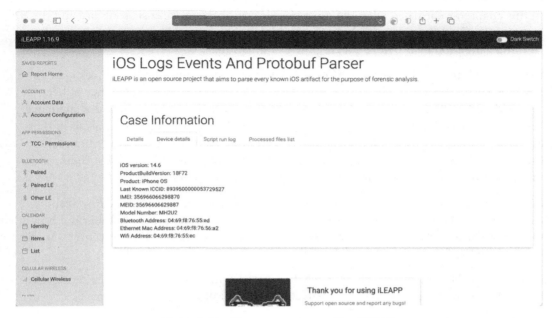

Figure 3.21 – The report generated by iLEAPP

The report will include all sorts of artifacts and useful evidence, including **accounts data**, **cellular data**, **locations**, **application data**, **device usage data**, **contacts**, **messaging**, and much, much more!

This open source software is such a powerful tool that I absolutely recommend you play around with it to understand its full potential.

Summary

In this chapter, we learned what the most popular commercial forensic tools are and the importance of validating results by using multiple tools, comparing their outputs, and running validation tests before starting the examination.

Keep in mind that although these tools are extremely useful and make the investigator's job a lot easier, the tool itself is not the evidence. The report is not the evidence either. The evidence is the evidence, and it's the examiner's job to understand how that evidence was created, what it represents, and what insights can be gained from the analysis of that evidence. Forensic software definitely has a place, but it should not substitute manually examining the artifacts. In other words, use these tools but don't blindly trust them, and make sure you understand what is happening behind the scenes.

Further on in the chapter, we concentrated on two of these tools, Cellebrite Physical Analyzer and Magnet AXIOM. We learned how to import data into these tools and how to use the software's features – such as the AppGenie or the Connections explorer – to dig deeper into the data and gain useful insights.

Finally, in the last part of this chapter, we discovered some useful open source scripts and used iLEAPP to extract and analyze artifacts from a full filesystem extraction.

In the next chapter, we will discuss the iOS filesystem and we'll learn where to find core iOS artifacts.

4
Working with Common iOS Artifacts

In previous chapters, we discussed in broad terms how the iOS operating system works and the different phases of the mobile examination workflow. Then, we learned all about different acquisition methods and how to extract the richest amount of data from a device. In the third chapter, we looked at forensic tools and continued our examination process by loading the data into the tool for analysis.

One of the most critical aspects of a mobile forensics investigation is validating your findings. We've already discussed the importance of tool validation in earlier chapters, but the process should be extended to ensure the integrity of the data collected and to understand and explain the context of the data, as this is essential for presenting it as evidence in court. This usually entails following the source file and manually viewing the artifacts in their native format.

In this chapter, we first look at the most common types of artifacts found on an iOS device and how you can view them in their native format. Then, we will dive deep into SQLite databases to learn how they manage data storage internally and what options we have to recover deleted records. Finally, we'll take a closer look at the filesystem to understand where system artifacts are located, what insights we can gain by analyzing this data, and where application-specific artifacts can be found.

In this chapter, we will cover the following topics:

- Understanding the importance of validation
- Working with iOS artifacts
- Locating common artifacts

Understanding the importance of validation

In *Chapter 3, Using Forensic Tools*, we learned about some of the features of software such as **Cellebrite Physical Analyzer** and **Magnet AXIOM**, and gained a better understanding of what data we can expect to see analyzed by these tools.

You may be wondering why an examiner would invest time in learning how to manually analyze data found on a device when these tools do all the hard work for you. Well, for starters, while this software is an essential item in the investigator's toolbox, the investigator should also understand the limitations of these tools and how to deal with artifacts that are not automatically parsed; while forensic tools claim to support a variety of different apps and artifacts, this does not mean that the products can actually parse *all* of the data that pertains to a specific application that is being examined. With the rate at which mobile apps are updated, it is quite common for a forensic tool to not support a recently updated application or, in some cases, only partially support it by providing some but not all of the available data. In such situations, the investigator must resort to manually examining the source file in its native format.

Another reason an investigator might want to look at the source file of an artifact is to validate their findings; even if a forensic tool has produced an appreciable output, it is important to cross-reference the data to the source files to understand the context of that data. For example, by analyzing the tables in an SQLite database, the investigator can understand not only *what* data is stored but also *how* that data is stored on the device, and *how* the operating system logs a particular event, such as an incoming phone call, text message, or notification.

If some key artifacts are found during the examination process that are fundamental to the overall investigation, the examiner should be prepared to answer questions such as the following:

- How did that data get there?

- What does that data tell us when we put it in context?

- Was that artifact the result of user activity or was it generated by the operating system?

- How did it interact with other data found on the device?

The answer to these questions can often lie in the source file of the artifact, so learning how to manually analyze such files is a must for the person responsible for the examination process of an iOS device.

The importance of **validation** cannot be stressed enough; using a validated methodology to examine a device, making sure tools are working correctly by validating their output, and validating your findings by diving deep into the source files to understand the context of the data can have a huge impact on the final outcome of an investigation. In some cases, this can be the difference between someone losing their job or not, or, in extreme cases, the difference between them going to jail or not.

Before we discuss where common artifacts are located on an iOS device, in the next section we will learn how to manually work with the most common file types you'll encounter in a typical examination.

Working with iOS artifacts

Generally speaking, the artifacts that can be found on an iOS device can be grouped into one of the following categories:

- SQLite databases

- Property lists

- Protocol buffers

- XML files

- Log files

While the last two files don't pose any kind of concern as they are essentially text files and, as such, can be viewed with pretty much any text editor, the others may be (and often are) stored in **binary format**, so they require specific tools or libraries to parse through the data.

Introducing SQLite

Almost every application on an iOS device, including system ones like **Messages**, **Contacts**, or **Email**, needs a place to store data for the long term. This is achieved by using **SQLite**, which is an open source, small, self-contained relational database. SQLite databases can be recognized by the `.sqlite` or `.sqlite3` file extensions, although some databases are given the `.db` extension, or other extensions as well.

The reason why SQLite is so popular among mobile devices is due to its simple architecture and great performance. The following are some of its features:

- **SQLite is self-contained**: The entire database is contained within a single file that integrates directly with applications. Its serverless architecture means that the database works as a standalone file, as opposed to the traditional client-server protocol.

- **SQLite is cross-platform**: The database resides in a single, cross-platform file that can be accessed by all operating systems supported by SQLite, including Windows, macOS, Linux, Android, iOS, BSD, Solaris, and so on.

- **SQLite is fully ACID-compliant**: This allows safe access to multiple applications or threads. It also supports most of the SQL query language, which is the main means of interacting with nearly all modern relational database systems.

Now that we've seen SQLite's features, let's take a look at how it stores data.

Tables, columns, and rows

The basic concepts of an SQLite database should be easy to visualize – a database contains one or more **tables**, which each contain data that is organized into **columns** and **rows**. A column represents a single data element, such as a *phone number* or *address*, while a row represents a set of values, one for each column.

SQLite supports five different data types:

- `INTEGER`
- `TEXT`
- `REAL`
- `BLOB`
- `NULL`

The first three types are self-explanatory. The **Binary Large Object (BLOB)** data type preserves any input exactly as is, without casting it as a certain type; BLOB data types are commonly used to store complex binary data structures such as **property lists** or **protocol buffers** in an SQLite record. The NULL data type simply stores an empty value.

To retrieve data from a database, you run a **query**, which is a set of logical instructions written in **SQL language** that parses through a given table to extract the data you want. The result of the query is actually represented as another table, as you can see in the following screenshot.

To understand what a query looks like, let's see a simple example. The following query extracts the last five messages from the sms.db database:

```
SELECT ROWID, text FROM message
ORDER BY ROWID DESC
LIMIT 5;
```

The output can be seen in the following screenshot:

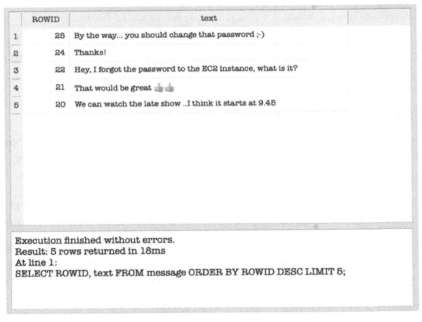

Figure 4.1 – The result of a query displayed in DB Browser for SQLite

Without going into too much detail, we will focus on this query for a moment to understand the basics of SQL language. Obviously, if you're doing a forensic examination of an SQLite database, you do not want to modify the data in any way. Therefore, all queries will probably start with the SELECT clause, which indicates that we want to read data from a table.

On the first line, we select which columns to include in the result (ROWID and text) and the name of the table – in this case, the message table. The second line of the query indicates the order in which the results should be displayed. In the example table, each SMS message is identified by a progressive ROWID column, so to display the most recent messages, we're ordering the results in descending order based on this column. As we're only interested in five messages, we use the LIMIT command to indicate how many rows should be displayed.

> **Tip**
>
> If you're new to SQL language, you can learn how to write the most common types of queries by visiting the SQLite website at https://www.sqlite.org/lang.html.

As a forensic examiner, the queries you run usually entail filtering and searching through the data, so you may want to look into commands such as CASE, WHEN, and WHERE. We'll see more complex queries over the course of the chapter.

Running SQL queries

Most forensic tools come with a built-in database viewer that allows the investigator to view the entire database and run queries directly within the tool itself; there are, however, other options:

- **The SQLite command-line utility**, which can be downloaded from http://www.sqlite.org, allows direct interaction with the database from the command line.

- Other free tools, such as **DB Browser for SQLite**, allow the user to view the database through a **Graphical User Interface (GUI)** and run queries on it. DB Browser for SQLite can be downloaded from https://sqlitebrowser.org.

The investigator should be familiar with the tools used to access the database directly, as these will prove to be huge timesavers when the scope of the examination is limited to one or more SQLite databases. Analyzing these databases with forensic tools such as Cellebrite Physical Analyzer or Magnet AXIOM results in the need to load and parse the entire extraction into memory; this can be very time-consuming, depending on the size of the data extracted.

Using the SQLite command-line tool

`sqlite3` is a command-line utility that is part of the SQLite library. macOS and most Linux distributions have it already installed, while Windows users can download the executable from SQLite's website, which is listed in the preceding section.

To open an SQLite database from the command line, just type the following:

```
sqlite3 filename.db
```

If a database with the specified name doesn't exist, SQLite will create it for you. Once you've opened a database, a SQL prompt will be displayed, where you can run queries and commands. There are a number of built-in commands you can issue to obtain basic information on the database and its tables.

If you're not familiar with the database layout, you can list all the tables in it by running the `.tables` command:

```
sqlite> .tables

attachment                  message
chat                        message_attachment_join
chat_handle_join            message_processing_task
chat_message_join           sync_deleted_attachments
deleted_messages            sync_deleted_chats
```

If you're interested in a specific table, type `.schema` followed by the name of the table to display the columns and data types of the table:

```
sqlite> .schema handle
CREATE TABLE handle (ROWID INTEGER PRIMARY KEY AUTOINCREMENT
UNIQUE, id TEXT NOT NULL, country TEXT, service TEXT NOT NULL);
```

By looking at the column names and types, you should be able to get a basic understanding of what data is stored in the table. In this example, every row in the `handle` table has an auto-incrementing `ROWID` column and three columns of `TEXT` type: `id`, `country`, and `service`.

If you want to retrieve data from the table, you use a `SELECT` query:

```
SELECT * FROM handle;
```

When you are finished, type `.exit` or `.quit` to terminate the SQLite session.

Pages, vacuuming, and write-ahead logs

One of the features of SQLite that makes it so interesting to forensic examiners is the possibility of recovering **deleted records** from a database. Depending on the scope of the database, this could mean recovering deleted text messages, browser history, or logs relating to device activity. To have a better understanding of how data recovery is possible, we need to take a step back and learn how SQLite manages `write` and `delete` operations under the hood.

We've already learned that, from a logical point of view, the data in a database is organized into tables that each contain columns and rows. This is a high-level abstraction layer that allows users to interact with a database with a simple data model that is easy to visualize, such as columns and rows; however, at a lower level, the SQLite library actually organizes data differently on the filesystem, storing data into **pages**. Pages are similar to blocks in a filesystem, and their purpose is to store data in binary format. Each page in an SQLite database can have a variable size, with the default size being 4096 bytes, and each page has a distinct number. The first page contains a 100-byte header, which can be analyzed by using a **hex viewer**, such as the `hexdump` command-line utility available on macOS and Linux.

For example, to view the header from an SQLite database called `sms.db`, we would execute the following command:

```
hexdump -n 100 -C sms.db
```

The `-n` argument specifies the number of bytes that should be displayed. As SQLite has a fixed-size header, we're only interested in the first 100 bytes. The `-C` argument tells the `hexdump` utility to also display data in string format:

```
00000000  53 51 4c 69 74 65 20 66  6f 72 6d 61 74 20 33 00  |SQLite format 3.|
00000010  10 00 02 02 00 40 20 20  00 00 00 13 00 00 00 43  |.....@  .......C|
00000020  00 00 00 00 00 00 00 00  00 00 00 50 00 00 00 04  |...........P....|
00000030  00 00 00 00 00 00 00 00  00 00 00 01 00 00 00 00  |................|
00000040  00 00 00 00 00 00 00 00  00 00 00 00 00 00 00 00  |................|
00000050  00 00 00 00 00 00 00 00  00 00 00 00 00 00 00 13  |................|
00000060  00 2e 24 80                                        |..$.|
00000064
```

Figure 4.2 – The output from the hexdump command

As you can see, the first 16 bytes contain the *SQLite 3 format* string. You can parse the rest of the header by using the following table as a reference:

Offset	Size	Description
0	16	The header string: "SQLite format 3\000"
16	2	The database page size in bytes.
18	1	File format write version. 1 for legacy; 2 for WAL.
19	1	File format read version. 1 for legacy; 2 for WAL.
20	1	Bytes of unused "reserved" space at the end of each page. Usually 0.
21	1	Maximum embedded payload fraction. Must be 64.
22	1	Minimum embedded payload fraction. Must be 32.
23	1	Leaf payload fraction. Must be 32.
24	4	File change counter.
28	4	Size of the database file in pages. The "in-header database size".
32	4	Page number of the first freelist trunk page.
36	4	Total number of freelist pages.
40	4	The schema cookie.
44	4	The schema format number. Supported schema formats are 1, 2, 3, and 4.
48	4	Default page cache size.
52	4	The page number of the largest root b-tree page when in auto-vacuum or zero otherwise.
56	4	The database text encoding. A value of 1 means UTF-8. A value of 2 means UTF-16le. A value of 3 means UTF-16be.
60	4	The "user version" as read and set by the user_version pragma.
64	4	True (non-zero) for incremental-vacuum mode. False (zero) otherwise.
68	4	The "Application ID" set by PRAGMA application_id.
72	20	Reserved for expansion. Must be zero.
92	4	The version-valid-for number.
96	4	SQLITE_VERSION_NUMBER

Figure 4.3 – The SQLite database header reference

To represent a table along with its data, SQLite organizes pages using a **balanced tree (B-tree)** data structure, which is a highly efficient way of storing data. Pages that actually contain data, also called **active pages**, are assigned to a node that serves the function of connecting pages to each other.

Active pages in the file are further divided into **cells**, which are segments of a page that contain the data for every row in the database. When new cells are added, SQLite will attempt to place them at the bottom of the page. The free space within the page before the first cell is called **unallocated space**. From a forensic viewpoint, unallocated space is of great interest, as it may be empty, but it may also contain previously deleted data or fragments of previously used pages.

When data is removed from the database, the corresponding cell or page is not actually deleted but merely *marked* as deleted. Pages that have been marked for deletion are called **free pages**, and SQLite manages these by adding them to another data structure, the **freelist**. Deleting individual records from a database creates gaps in a page; these spaces are called **free blocks** and are tracked by SQLite by adding them to a linked list.

As you can see from the previous table, the database header at offset 32 tells us the number of the first page in the free-list, while the total number of free pages can be read by looking at the value at offset 36. Every page in a database also has an 8 or 12-byte header, depending on the type of page. The following table illustrates the format of the page header:

Offset	Size	Description
0	1	The one-byte flag at offset 0 indicating the b-tree page type. • A value of 2 (0x02) means the page is an interior index b-tree page. • A value of 5 (0x05) means the page is an interior table b-tree page. • A value of 10 (0x0a) means the page is a leaf index b-tree page. • A value of 13 (0x0d) means the page is a leaf table b-tree page.
1	2	The two-byte integer at offset 1 gives the start of the first freeblock on the page, or is zero if there are no freeblocks.
3	2	The two-byte integer at offset 3 gives the number of cells on the page.
5	2	The two-byte integer at offset 5 designates the start of the cell content area. A zero value for this integer is interpreted as 65536.
7	1	The one-byte integer at offset 7 gives the number of fragmented free bytes within the cell content area.
8	4	The four-byte page number at offset 8 is the right-most pointer. This value appears in the header of interior b-tree pages only and is omitted from all other pages.

Figure 4.4 – The SQLite page header reference

With all this information in mind, we could manually parse through the file with a hex viewer and look out for free pages that contain data that was deleted from the database. Thankfully, there are tools that automate this task!

Vacuuming

You can confirm the fact that SQLite retains deleted pages by checking that the database file size does not change when data is removed. As a result of this behavior, under normal circumstances, the file can only grow in size as new data is written to the database. Additionally, as new records are added and deleted from the database, the data can become fragmented because free pages will be scattered and mixed all across the file. This means that the actual parts of a database that hold a particular table will not be stored contiguously within the file, which affects performance.

The following diagram illustrates what happens when data is written to and deleted from the database, resulting in a fragmented file:

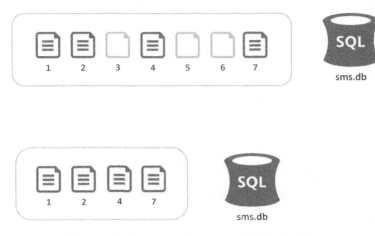

Figure 4.5 – Pages in a fragmented SQLite database

The process of **vacuuming** an SQLite database solves these problems by reading the logical data from the database (tables, columns, and rows) and writing it to a temporary file, ignoring free pages. As a result of this process, the database file is rebuilt from scratch, active pages are repacked, and data within the file is defragmented. Once the process is complete, the contents of the temporary file will be copied back into the original database, overwriting it.

The following diagram shows the same database after running the VACUUM command; the records stored in the database are obviously unchanged, but now the active pages are stored contiguously and the free pages are not present:

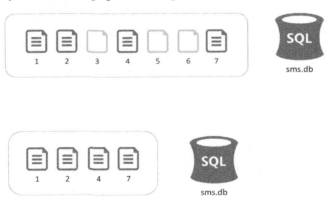

Figure 4.6 – Pages in an SQLite database after the vacuuming process

It should be clear that recovering deleted records from a database is nearly impossible once the vacuuming process is complete. Research has shown that iOS periodically runs the VACUUM command for most SQLite databases. At the time of writing, however, it is not clear exactly when this happens, as it seems to depend heavily on the device model and iOS version.

Write-ahead logging

Up to this point, we have focused on analyzing the main database file to understand how the data is stored in that file and where to look for deleted records. However, there are other files that are of interest from a forensic perspective that should not be overlooked, such as SQLite **temporary files**. The most common type of temporary file you will find on an iOS device is a journaling file called the **Write-Ahead Log (WAL)**.

WAL files can be easily identified by their filename, since the -wal string is appended to the name of the database. So, for example, if we are working on an SQLite database called sms. db, the WAL file will be called sms.db-wal, and it will be created in the same directory as the main database file. These temporary files will not always be present, as only databases that have their journaling mode set to WAL will use the write-ahead log method.

From the research that has been carried out, it's safe to say that most databases on an iOS device have WAL mode enabled. If this is the case, when data is added, modified, or deleted, the transaction is stored in the WAL file rather than directly in the main SQLite database. Similarly, when reading data from the database, the SQLite engine determines where the most recent version of a particular record is stored and reads it from the appropriate file:

Figure 4.7 – New records added to the database are appended to the WAL file

There are many reasons why an application would want to enable WAL mode in its database. The most important reason is **performance**; pages are written to the WAL file in sequential order, and every change to the database results in a single disk write. Additionally, because of the separate files, an application using multiple threads will be able to read from the database while writing to it.

At some point in time, the data in the WAL file will have to be transferred back into the main database. This process is called a **checkpoint**. Typically, SQLite automatically performs a checkpoint when the WAL file reaches a certain size (by default, this is 1,000 pages) or when the last database connection is closed:

Figure 4.8 – A checkpoint transfers data from the WAL file back into the main database

---

Tip

It's important to know that SQLite does an automatic checkpoint when all connections to the database have been closed cleanly. So, if you close a database with WAL enabled when using a tool like DB Viewer, the contents of the WAL file will be transferred to the main database and the WAL file will be removed.

As WAL files grow in size, it's quite common for them to become larger than the main database itself, so these should definitely not be overlooked during the examination process, as they may contain huge amounts of data.

The structure of these files is fairly simple – a WAL file consists of a 32-byte header followed by zero or more **frames**. Each frame records the revised contents of a single page from the database file. The following table shows what data we can find in the file header:

Offset	Size	Description
0	4	Magic number. 0x377f0682 or 0x377f0683
4	4	File format version. Currently 3007000.
8	4	Database page size. Example: 1024
12	4	Checkpoint sequence number
16	4	Salt-1: random integer incremented with each checkpoint
20	4	Salt-2: a different random number for each checkpoint
24	4	Checksum-1: First part of a checksum on the first 24 bytes of header
28	4	Checksum-2: Second part of the checksum on the first 24 bytes of header

Figure 4.9 – The WAL file header

Each frame within a WAL file contains a 24-byte frame header, followed by the new or altered database page. The size of the page can be determined by looking at the file header. The same page can appear multiple times in the WAL file because every time a page needs to be updated, the latest version is read (either from the WAL or main database file) and then changes are appended to the end of the WAL file.

Figure 4.10 shows the format of the frame header:

Offset	Size	Description
0	4	Page number
4	4	The size of the database file in pages after the commit
8	4	Salt-1 copied from the WAL header
12	4	Salt-2 copied from the WAL header
16	4	Checksum-1: Cumulative checksum up through and including this page
20	4	Checksum-2: Second half of the cumulative checksum.

Figure 4.10 – The WAL frame header

It should be noted that the only way to view all the data present in a WAL file is to either manually analyze the frames with a hex viewer or use a forensic tool with built-in support for SQLite data recovery. Using non-forensic tools (such as the SQLite command-line tool or DB Browser) will not display all the data but instead display either the live state of the database or the state of the database before the first transaction in the WAL file.

Recovering deleted data

Now that we've seen how SQLite manages data storage behind the scenes, we can focus on attempting recovery of deleted records. Building on what we learned in the previous section, deleted data may be found in any of the following locations:

- Unallocated space
- Free pages
- Free blocks
- WAL files

We'll start by manually analyzing the database and then we'll see some automated tools that will do the job for us.

Analyzing the database with a hex viewer

The most common method to locate deleted data in an SQLite database is to view its contents using a hex editor. Simply skimming through the file with a tool such as **Hex Fiend** or **HxD** will display all the data stored in it, including unallocated space and free pages:

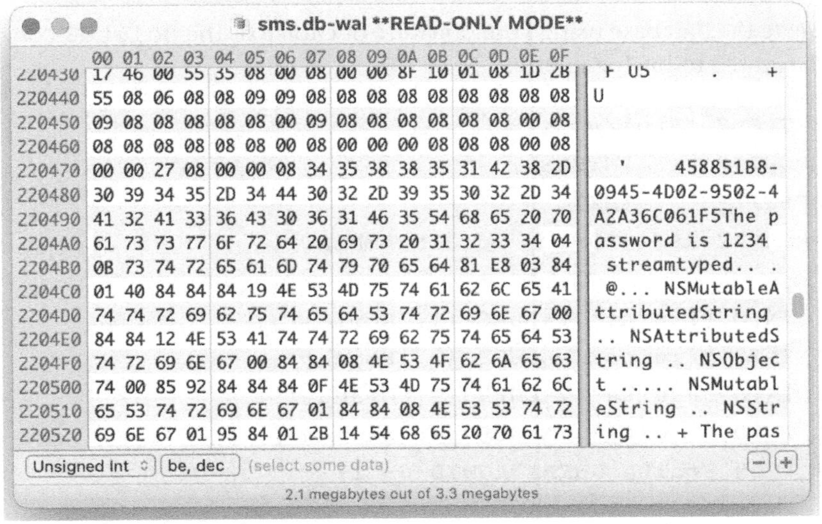

Figure 4.11 – Using a hex viewer to display the contents of an SQLite file

By analyzing the database header to understand the page size and location of free pages and free blocks, the examiner can use the tool of their choice to highlight a specific page in the file by specifying the offset and length, effectively isolating the page from the rest of the data. The page can then be analyzed by displaying its contents in string format.

The following steps describe the process of manually parsing through pages of an SQLite database:

1. Read the database header and identify the page size and number of pages.

2. Work out the offset location of each page.

3. Analyze the page header.

4. If it's an active page, search for any useful evidence in unallocated space or free blocks. If it's a free page, analyze the entire page.

5. Continue the process for each page in the database.

The same principles apply to WAL files; as the file format is well documented, the examiner can open the WAL using a hex viewer, calculate the offset of each frame, isolate each individual frame, and view the data by converting it to a UTF-8 string to identify any readable strings.

As an example, we're going to create a new database named `test.db` that contains a single table called `Fruits`. Then, we'll populate the database with a few records, delete a row of data, and analyze the file with a hex viewer. For simplicity, the database will not use write-ahead logging.

You can create the database using your software of choice or the `sqlite3` command-line tool. Then, run the following queries:

```
CREATE TABLE "Fruits" (
    "ROWID"      INTEGER,
    "Fruit"      TEXT,
    PRIMARY KEY("ROWID" AUTOINCREMENT)
);
INSERT INTO "Fruits" VALUES (1,'Apple');
INSERT INTO "Fruits" VALUES (2,'Peach');
INSERT INTO "Fruits" VALUES (3,'Orange');
INSERT INTO "Fruits" VALUES (4,'Banana');
DELETE FROM Fruits WHERE ROWID == 1;
```

As you can see from the following screenshot, the table now contains three rows, as expected:

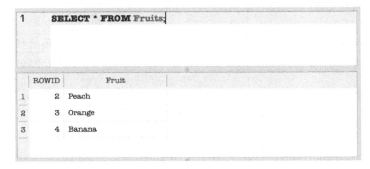

Figure 4.12 – The table contains three rows of data

The first step in our examination is to open the file with a hex viewer and analyze the 100-byte header to extract any useful information from the database:

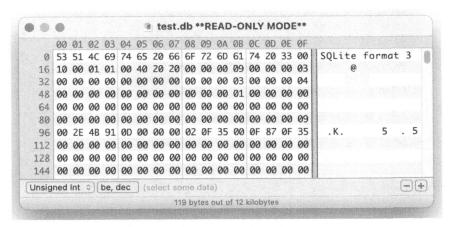

Figure 4.13 – The SQLite database header

The previous screenshot shows three highlighted data points in the header:

- At offset 16, we can see the page size, which is 0x1000 or 4096 in decimal format.

- At offset 28, we find the number of pages, which is 3.

- At offset 36, the number of free pages is 0.

Since there are no free pages, our examination will include analysis of active pages, unallocated space, and free blocks. Now that we know the page size and the number of pages, we can easily calculate the offset of each page:

Page	Offset (Dec)	Offset (HEX)
1	0	0x0000
2	4096	0x1000
3	8192	0x2000

Table 4.1 – The decimal offset for each page

We will focus on the analysis of page 2. To isolate it from the rest of the data, make a new selection starting at offset 4096 and spanning for 4096 bytes, and copy the data to a new window in your editor. From now on, the offsets will be relative to the page:

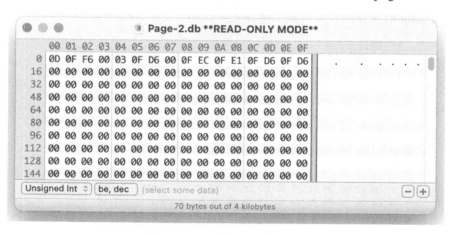

Figure 4.14 – The page header

Now that we have loaded the second page into our hex editor, the next step involves examining the page header:

- At offset 01, we can read the location of the first free block, which is 0x0FF6 or 4086 in decimal format.

- The value at offset 04 indicates the number of active cells on the page, 3.

- By looking at offset 05, we can find the location of the first non-empty data cell, which is 0x0FD6 or 4054.

- Finally, the space between the header and the first data cell is unallocated space.

With all this information in mind, we can highlight the free block that starts at offset `4086` and ends at the bottom of the page; the right pane of the hex viewer displays the data as a UTF-8 string:

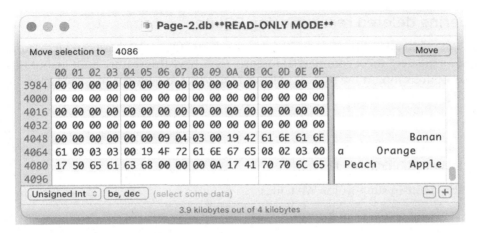

Figure 4.15 – The free block shows previously deleted data

As you can see, the record named **Apple** that was previously deleted from the database is still in the file, on the right in the free block of the second page.

Carving for strings

Data carving is the process of searching for particular strings or bytes within a file; the examiner first determines a string or pattern to search for and then, using a hex viewer or a command-line tool, initiates a search across a file for that string or pattern. This process is a great alternative to manually parsing through an SQLite database, as it allows the investigator to instantly verify whether a given record can be found in the file, including any locations where deleted data is normally hidden.

The `strings` tool is a command-line utility that performs string carving in a binary file and prints the result to the screen. Displaying all the strings that can be found in an SQLite database is as simple as running the following command:

```
strings sms.db
```

This tool can be combined with other commands, such as `grep`, to search for a particular string or pattern. The following command will search for the `Apple` word in the database we used for the previous example:

```
strings test.db | grep Apple
```
```
Apple
```

As you can see, the `Apple` string was printed to screen, and this confirms that it was found in the SQLite database. This simple tool can be a life-saving hack to show all the strings that are stored in a database, including deleted data!

Recovering deleted records using FQLite

The task of manually recovering deleted data from an SQLite database can be a daunting process; fortunately, most commercial forensic tools have this feature built in, but there are other options too. At the time of writing, FQLite is probably the most complete open source SQLite recovery tool, for the following reasons:

- It's written in Java, so you can run it from any OS.
- It supports the recovery of deleted records from all database pages, including free blocks and unallocated space.
- It has built-in support for WAL files.
- Recovered records can be exported in CSV format.

To download FQLite, visit `https://www.staff.hs-mittweida.de/~pawlaszc/fqlite/` or head over to the GitHub repository that is located at `https://github.com/pawlaszczyk/fqlite`.

We will now briefly go through the process of recovering deleted data from the `sms.db` SQLite database:

1. Launch FQLite and select the database from which recovery should be attempted by going to **File | Open Database**.

2. FQLite will now process the file and analyze the database, searching for deleted records. You can follow the progress by looking at the log panel at the bottom of the screen.

3. Once FQLite is done, from the left panel, choose the database or WAL file you want to examine.

4. FQLite will display a table with all the data that was found in the database, including deleted records:

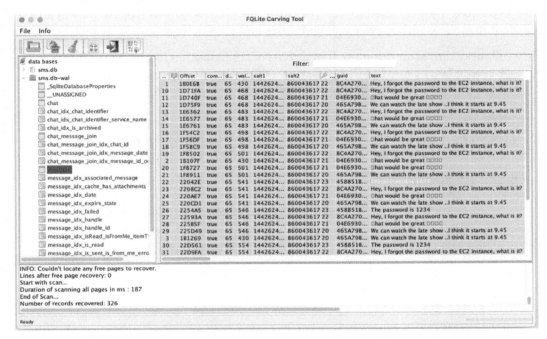

Figure 4.16 – FQLite recovers deleted records from an SQLite database

By now, you should have a good understanding of how SQLite works, how an investigator can examine a database through the command-line tool, and which are the most common techniques for data recovery. We'll now take a step forward and look at another popular data structure.

Working with property lists

Property lists, commonly referred to as **plists**, are one of the favorite data structures used in iOS devices. They are used to store, organize, and access various types of data in an efficient manner, such as device configurations and user settings.

In a full filesystem acquisition, we find dozens of configuration files stored as plists in `/private/var/mobile/Library/Preferences/`, such as `com.apple.DictionaryServices.plist`, as shown here:

```xml
<?xml version="1.0" encoding="UTF-8"?>
<!DOCTYPE plist PUBLIC "-//Apple//DTD PLIST 1.0//EN" "http://
www.apple.com/DTDs/PropertyList-1.0.dtd">
<plist version="1.0">
<dict>
    <key>DCSAssetPreferenceKeyDownloadedDictionaries</key>
    <array>
        <string>Apple Dictionary.dictionary</string>
        <string>Italian.dictionary</string>
        <string>Italian - English.dictionary</string>
    </array>
</dict>
</plist>
```

plists can be stored in two different formats:

- An XML-based format
- A binary-encoded format, also known as **Binary-PLIST (BPLIST)**

While the XML-encoded plist can be easily displayed with any text editor, the binary-encoded format cannot be displayed in its native format but must be converted to XML. We can do this by using the `plutil` tool, which is already installed on macOS. In other OSes, the tool will be available after installing **iTunes**.

To convert a bplist into an XML-encoded plist, run the following command:

```
plutil -convert xml1 filename.plist
```

In the previous part of the chapter, we learned that SQLite databases can also contain BLOBs, which are records of binary data. It's quite common on iOS devices to see bplists stored inside BLOBs; in this scenario, the examiner will have to export the BLOB to a file in binary format and then convert the bplist into an XML-encoded file using the `plutil` tool.

Let's see how this works.

The following screenshot shows the `applicationState.db` SQLite database using DB Browser. As you can see, the `kvs` table has a column called `value`, which contains BLOBs of binary data:

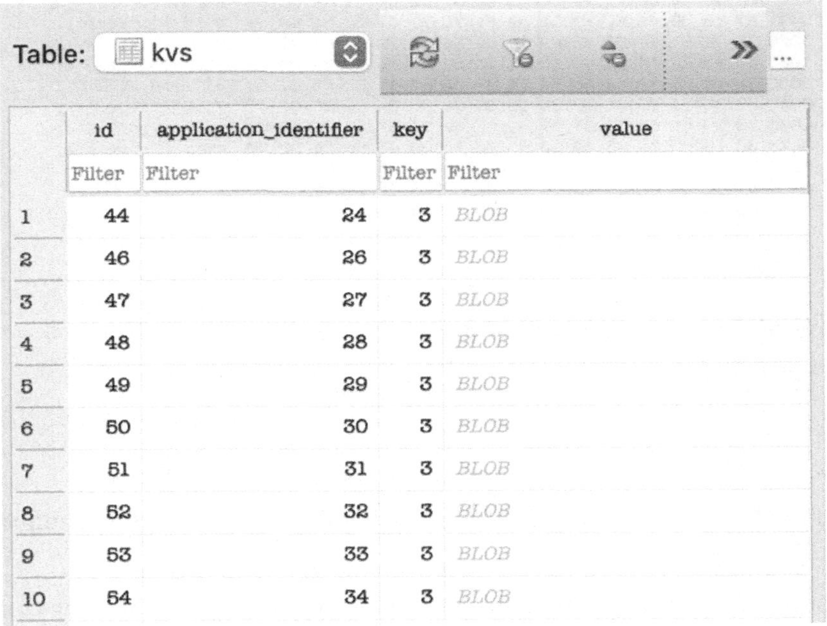

	id	application_identifier	key	value
	Filter	Filter	Filter	Filter
1	44	24	3	*BLOB*
2	46	26	3	*BLOB*
3	47	27	3	*BLOB*
4	48	28	3	*BLOB*
5	49	29	3	*BLOB*
6	50	30	3	*BLOB*
7	51	31	3	*BLOB*
8	52	32	3	*BLOB*
9	53	33	3	*BLOB*
10	54	34	3	*BLOB*

Figure 4.17 – A SQLite database containing BLOBs of binary data

DB Browser allows us to view the contents of the BLOB in a hex viewer. Looking at the first few bytes, we see the bplist00 string, so we now know for sure that the BLOB contains a bplist:

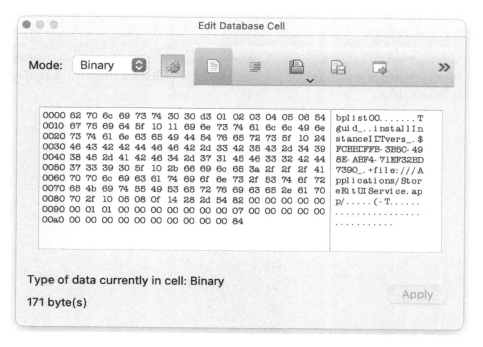

Figure 4.18 – The hex viewer shows the bplist in binary format

Now, select the **Export to File** icon and save the BLOB into a file. In this example, we're calling the file data.plist.

Finally, we can convert the exported bplist to a plist by running the following command:

```
plutil -convert xml1 data.plist
```

We can now examine the plist with an editor or any text viewer.

Working with protocol buffers

Protocol buffers (**protbufs**) are a language-agnostic method developed by Google to serialize data structures to binary format and are sometimes used as an alternative to XML files or plists.

Although Protobufs are not as common on iOS devices, there are still some apps that use them to store data so an investigator should have at least a basic understanding of how to work with these files.

As protobufs are stored in binary format, they aren't human-readable; the `protoc` command-line tool allows you to display the contents of the file and gives you a general idea of how the data is structured.

> **Tip**
>
> The `protoc` tool is part of the protocol buffers package and can be downloaded from the GitHub repository located at `https://github.com/protocolbuffers/protobuf`.

Once the `protoc` tool has been installed, the contents of a protobuf can be printed to the screen by running the following command:

```
protoc --decode_raw < [protobuf_blob_file]
```

Examples of applications that make use of protocol buffers include Apple **Notes**, Apple **Maps**, and the **Spotify** application.

Now that we have a better understanding of what artifacts look like and how these can be manually analyzed, the next section will provide an exhaustive list of the most common evidence locations on iOS devices and what insights we can expect to gain.

Locating common artifacts

Application-related artifacts are essential for an iOS investigation, but device settings, logs, and user-generated content are also important. In this final section of the chapter, we'll look into some common locations within the iOS filesystem that the examiner can quickly review to gather more information:

- The starting point for any iOS examination will most likely be `/private/var/mobile/Library/`, as this folder contains artifacts that relate to device information as well as data pertaining to the user's iCloud account. *Table 4.2* illustrates some of the files that may be of interest.

- `/private/var/mobile/Library/Preferences/` contains device configuration files and user-defined settings, such as language, device name, time settings, and so on. Most of the artifacts will be plists, either in XML or binary format.

- Artifacts relating to the SIM card such as the phone number, IMEI, and network carrier can be found by analyzing the plists located at `/private/var/wireless/Library/Preferences/`.

- `/private/var/preferences/SystemConfiguration/` contains cellular information and network settings, including WiFi and VPN data.

The following table shows some of the most common device-related artifacts. All paths are relative to `/private/var/`:

Path	Description
installd/Library/MobileInstallation/LastBuildInfo.plist	OS version
mobile/Library/Preferences/com.apple.springboard.plist	Order of apps
mobile/Library/Preferences/com.apple.mobilegestalt.plist	Device name
mobile/Library/Preferences/com.apple.Preferences.plist	Disk usage
mobile/Library/Preferences/com.apple.purplebuddy.plist	Language
mobile/Library/Preferences/com.apple.commcenter.shared.plist	Phone number
mobile/Library/Preferences/com.apple.corerecents.recentsd.plist	iCloud data
preferences/SystemConfiguration/com.apple.networkidentification.plist	Network data
preferences/SystemConfiguration/NetworkInterfaces.plist	WiFi data
preferences/SystemConfiguration/preferences.plist	Cellular + WiFi

Table 4.2 – Common iOS device artifacts

Now that we know where to look out for settings and logs, we'll take a quick look at where to find data generated by the user, such as messages or calls. *Table 4.3* illustrates some of the most popular files. As always, the paths are relative to /private/var/:

Path	Description
mobile/Library/Mail/Recents.db	Recent SMS and email metadata
mobile/Media/Recordings/Recordings.db	Audio recordings
mobile/Media/PhotoData/Photos.sqlite	Photo categorization
mobile/Library/CallHistoryDB/CallHistory.storedata	Call log
mobile/Library/SMS/sms.db	SMS/MMS/iMessage
mobile/Library/Safari/History.db	Browsing history
mobile/Media/DCIM/*	Photos
mobile/Library/Accounts/Accounts3.sqlite	Account details

Table 4.3 – Common iOS user artifacts

It's important to understand that these tables only include some of the most popular artifacts, but there are many, many more files that could be of interest for the investigation. The examiner should always take an in-depth look at the entire filesystem to gain all available insights from the data.

Summary

In this chapter, we learned which are the most common types of artifacts found on an iOS device and how to analyze these files.

First, we introduced databases and learned how SQLite organizes data into tables, columns, and rows. Then, we took a deep dive into SQLite's internal architecture to understand how records are organized at a lower level and where deleted records can be found. We discussed possible options to attempt the recovery of deleted data, such as manually analyzing the database through a hex viewer or using tools such as FQLite.

Further on in the chapter, we talked about property lists and protocol buffers, which can also be found on iOS devices in XML or binary format. To be readable, these files first need to be decoded.

Finally, in the last part of the chapter, we outlined some common locations where artifacts can be found and listed some essential files that should be considered in every investigation. In the next chapter, we will discuss pattern-of-life forensics.

5
Pattern-of-Life Forensics

In the previous chapter, we learned all about different kinds of artifacts that can be found on iOS devices, such as SQLite databases and plists, and how to manually analyze these files. In this chapter, we will use this knowledge to work with some of the most interesting databases from a forensics perspective, such as the **KnowledgeC** database, which is the go-to solution for pattern-of-life forensics.

Pattern-of-life data is all about the habits that the device owner carries out in their day-to-day life. When it comes to smartphones, this includes what apps have been used at any given point in time and for how long, when the device was unlocked, what the battery temperature was, and what webpage the user was browsing.

We'll start the chapter by defining pattern-of-life forensics to get a better understanding of what kind of data we may encounter in an iOS device investigation. We will then discuss timestamps and how to convert them between different time zones. Then, we will take an in-depth look at KnowledgeC, power logs, and device events, and we will learn how to identify user interaction. Finally, we will introduce Apollo, an open source tool that greatly simplifies the process of locating and reviewing pattern-of-life artifacts.

In this chapter, we will cover the following topics:

- Introducing pattern-of-life forensics
- Working with timestamps
- Logs, events, and user interaction
- Introducing Apollo

Introducing pattern-of-life forensics

If you have never had the opportunity to take a close look at an iOS device's pattern-of-life data, you'll likely be surprised by the amount and variety of data that is collected, stored, and processed during normal smartphone use. Typically, this data is used by the operating system to provide customized recommendations to the user, such as Siri's suggestions.

What exactly is pattern-of-life forensics? This data is all about **user behavior** and **device usage**, and it allows the investigator to answer questions such as the following:

- What has the user been using the device for?
- What have they accessed?
- Who have they communicated with?

From a forensic perspective, analyzing pattern-of-life data is extremely useful, not only to identify all activities performed on the device in a given period of time but also to build a profile of the device owner; by analyzing the data collected by iOS, the investigator will gain a deep understanding of the owner's habits, such as which apps are used when the user wakes up, which Wi-Fi networks the device connects to most often, web history, and notifications. Building a profile of the activity that can be considered normal allows the investigator to instantly detect **patterns of abnormal behavior** that may be of interest to the investigation.

Surprisingly, pattern-of-life data gets very little attention from the forensic community, mostly because of the challenges in obtaining the relevant SQLite databases from the device; this data is not accessible during normal use of the device and can only be accessed through a **full filesystem acquisition**. Clearly, this limits the range of devices from which this kind of data can be extracted, but the **checkm8 exploit** and other techniques such as **agent-based acquisitions** that rely on public software vulnerabilities allow investigators to access user activity and behavior from most iOS devices.

Meaningful SQLite databases

The following is a list of the most common databases relevant to pattern-of-life forensics. We will take an in-depth look at each of these later on in the book:

- The primary source for user and device activity is the `KnowledgeC.db` SQLite database, which can be found on both macOS and iOS devices. On iOS, it is located at `/private/var/mobile/Library/CoreDuet/Knowledge/` and can be accessed only through a full filesystem acquisition. This database typically contains hundreds of thousands of records pertaining to device events and user activity.

- The `interactionC.db` SQLite database keeps track of recent interactions between the device owner and their contacts, such as SMS messages or calls. It's not exactly clear what the retention period is for this database, as the data is not consistent among different devices, but generally speaking, an investigator will find entries for the last six months. Although `interactionC.db` does not contain the actual contents of the conversations, it contains metadata that can be correlated with other artifacts. The database can be found at `/private/var/mobile/Library/CoreDuet/People/`.

- The `CurrentPowerlog.PLSQL` file, located at `/private/var/containers/Shared/SystemGroup/UUID/Library/BatteryLife/`, tracks data related to battery life, such as usage and temperature.

- Another interesting database that can help an investigator understand what processes were running on a device at a certain point in time is the `DataUsage.sqlite` database, which is located at `/private/var/wireless/Library/Databases/`. This database stores network usage stats for every process.

- One of the most important subjects pertaining to pattern-of-life forensics is location data; on iOS, there is more than one file that tracks where a user is located at any given point in time, showing which places a user visits more often, such as the `cache_encrypted.db` database located at `/private/var/root/Library/Caches/locationd/` or the `consolidated.db` database. Every database contains data with different granularity and levels of detail, and we'll look into this topic thoroughly in the next chapter.

Now that we've learned which are the most common sources of pattern-of-life data, you may be wondering what exactly we can expect to see tracked in these databases. The following screenshot shows some of the most interesting pattern-of-life artifacts by viewing them in Cellebrite Physical Analyzer:

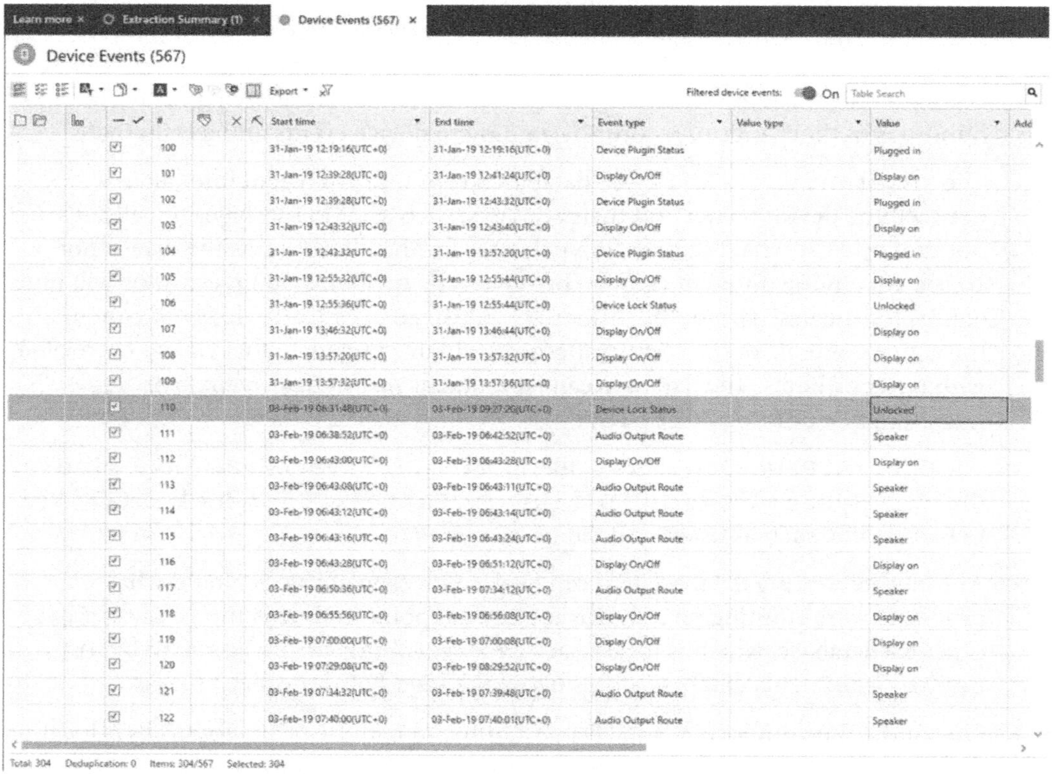

Figure 5.1 – Device events in Cellebrite Physical Analyzer

As you can see, `KnowledgeC.db` records every time the device was plugged in, unplugged, locked and unlocked, when the display was activated, if the speakers were on or off, and so on.

Before we dive deep into analyzing this database, we'll take a look at how iOS databases and log files represent the date and time of a specific event and how to convert between different timestamp formats.

Working with timestamps

Before jumping into the analysis of SQLite databases, it's important to understand how iOS stores date and time records, and this is achieved by using **timestamps**. A timestamp is a numerical representation of a date and time, usually in the form of the number of seconds elapsed since a certain point in time called an *epoch*.

Generally speaking, timestamps found on iOS devices are presented either as a **Unix timestamp** or a **Mac timestamp**. The investigator should understand what timestamp format is used by each database to ensure that forensic tools display the date and time correctly.

Unix timestamps

A Unix timestamp is a 10-digit number that represents time as the number of seconds elapsed since 01/01/1970 00:00:00. This timestamp can be easily converted to a readable string by using online converters, such as www.epochconverter.com.

As an example, we will use an online tool to convert a Unix timestamp, 1633614474, to a readable string:

Convert epoch to human-readable date and vice versa

| 1633614474 | | Timestamp to Human date | [batch convert] |

Supports Unix timestamps in seconds, milliseconds, microseconds and nanoseconds.

Assuming that this timestamp is in **seconds**:
GMT: Thursday 7 October 2021 13:47:54
Your time zone: giovedì 7 ottobre 2021 15:47:54 GMT+02:00 DST
Relative: A few seconds ago

Figure 5.2 – Converting a Unix timestamp to a string

Now that we know what a Unix timestamp is, let's see how we can convert it to a readable string using a SQL query.

In the example below, we have a single table called Events that has three columns: id, uuid, and timestamp. The timestamp is in Unix format:

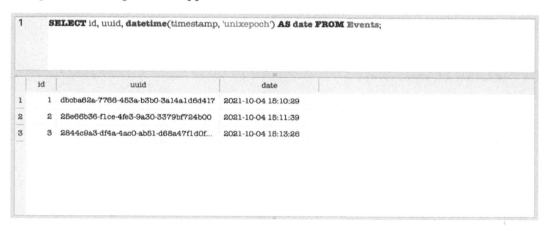

```
1    SELECT * FROM Events;
```

	id	uuid	timestamp
1	1	dbcba62a-7766-453a-b3b0-3a14a1d6d417	1633360229
2	2	25e66b36-f1ce-4fe3-9a30-3379bf724b00	1633360299
3	3	2844c9a3-df4a-4ac0-ab51-d68a47f1d0f3...	1633360406

Figure 5.3 – The Events table in a SQLite database

To convert the Unix timestamp to a human-readable string, run the following query:

```
SELECT id, uuid, datetime(timestamp, 'unixepoch') AS date FROM
Events;
```

The datetime SQL function converts the numeric value in the timestamp column to a string. The resulting time is supplied in UTC format:

```
1    SELECT id, uuid, datetime(timestamp, 'unixepoch') AS date FROM Events;
```

	id	uuid	date
1	1	dbcba62a-7766-453a-b3b0-3a14a1d6d417	2021-10-04 15:10:29
2	2	25e66b36-f1ce-4fe3-9a30-3379bf724b00	2021-10-04 15:11:39
3	3	2844c9a3-df4a-4ac0-ab51-d68a47f1d0f...	2021-10-04 15:13:26

Figure 5.4 – Converting a timestamp to a string

To display the string in local time format, run this query instead:

```
SELECT id, uuid, datetime(timestamp, 'unixepoch', 'localtime')
AS date FROM Events;
```

The time zone will reflect the settings of the device that is being used, usually the investigator's workstation.

Mac timestamps

Another commonly used timestamp format is Mac absolute time, which is defined as the number of seconds elapsed since the Mac epoch on 01/01/2001 00:00:00. A Mac timestamp can be converted to a human-readable string by using online converters or simply by adding the number of seconds since the **Unix epoch** (978307200) to the Mac timestamp and then converting it to a string.

The following query illustrates the process of converting a Mac timestamp to a string in the local time zone:

```
SELECT id, uuid, datetime(timestamp + 978307200, 'unixepoch',
'localtime') AS date FROM Events;
```

Mac timestamps are commonly used in iOS pattern-of-life data, such as in the KnowledgeC.db database.

Logs, events, and user interaction

At the start of this chapter, we introduced pattern-of-life forensics, and we learned how iOS stores and analyzes a number of user events and device events. Then, we went through the most common sources of data, such as the KnowledgeC.db database, and learned how iOS represents time through Unix timestamps and Mac absolute time.

Now, we'll take an in-depth look at one of the most forensically interesting SQLite databases you will find on an iOS device.

The KnowledgeC database

KnowledgeC.db is the SQLite database that tracks almost all activity and device events, ranging from battery level to what music was played. The database is located at /private/var/mobile/Library/CoreDuet/Knowledge/, and it is only accessible through a full filesystem acquisition. The database is made of 16 tables, although most of the useful data is concentrated in one of them, the ZOBJECT table.

The following screenshot shows the database schema:

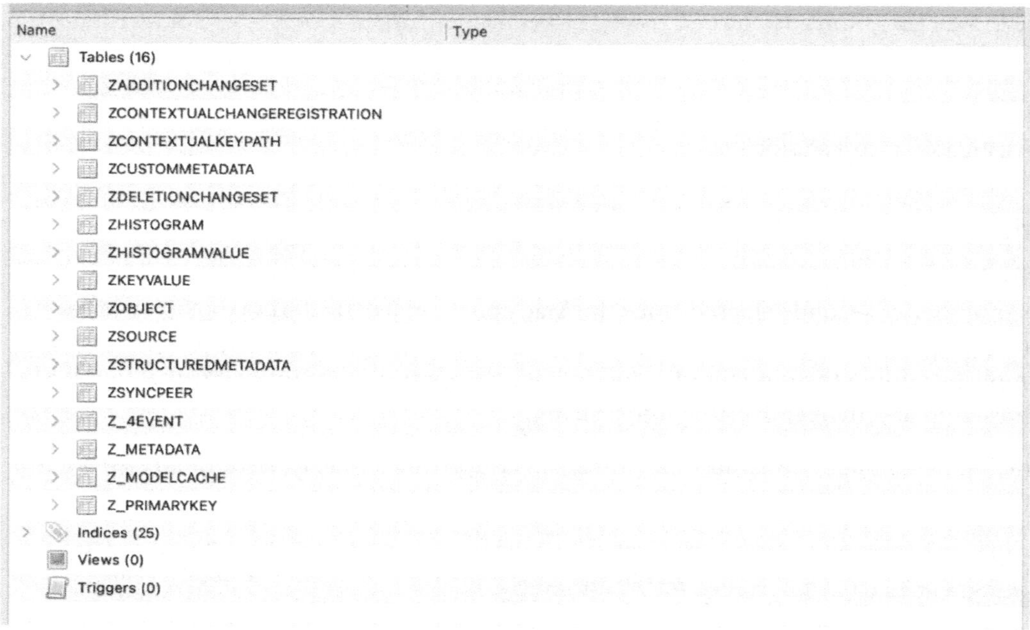

Name	Type
∨ 🔲 Tables (16)	
> 🔲 ZADDITIONCHANGESET	
> 🔲 ZCONTEXTUALCHANGEREGISTRATION	
> 🔲 ZCONTEXTUALKEYPATH	
> 🔲 ZCUSTOMMETADATA	
> 🔲 ZDELETIONCHANGESET	
> 🔲 ZHISTOGRAM	
> 🔲 ZHISTOGRAMVALUE	
> 🔲 ZKEYVALUE	
> 🔲 ZOBJECT	
> 🔲 ZSOURCE	
> 🔲 ZSTRUCTUREDMETADATA	
> 🔲 ZSYNCPEER	
> 🔲 Z_4EVENT	
> 🔲 Z_METADATA	
> 🔲 Z_MODELCACHE	
> 🔲 Z_PRIMARYKEY	
> 🔖 Indices (25)	
🖼 Views (0)	
📄 Triggers (0)	

Figure 5.5 – The schema of the KnowledgeC database

It's important to keep in mind that data in this database will only be stored for approximately four weeks before being purged on a first in-first out basis, so if pattern-of-life data is an essential part of the investigation, the device should be acquired as soon as possible.

The main table of interest from a forensic perspective is the ZOBJECT table, which contains a row for each event or interaction with data spread over 40 columns. We will briefly go over the most interesting columns to understand how this table logs events:

- Each row contains a ZCREATIONDATE column that records a timestamp (in MAC format) of when the entry was written to the database.

- The ZSTARTDATE and ZENDDATE columns contain a timestamp for the start and end times of the event.

- The ZSTARTDAYOFWEEK column indicates what day the event occurred.

- The GMT offset in seconds is indicated in the ZSECONDSFROMGMT column.

- The ZSTREAMNAME column indicates the type of event that occurred.

- The ZVALUESTRING column shows the bundle ID for the application relevant to the event.

To gain a better understanding of what kind of events will be logged by this database, we'll analyze the ZSTREAMNAME column and check its values. You can see a list of the event types by running the following SQL query:

```
SELECT DISTINCT ZOBJECT.ZSTREAMNAME FROM ZOBJECT ORDER BY
ZSTREAMNAME;
```

On one of the latest iOS devices running iOS 14.6, this query resulted in more than 50 different event types. The following is a list of some of the most common event types and how to interpret data from the ZOBJECT table.

/device/batteryPercentage

The batteryPercentage stream type indicates the charge level of the device's battery. The percentage value is stored in the ZVALUEDOUBLE column.

/device/isPluggedIn

This event indicates whether the device was plugged in and charging or not. The ZVALUEINTEGER column will indicate 0 if the device was unplugged or 1 if the device was plugged in.

/displayIsBacklit

This event stream indicates whether the backlight was lit or not. The ZVALUEINTEGER column will indicate 0 if the backlight was off or 1 if the backlight was on. This event can be useful to detect human interaction while the device is locked; simply tapping the screen will light up the display, resulting in this event being triggered.

/device/isLocked

The isLocked stream type indicates whether the device is passcode-locked or not. The locked status is stored in the ZVALUEINTEGER column; a value of 0 indicates that the device is locked, while a value of 1 indicates an unlocked device.

/app/inFocus

This event stream indicates which application is active and running in the foreground. The ZVALUESTRING column stores the name of the app. The inFocus event can be analyzed to track application usage in great detail.

/notification/usage

This event stream indicates push notification activity. The ZVALUESTRING column shows what kind of activity was logged, such as *receive*, *clear*, and *dismiss*. This event can also be useful to identify user activity, such as the user dismissing a notification when the device is locked.

/app/webUsage

This event indicates which app is using the internet connection. The ZVALUESTRING column shows the name of the application.

/display/orientation

The orientation event indicates a change in the device's orientation. The ZVALUEINTEGER column will indicate 0 if the device is in portrait mode or 1 if the device is in landscape mode.

/media/nowPlaying

This event indicates that multimedia is playing on the device. The ZVALUESTRING column will display information on the app that is playing it, such as YouTube or Apple Music.

By now, you should have a rough idea of what kind of events are logged in the KnowledgeC.db database and how to analyze such records. We will now look into more advanced topics, such as analyzing application usage in detail.

Analyzing application usage

One of the most valuable insights that can be gained by analyzing pattern-of-life data is application usage. By analyzing the /app/inFocus event stream from the ZOBJECT table, the investigator will be able to identify what apps were being used on a device in a certain time span and for how long.

As an example, we'll run a query to identify what applications were used over a 48-hour time span, starting from 24/05/2021 00:00:00 up to 26/05/2021 00:00:00.

First, we need to convert our date and time to a Mac absolute timestamp:

Result

Conversion of date and time: **Monday, 2021-05-24 00:00:00 UTC**

Date and Time:	**Monday, 2021-05-24 00:00:00 UTC**
UNIX Epoch Time:	**1621814400**
UNIX Epoch Time (Hex):	**60AAEC80**
CF Absolute Time:	**643507200**

Figure 5.6 – Converting date and time to a MAC timestamp using
https://www.gaijin.at/en/tools/time-converter

Now that we have our Mac absolute timestamps, we want to query KnowledgeC.db for all /app/inFocus events that occurred between the 643507200 timestamp and the 643680000 timestamp. To do so, run the following query:

```
SELECT
datetime(ZOBJECT.ZSTARTDATE+978307200,'UNIXEPOCH', 'LOCALTIME')
as "START",
datetime(ZOBJECT.ZENDDATE+978307200,'UNIXEPOCH', 'LOCALTIME')
as "END",
ZOBJECT.ZSECONDSFROMGMT/3600 AS "GMT OFFSET",
(ZOBJECT.ZENDDATE-ZOBJECT.ZSTARTDATE) as "USAGE IN SECONDS",
ZOBJECT.ZSTREAMNAME,
ZOBJECT.ZVALUESTRING
FROM ZOBJECT
WHERE ZSTREAMNAME IS "/app/inFocus"
AND ZOBJECT.ZSTARTDATE > 643507200
AND ZOBJECT.ZSTARTDATE < 643680000
ORDER BY "START";
```

First, we use the datetime SQL command to select the start and end timestamps and convert them to a readable string. Then, we calculate the GMT offset in hours and the duration of the event in seconds. Finally, we filter down the results by only selecting /app/inFocus events that occurred between the timestamps we calculated previously.

The resulting dataset is shown below:

	START	END	GMT OFFSET	USAGE IN SECONDS	ZSTREAMNAME	ZVALUESTRING
1	2021-05-24 08:36:56	2021-05-24 08:37:10	2	14	/app/inFocus	com.apple.mobilesafari
2	2021-05-24 08:37:10	2021-05-24 08:37:12	2	2	/app/inFocus	com.apple.CoreAuthUI
3	2021-05-24 08:37:12	2021-05-24 08:37:32	2	20	/app/inFocus	com.apple.mobilesafari
4	2021-05-24 08:37:32	2021-05-24 08:37:34	2	2	/app/inFocus	us.zoom.videomeetings
5	2021-05-24 08:37:34	2021-05-24 08:37:37	2	3	/app/inFocus	com.apple.mobilesafari
6	2021-05-24 08:37:37	2021-05-24 08:38:13	2	36	/app/inFocus	us.zoom.videomeetings
7	2021-05-24 08:38:13	2021-05-24 10:56:11	2	8278	/app/inFocus	us.zoom.videomeetings
8	2021-05-24 10:56:15	2021-05-24 10:58:45	2	150	/app/inFocus	com.apple.mobilesafari
9	2021-05-24 10:56:17	2021-05-24 10:56:18	2	1	/app/inFocus	com.apple.PDFKit.PDFExtensionView
10	2021-05-24 10:56:19	2021-05-24 10:56:21	2	2	/app/inFocus	com.apple.PDFKit.PDFExtensionView
11	2021-05-24 10:58:45	2021-05-24 10:58:46	2	1	/app/inFocus	com.apple.CoreAuthUI
12	2021-05-24 10:58:46	2021-05-24 10:58:56	2	10	/app/inFocus	com.apple.mobilesafari

Figure 5.7 – The query result shows application usage

As you can see, we have a detailed breakdown of what applications were used on the device, the date and time of the event, and how long the app was used. For example, you can see that on this day, I briefly navigated the web using Safari, then attended a 2-hour Zoom meeting, and finally viewed a PDF file from a website in Safari.

Another insight that can be useful for the investigation is analyzing the user's behavior and determining whether they were engaged in any long task, such as watching a movie. We can achieve this by ordering the result in descending order based on the USAGE column. In the following example, I have also removed all time constraints:

```
SELECT
datetime(ZOBJECT.ZSTARTDATE+978307200,'UNIXEPOCH', 'LOCALTIME')
as "START",
datetime(ZOBJECT.ZENDDATE+978307200,'UNIXEPOCH', 'LOCALTIME')
as "END",
ZOBJECT.ZSECONDSFROMGMT/3600 AS "GMT OFFSET",
(ZOBJECT.ZENDDATE-ZOBJECT.ZSTARTDATE) as "USAGE IN SECONDS",
ZOBJECT.ZSTREAMNAME,
ZOBJECT.ZVALUESTRING
FROM ZOBJECT
WHERE ZSTREAMNAME IS "/app/inFocus"
ORDER BY "USAGE IN SECONDS" DESC;
```

Below, you can see the resulting data:

	START	END	GMT OFFSET	USAGE IN SECONDS	ZSTREAMNAME	ZVALUESTRING
1	2021-05-24 08:38:13	2021-05-24 10:56:11	2	8278	/app/inFocus	us.zoom.videomeetings
2	2021-06-06 14:53:43	2021-06-06 17:07:49	2	8046	/app/inFocus	com.apple.mobilesafari
3	2021-05-26 16:25:19	2021-05-26 18:38:19	2	7980	/app/inFocus	us.zoom.videomeetings
4	2021-06-02 11:03:58	2021-06-02 12:31:20	2	5242	/app/inFocus	com.apple.mobilesafari
5	2021-05-25 14:57:21	2021-05-25 16:23:48	2	5187	/app/inFocus	com.apple.mobilesafari
6	2021-05-24 13:37:35	2021-05-24 14:58:41	2	4866	/app/inFocus	com.apple.mobilesafari
7	2021-06-13 18:02:54	2021-06-13 19:23:42	2	4848	/app/inFocus	com.apple.mobilesafari
8	2021-06-13 16:44:36	2021-06-13 18:02:54	2	4698	/app/inFocus	com.apple.mobilesafari
9	2021-05-29 10:52:03	2021-05-29 12:09:21	2	4638	/app/inFocus	com.google.ios.youtube
10	2021-05-31 17:47:34	2021-05-31 19:04:05	2	4591	/app/inFocus	us.zoom.videomeetings
11	2021-06-01 22:03:57	2021-06-01 23:19:53	2	4556	/app/inFocus	com.netflix.Netflix
12	2021-06-06 11:15:07	2021-06-06 12:30:11	2	4504	/app/inFocus	com.apple.mobilesafari

Figure 5.8 – Analyzing long tasks

As you can see, I was engaged in quite a few long-running tasks, such as Zoom meetings, web browsing, and playing media on YouTube and Netflix. Now, let's suppose we want to dig deeper into the data and analyze what happened on the evening of 1 June, 2021. From the previous query result, we can see that on that evening, I was using Netflix. But what exactly was I watching?

First, we'll calculate the Mac timestamps for the date and time, and then run the following query:

```
SELECT
datetime(ZOBJECT.ZSTARTDATE+978307200,'UNIXEPOCH', 'LOCALTIME')
as "START",
datetime(ZOBJECT.ZENDDATE+978307200,'UNIXEPOCH', 'LOCALTIME')
as "END",
ZOBJECT.ZSECONDSFROMGMT/3600 AS "GMT OFFSET",
(ZOBJECT.ZENDDATE-ZOBJECT.ZSTARTDATE) as "USAGE IN SECONDS",
ZOBJECT.ZSTREAMNAME,
ZOBJECT.ZSTRUCTUREDMETADATA,
ZOBJECT.ZVALUESTRING
FROM ZOBJECT
WHERE ZOBJECT.ZSTARTDATE > 644266800
AND ZOBJECT.ZSTARTDATE < 644277599
ORDER BY "START";
```

The result is shown below:

	START	END	GMT OFFSET	USAGE IN SECONDS	ZSTREAMNAME	ZSTRUCTUREDMETADATA
123	2021-06-01 22:03:04	2021-06-01 22:03:58	2	54	/media/nowPlaying	5149
124	2021-06-01 22:03:39	2021-06-01 22:03:57	2	18	/app/inFocus	428
125	2021-06-01 22:03:39	2021-06-01 23:19:53	2	4874	/app/usage	15
126	2021-06-01 22:03:40	2021-06-01 22:03:56	2	16	/display/orientation	NULL
127	2021-06-01 22:03:57	2021-06-01 23:19:53	2	4856	/app/inFocus	NULL
128	2021-06-01 22:03:58	2021-06-01 22:03:59	2	1	/media/nowPlaying	51731
129	2021-06-01 22:03:59	2021-06-01 22:04:00	2	1	/media/nowPlaying	51732
130	2021-06-01 22:04:00	2021-06-01 22:04:01	2	1	/media/nowPlaying	51733
131	2021-06-01 22:04:01	2021-06-01 23:19:29	2	4528	/media/nowPlaying	51732
132	2021-06-01 22:04:12	2021-06-01 23:19:48	2	4536	/display/orientation	NULL
133	2021-06-01 22:06:20	2021-06-01 22:08:20	2	120	/device/batteryPercentage	NULL
134	2021-06-01 22:07:00	2021-06-01 22:07:00	2	0	/dasd/batterytemperature	NULL

Figure 5.9 – The query result shows user interaction in the time span of interest

By analyzing the resulting dataset, we can see that the Netflix app was launched, a /media/nowPlaying event was triggered, and the device was rotated into landscape mode. To understand what was playing on Netflix, we need to analyze the metadata associated with the event. In this case, the associated ID is 51732, which we will use to query the ZSTRUCTUREDMETADATA table:

```
SELECT
Z_PK AS "ID",
Z_DKNOWPLAYINGMETADATAKEY__TITLE
FROM ZSTRUCTUREDMETADATA
WHERE "ID" = "51732";
```

The result, shown in the following screenshot, displays the name of the application that was playing, Netflix, and the name of the movie I was watching:

	ID	Z_DKNOWPLAYINGMETADATAKEY__TITLE
1	51732	Netflix - Quo Vado?

Figure 5.10 – The metadata associated with the /media/nowPlaying event

As you can see from these simple examples, the investigator has the ability to analyze the user's behavior in great detail and understand not only what application the user was using but also what exactly the user was doing with a particular application. For example, by customizing SQL queries, it is possible to learn what website the user visited or what PDF file the user was reading. We will look at these use cases in detail over the course of the next chapters.

> **Tip**
> Gaining insights from pattern-of-life data would not be possible without the generous contributions from the **Digital Forensics and Incident Response** (**DFIR**) community. In particular, most of the queries used in this chapter are based on the research carried out by Sarah Edwards (@iamevltwin). You can view her blog by going to https://www.mac4n6.com.

Analyzing user interaction

In any kind of digital investigation involving a smart device, typically one of the first questions investigators want to answer is when the device was used and when human-device interaction occurred. This can easily be discovered by looking out for events that require human interaction, such as unlocking the device or activating the screen.

The following query shows when the device was locked or unlocked:

```sql
SELECT
datetime(ZOBJECT.ZSTARTDATE+978307200,'UNIXEPOCH', 'LOCALTIME')
as "DATE / TIME",
ZOBJECT.ZSECONDSFROMGMT/3600 AS "GMT OFFSET",
CASE ZOBJECT.ZVALUEINTEGER
        WHEN '0' THEN 'UNLOCKED'
        WHEN '1' THEN 'LOCKED'
     END "IS LOCKED"
FROM ZOBJECT
WHERE ZOBJECT.ZSTREAMNAME LIKE "/device/isLocked"
ORDER BY "DATE / TIME";
```

The result is shown in the following screenshot:

	DATE / TIME	GMT OFFSET	IS LOCKED
1	2021-05-23 14:49:13	2	LOCKED
2	2021-05-23 15:41:55	2	UNLOCKED
3	2021-05-23 15:58:59	2	LOCKED
4	2021-05-23 16:08:33	2	UNLOCKED
5	2021-05-23 16:52:36	2	LOCKED
6	2021-05-23 22:11:48	2	UNLOCKED
7	2021-05-23 22:50:47	2	LOCKED
8	2021-05-23 22:54:20	2	UNLOCKED
9	2021-05-23 23:23:24	2	LOCKED
10	2021-05-23 23:33:14	2	UNLOCKED
11	2021-05-24 00:08:13	2	LOCKED
12	2021-05-24 00:10:48	2	UNLOCKED

Figure 5.11 – The query shows the device lock status

If, however, we want to find out every time the screen was activated, even if the device was not unlocked, we can do so by running this query:

```
SELECT
datetime(ZOBJECT.ZSTARTDATE+978307200,'UNIXEPOCH', 'LOCALTIME')
as "DATE / TIME",
ZOBJECT.ZSECONDSFROMGMT/3600 AS "GMT OFFSET"
FROM ZOBJECT
WHERE ZOBJECT.ZSTREAMNAME LIKE "/display/isBacklit"
AND ZOBJECT.ZVALUEINTEGER = '1'
ORDER BY "DATE / TIME";
```

The resulting records will show when the display was activated. The queries used in these examples should be straightforward to understand and can easily be customized to match other events that can be of interest to the investigation.

We will now look into another option to analyze pattern-of-life data, using an open source tool.

Introducing Apollo

So far, we have learned how to manually analyze pattern-of-life data by querying the SQLite databases. However, there is another option that automates the process and allows the investigator to look at all the data in a unified database.

Apollo, which stands for **Apple Pattern of Life Lazy Output'er**, is a Python script developed by Sarah Edwards (`@iamevltwin`) that correlates multiple sources of data into a unified **timeline**, simplifying the examiner's job of finding out what exactly was happening on the device.

The tool consists of dozens of highly configurable modules that each query a specific iOS database to extract data and events. The main Python script then compiles the results of each module into a unified **CSV** file or SQLite database.

We'll now go over the steps required to download the tool, run it, and export the results into a single SQLite database:

1. To download Apollo, head over to its GitHub repository located at `https://github.com/mac4n6/APOLLO` and download the latest version as a ZIP archive or by cloning the repository by running the `git clone` command.

2. Next, run the tool by specifying the export format, the location of the modules directory, and the location of the data that should be analyzed, such as the folder that contains the SQLite databases or the full filesystem extraction. For example, running `python apollo.py -output sql modules/ fs-extraction/` will run Apollo in SQL mode, analyzing the files in the `fs-extraction` folder and running all modules found in the `modules` folder. Apollo can be run using different options too; for a full list of all available command-line options, you can refer to the project's GitHub page.

3. When the tool ends the process, the results will be stored in a file called `apollo.db`.

4. You can then proceed to analyze the SQLite database using your tool of choice, such as **DB Browser**.

The following screenshot shows the output database in DB Browser:

	Key ▾¹	Activity	Output	Database	
	Filter	Filter	Filter	Filter	Filter
106553	2021-06-19 07:53:52	Device/App Assertions	[...	tmp_apollo/private/var/containers/Shared/SystemGroup/...	modul
106554	2021-06-19 07:53:52	WiFi Connection	[...	tmp_apollo/private/var/containers/Shared/SystemGroup/...	modul
106555	2021-06-19 07:53:52	WiFi Connection	[...	tmp_apollo/private/var/containers/Shared/SystemGroup/...	modul
106556	2021-06-19 07:53:52	WiFi Connection	[...	tmp_apollo/private/var/containers/Shared/SystemGroup/...	modul
106557	2021-06-19 07:53:52	Process ID	[...	tmp_apollo/private/var/containers/Shared/SystemGroup/...	modul
106558	2021-06-19 07:53:52	Process ID	[...	tmp_apollo/private/var/containers/Shared/SystemGroup/...	modul
106559	2021-06-19 07:53:52	Battery Level UI	[...	tmp_apollo/private/var/containers/Shared/SystemGroup/...	modul
106560	2021-06-19 07:53:56	Battery Level	[...	tmp_apollo/private/var/mobile/Library/CoreDuet/...	modul
106561	2021-06-19 07:54:12	Battery Level	[...	tmp_apollo/private/var/containers/Shared/SystemGroup/...	modul
106562	2021-06-19 07:57:09	Battery Level	[...	tmp_apollo/private/var/containers/Shared/SystemGroup/...	modul
106563	2021-06-19 07:57:09	WiFi Connection	[...	tmp_apollo/private/var/containers/Shared/SystemGroup/...	modul
106564	2021-06-19 07:57:09	WiFi Connection	[...	tmp_apollo/private/var/containers/Shared/SystemGroup/...	modul
106565	2021-06-19 07:58:55	Routined Location	[...	tmp_apollo/private/var/mobile/Library/Caches/...	modul
106566	2021-06-19 07:59:54	App Usage by Hour	[...	tmp_apollo/private/var/containers/Shared/SystemGroup/...	modul
106567	2021-06-19 07:59:54	App Usage by Hour	[...	tmp_apollo/private/var/containers/Shared/SystemGroup/...	modul
106568	2021-06-19 07:59:54	App Usage by Hour	[...	tmp_apollo/private/var/containers/Shared/SystemGroup/...	modul
106569	2021-06-19 07:59:54	App Usage by Hour	[...	tmp_apollo/private/var/containers/Shared/SystemGroup/...	modul
106570	2021-06-19 07:59:54	App Usage by Hour	[...	tmp_apollo/private/var/containers/Shared/SystemGroup/...	modul
106571	2021-06-19 07:59:54	App Usage by Hour	[...	tmp_apollo/private/var/containers/Shared/SystemGroup/...	modul
106572	2021-06-19 07:59:54	App Usage by Hour	[...	tmp_apollo/private/var/containers/Shared/SystemGroup/...	modul
106573	2021-06-19 07:59:54	App Usage by Hour	[...	tmp_apollo/private/var/containers/Shared/SystemGroup/...	modul
106574	2021-06-19 07:59:54	App Usage by Hour	[...	tmp_apollo/private/var/containers/Shared/SystemGroup/...	modul
106575	2021-06-19 07:59:54	App Usage by Hour	[...	tmp_apollo/private/var/containers/Shared/SystemGroup/...	modul

|◀ ◀ 106553 - 106576 of 209564 ▶ ▶| Go to: 1

Figure 5.12 – The Apollo database displayed in DB Browser

The database consists of a single table, APOLLO, which contains a timeline of all the data that was processed by the tool's modules. The following is a brief description of the table's columns:

- The Key column contains the timestamp of when the event occurred, displayed as a human-readable string.

- The Activity column shows a simple description of what kind of event was logged.

- The Output column contains a JSON object with all the data pertaining to a specific event.

- The Database column indicates from which database the event was extracted.

- The Module column indicates the name of the module that was responsible for extracting and analyzing the event.

Typically, the `Output` command will contain most of the interesting data from a forensic perspective. The following figure shows what the JSON object looks like for a `Battery Level` event:

```
 1  {
 2      "ADJUSTED_TIMESTAMP": "2021-06-19 07:57:09",
 3      "LEVEL": 31.0,
 4      "RAW LEVEL": 31.226496962684408,
 5      "IS CHARGING": 0,
 6      "FULLY CHARGED": 0,
 7      "ORIGINAL_TIMESTAMP": "2021-04-26 05:35:55",
 8      "OFFSET_TIMESTAMP": "2021-04-28 15:48:55",
 9      "TIME_OFFSET": 4674074.367777824,
10      "PLBATTERYAGENT_EVENTBACKWARD_BATTERY TABLE ID":
        480012
11  }
```

Figure 5.13 – The JSON object stored in Apollo's Output column

The beauty of Apollo is that it is a fully modular and customizable tool that allows the investigator to extract all pattern-of-life data or choose to only include some artifacts by using the appropriate modules. Condensing the result into a single file means that the investigator gains the ability to view a timeline of events that can be easily filtered down based on date and time or by searching for a specific event.

Apollo is under active development and modules are continually being added and updated. Finally, it should be noted that the tool not only supports iOS but also allows the analysis of pattern-of-life data from MacOS devices and others.

Summary

In this chapter, we learned what pattern-of-life forensics is and how an investigator can benefit from analyzing such data to visualize user behavior and detect abnormal patterns.

First, we introduced some of the databases that contain relevant data, such as `KnowledgeC.db` and `InteractionC.db`. Then, we learned how a device handles date and time, and the differences between Unix and Mac timestamps. We also learned how to convert a specific date and time to a timestamp and vice versa.

Later in the chapter, we focused on the most popular database found on an iOS device by performing a full filesystem acquisition – `KnowledgeC.db`. We learned which are the most data-rich tables and how the data is organized in different columns. Then, we described some of the most interesting events logged by this database and introduced SQL queries that can be used to query the database for application usage and user interaction.

Finally, in the last section of this chapter, we introduced an open source tool, Apollo, that greatly simplifies the process of analyzing pattern-of-life data by aggregating the results into a single database.

In the next chapter, we will dive deep into location forensics.

6
Dissecting Location Data

In the previous chapter, we learned all about pattern-of-life artifacts that can be found on iOS devices, such as application usage and system events, and how to manually analyze databases and logs. In this chapter, we will focus on one of the most interesting types of data that can be found on a mobile device, which is location data.

Mobile devices store a wealth of location data, such as data pertaining to cell towers, Wi-Fi networks, and Bluetooth devices that come into close proximity with the device. Location artifacts can also be extracted from third-party applications or multimedia files.

We'll start the chapter by learning what location data is, how a device determines its position, and where this data is stored. We will learn the differences between GPS, cell tower triangulation, and Wi-Fi locations. Then, we will take an in-depth look at some of the SQLite databases that store location data, and we will learn how to analyze them to gain meaningful insights. Finally, we will learn how forensic tools such as Cellebrite Physical Analyzer and Apollo can speed up the process of analyzing location data.

In this chapter, we will cover the following topics:

- Introducing location data
- GPS fixes, cell towers, and Wi-Fi networks
- Locating location artifacts
- Analyzing location data using forensic tools

Introducing location data

The investigation of a device's location data can serve many different facets of an event or series of events. Obtaining information pertaining to the device's location, such as **cell tower** data or **GPS fixes**, can help identify whether a device's owner was at a geographic location at a particular date and time, as well as the owner's route of travel.

The device's location is calculated by **Location Services**, which is an iOS API that is used by all applications that require location data. This means that when developers are creating an iOS app, they don't need to write everything from scratch but can get a device's location simply by requesting it from Location Services.

Typically, a geographic location is expressed in coordinates, such as **latitude** and **longitude**. Additionally, Location Services also determines the device's **altitude** and the radius of how accurate the location is, expressed in meters. This is known as **horizontal accuracy**.

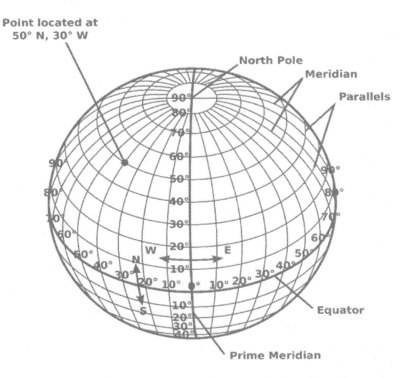

Figure 6.1 – Geographic locations are expressed using latitude and longitude

In the following part of the chapter, we will learn how Location Services works to determine the device's position.

GPS fixes, cell towers, and Wi-Fi networks

The Location Services iOS API uses a collection of technologies known as **Assisted GPS** (**A-GPS**) to determine the device's position. The main reason why mobile devices use A-GPS instead of only traditional satellite GPS is that the latter does not perform well inside buildings; it is also slower than other technologies and quickly drains a device's battery. A-GPS works by augmenting satellite GPS by using external sources (such as cell towers) that enhance the speed, quality, and precision of satellite signals. Data received by external sources is then consolidated to figure out the device's precise location.

The following is a list of sources that power A-GPS:

- Satellite GPS
- Cell towers
- Wi-Fi networks
- Bluetooth devices

We will look into these in more detail in the following sections.

You may be wondering how an iOS device manages to resolve locations from Wi-Fi networks or cell towers; this is implemented by Apple using a **peer-based mechanism** where each iOS device contributes to create a map of networks and devices.

In general, this mechanism consists of three steps:

1. If Location Services is enabled, each iOS device periodically collects and stores the current GPS position and a list of surrounding cell towers and Wi-Fi hotspots.
2. This data is then sent to Apple servers anonymously, where it is consolidated with other collected information and third-party providers.
3. The data is synced back to the iOS device when a location service requests the device's position.

For instance, if a location service requests the device's position and satellite GPS is unavailable, iOS will scan for nearby cell towers and query Apple's peer-generated map to find any geolocation coordinates associated with those cell towers. Through this mechanism, Location Services can get a rough position in a few seconds and then report a more accurate GPS-sourced location when available.

Every iOS device also has an internal cache that stores a large quantity of locations, cell towers, and Wi-Fi networks; by accessing the local cache, the device is able to resolve locations from Wi-Fi networks without needing a data connection. To keep this data up to date, the cache database is purged periodically.

Other than this peer-based mechanism, Apple also relies on external sources to translate cell towers and wireless networks into physical locations; wardriving, for instance, is the act of searching for radio signals by a person usually moving in a vehicle, using a laptop or smartphone, recording their own GPS coordinates together with the data pertaining to the radio signals.

Satellite GPS

Traditional GPS, also known as satellite GPS, is the most accurate source of location data for iOS devices.

This technology is based on a network of over 30 satellites orbiting the earth at an altitude of 20,000 kilometers. Each satellite emits a signal that is transmitted to earth via radio waves, which contains the satellite's identifier, its current position, and a timestamp. Therefore, when a device intercepts a satellite signal, it uses the time difference between the time of signal reception and the broadcast time to compute the distance, or range, from the receiver to the satellite. The device then uses the calculated distance and the satellite's location to calculate its approximate position.

It should be noted that to calculate a precise location, the receiver must be locked on to the signal of at least three satellites. With four or more satellites in view, the receiver can determine its 3D position: **latitude**, **longitude**, and **altitude**.

Certain atmospheric factors and other error sources can affect the accuracy of the device's GPS receiver; however, receivers are typically accurate to within 10 meters.

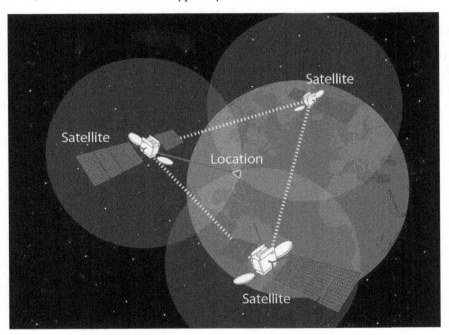

Figure 6.2 – GPS satellite triangulation calculates the receiver's location

From a forensic perspective, GPS location data is stored in the `Cache.sqlite` database located at `/private/var/mobile/Library/Caches/com.apple.routined/`. There are many more databases of interest that contain valuable location data. We will look into these in detail later on in the chapter.

Cell towers

Cell towers are another source of data that can be used by an iOS device to calculate its position. This process is called **trilateration** and, compared to GPS, it is less precise but much faster and has little to no impact on battery life.

The accuracy of trilateration depends on the quality of the signal and the number of cell towers in close proximity to the device. A higher number of towers entails a higher confidence level in the calculated geolocation.

A deep understanding of the process is beyond the scope of this book, but put simply, trilateration is the process whereby a device picks up the radio signal that is broadcasted by a cell tower and evaluates a value called the **Received Signal Strength Indicator (RSSI)** to estimate the distance from the cell tower to which it is connected. The lower the signal, the further the device is from the tower.

As radio waves can be affected by objects, effectively weakening the signal, the distance between the device and the tower is only an approximation. If the location is served by more than one tower, the device can pinpoint its location more precisely by picking up the signal from the *secondary* towers, even if it's not effectively connected to these towers.

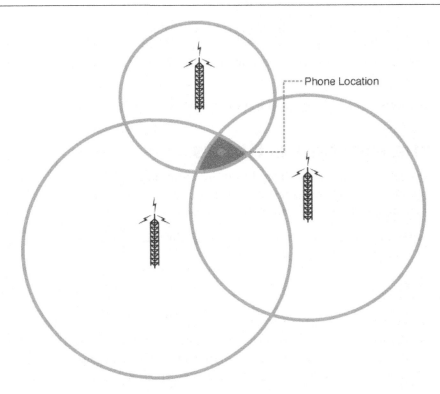

Figure 6.3 – Cell tower trilateration process

It's easy to see how the accuracy of the trilateration process varies so much depending on the location and density of the cell towers.

Wi-Fi and Bluetooth

Wi-Fi networks and hotspots are also part of the A-GPS technology and can be used in combination with cell towers and satellite GPS to pinpoint a device's location.

Similar to cell towers, Wi-Fi hotspots also broadcast a radio signal and the strength of this signal can be measured through the RSSI. Mobile devices are constantly scanning for wireless hotspots, searching for known networks, so it makes sense to use these to calculate a device's whereabouts. The range of a Wi-Fi signal is only about 70 m outdoors and 40-50 m indoors, so if a device picks up the signal, it must be physically near to the hotspot.

With this in mind, it's clear how mobile devices can evaluate the RSSI of Wi-Fi networks to establish an approximate distance between the device and the hotspot. Then, iOS resolves this data to a physical location using the peer-based mechanism described earlier on.

Bluetooth beacons can also be used in a similar way.

Locating location artifacts

In the first part of this chapter, we introduced the Location Services API and learned how iOS uses different technologies to assess its position. Now, we'll take an in-depth look at the SQLite databases where geolocation data is stored.

The following is a list of files of interest that can only be found in a full filesystem extraction:

- `/private/var/mobile/Library/Caches/com.apple.routined/ Cache.sqlite`

  This is the primary storage means for iOS location data. The ZRTCLLOCATIONMO table contains several useful records, such as GPS coordinates, timestamps, and a horizontal accuracy value, which is an indicator of how accurate the device believes the GPS coordinates to be. The ZRTWIFIACCESSPOINTMO table stores a list of Wi-Fi networks that the device has scanned. Generally speaking, data contained in this database should be considered up to date and accurate.

- `/private/var/mobile/Library/Caches/com.apple.routined/ Local.sqlite`

  This SQLite database is identical to the Cache.sqlite database in its structure. Depending on the iOS version, the ZRTLEARNEDLOCATIONOFINTERESTMO table usually contains details for any *frequent locations*, which we will look into later on.

- `/private/var/mobile/Library/Caches/com.apple.routined/ Cloud-V2.sqlite`

  As the name suggests, this database stores location data that should be synced to iCloud.

- `/private/var/root/Library/Caches/locationd/cache_ encryptedB.db`

This database contains harvested location data received by Apple, such as radio cells and Wi-Fi networks; these records refer to cell towers in close proximity to the device, although the accuracy of these geo-cordinates should always be checked.

- `/private/var/root/Library/Caches/locationd/cache_encryptedC.db`

  This database stores data received from the device's accelerometer, such as motion data and generic health-related artifacts.

- `/private/var/root/Library/Caches/locationd/consolidated.db`

  Finally, this database is used by the GeoFence API, and any application that creates a geofence will be stored here.

To gain a better understanding of how location-related data is stored in these databases, we'll analyze each of them separately and we'll learn what queries can be used to extract meaningful insights.

Analyzing location data

As we've already learned, iOS devices track a multitude of different location-related artifacts. The investigator should have a clear understanding of how and where these are stored and which ones are locations that the user actually visited, versus locations that were simply in close proximity to the device.

The first step in a forensic analysis of location data is the `Cache.sqlite` database. This database contains an extremely accurate history of coordinates provided by the device's GPS receiver. Typically, this data is stored for just over a week.

We're going to start by looking at the `ZRTCLLOCATIONMO` table. The following is the table's structure:

- `ZLATITUDE` and `ZLONGITUDE` store the geocoordinates.
- The `ZALTITUDE` column indicates an estimate of the altitude. This data is provided by the device's accelerometer.
- The `ZHORIZONTALACCURACY` column indicates how accurate the device believes the coordinates to be, expressed in meters.
- `ZVERTICALACCURACY` indicates the altitude's accuracy, in meters.
- The `ZTIMESTAMP` column stores the timestamp, in Mac Absolute Time format.

A full history of the device's location data can be obtained by running the following query:

```sql
SELECT
        DATETIME(ZTIMESTAMP + 978307200, 'UNIXEPOCH') AS
"TIMESTAMP",
        ZLATITUDE AS "LATITUDE",
        ZLONGITUDE AS "LONGITUDE",
        ZALTITUDE AS "ALTITUDE",
        ZSPEED AS "SPEED (M/S)",
        ZSPEED*2.23694 AS "SPEED (MPH)",
        ZSPEED*3.6 AS "SPEED (KMPH)",
        ZHORIZONTALACCURACY AS "HORIZONTAL ACCURACY",
        ZVERTICALACCURACY AS "VERTICAL ACCURACY"
    FROM
        ZRTCLLOCATIONMO;
```

First, we use the `datetime` SQL command to convert the Mac Absolute timestamp to a readable string. Then, we select the relevant columns from the table and calculate the speed at which the device was moving.

The following figure shows the query results:

	TIMESTAMP	LATITUDE	LONGITUDE	ALTITUDE	SPEED (M/S)	SPEED (MPH)	SPEED (KMPH)	HORIZO
1	2020-04-12 08:28:48	35.6578612348278	-78.8705126020217	102.232818603516	-1.0	-2.23694	-3.6	
2	2020-04-12 08:28:49	35.6578694814717	-78.8705127743498	102.232818603516	-1.0	-2.23694	-3.6	
3	2020-04-12 08:28:51	35.6553155556039	-78.8704595665105	102.232818603516	-1.0	-2.23694	-3.6	19
4	2020-04-12 08:28:51	35.6513724593481	-78.8703774158301	102.232818603516	-1.0	-2.23694	-3.6	19
5	2020-04-12 08:28:51	35.653168602849	-78.8704148367899	102.232818603516	-1.0	-2.23694	-3.6	19
6	2020-04-12 08:32:23	35.6558862343305	-78.8704714569495	102.232818603516	-1.0	-2.23694	-3.6	
7	2020-04-12 08:32:24	35.6568810173752	-78.8704921817063	102.232818603516	-1.0	-2.23694	-3.6	
8	2020-04-12 08:32:22	35.6457080733981	-78.8702594108219	102.232818603516	-1.0	-2.23694	-3.6	
9	2020-04-12 08:33:54	35.6574534521418	-78.8705041068972	102.232818603516	-1.0	-2.23694	-3.6	
10	2020-04-12 08:35:33	35.6528454092581	-78.8704081031046	102.232818603516	-1.0	-2.23694	-3.6	19
11	2020-04-12 08:35:30	35.6575081235283	-78.8705052462567	102.232818603516	-1.0	-2.23694	-3.6	
12	2020-04-12 08:35:30	35.6571394683115	-78.8704975656647	102.232818603516	-1.0	-2.23694	-3.6	

Figure 6.4 – The query results show the device's location

As you can see, location artifacts provide the investigator with an accurate idea of where a certain user's device was at a given moment. Typically, this data is extremely granular and it's not uncommon to see entries logged every second. The differences in the data's granularity can be explained by the fact that GPS is not available everywhere, so on these occasions, the device reverts to using Wi-Fi networks and cell towers to establish its position, if there are any in close proximity.

Once the investigator has acquired a list of geocoordinates, these can be used with a map provider to obtain visual feedback of the device's whereabouts.

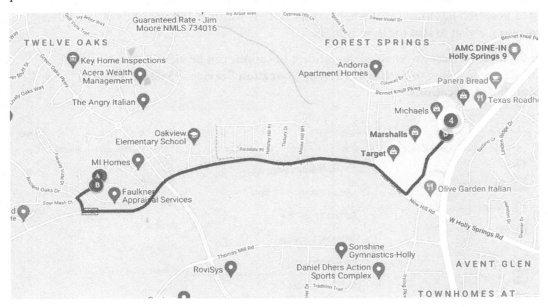

Figure 6.5 – The query results are mapped out to determine the user's journey

It should be noted that different databases store different types of location data that can be more or less accurate. From research that has been conducted, this data, which is known as **routined location data,** has proven to be highly accurate.

Understanding Significant Locations

With the release of iOS 8, Apple introduced a feature known as **Frequent Locations**, which was renamed to **Significant Locations** starting from iOS 10. Essentially, every time a device visits a location, a record is stored in a SQLite database with details from the device's journey. When the device has returned to the same location enough times, that becomes a *significant location*.

As of today, it is still unclear how the algorithm that Apple uses works and how many visits to a specific location are required for it to be considered significant. In terms of area, research has found that whenever a device is within a 250 m radius of a significant location, a visit to that location is logged.

If location services are enabled, Significant Locations can be viewed directly from the device by going to **Settings | Privacy | Location Services | System Services | Significant Locations**.

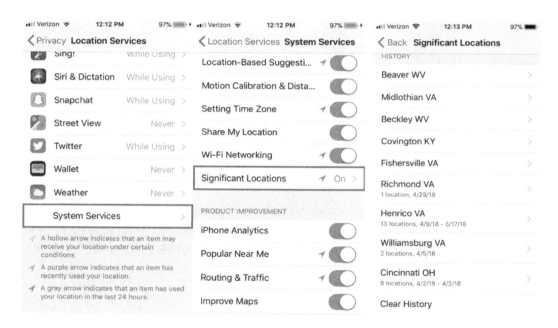

Figure 6.6– Significant Locations can be viewed directly on the device

Please keep in mind that since iOS 15, viewing Significant Locations on the device only shows a summary of these locations. The complete data will be available only from a full filesystem extraction.

From a forensics point of view, frequent location data is invaluable, as it allows an investigator to understand what locations a user visited often. Also, data pertaining to significant locations typically goes way back in time.

To view this data, we're going to run the following query on the `Local.sqlite` database:

```
SELECT
        DATETIME(ZRTLEARNEDLOCATIONOFINTERESTVISITMO.ZENTRYDATE
+ 978307200, 'UNIXEPOCH') AS "ENTRY",
        DATETIME(ZRTLEARNEDLOCATIONOFINTERESTVISITMO.ZEXITDATE
+ 978307200, 'UNIXEPOCH') AS "EXIT",
        (ZRTLEARNEDLOCATIONOFINTERESTVISITMO.ZEXITDATE-ZRTLE
ARNEDLOCATIONOFINTERESTVISITMO.ZENTRYDATE)/60.00 AS "DURATION
(MINUTES)",
        ZRTLEARNEDLOCATIONOFINTERESTMO.ZLOCATIONLATITUDE AS
"LATITUDE",
        ZRTLEARNEDLOCATIONOFINTERESTMO.ZLOCATIONLONGITUDE AS
"LONGITUDE",
        ZRTLEARNEDLOCATIONOFINTERESTVISITMO.
ZLOCATIONUNCERTAINTY AS "LOCATION UNCERTAINTY",
        ZRTLEARNEDLOCATIONOFINTERESTVISITMO.ZDATAPOINTCOUNT AS
"DATA POINTS"
    FROM
        ZRTLEARNEDLOCATIONOFINTERESTVISITMO
    LEFT JOIN
        ZRTLEARNEDLOCATIONOFINTERESTMO
        ON ZRTLEARNEDLOCATIONOFINTERESTMO.Z_PK =
ZRTLEARNEDLOCATIONOFINTERESTVISITMO.ZLOCATIONOFINTEREST;
```

Although this query may seem complicated, it's actually a lot easier if we break it down into logical steps: first, we use the `datetime` SQL command to convert the timestamps into readable strings. The `Entry` field refers to when the device visited the significant location, and the `Exit` field indicates when the device left the location. Then, we calculate the duration (`Duration`) of the visit and print `Latitude`, `Longitude`, and `Uncertainty`. Finally, we print the number of data points (`Data Points`) for that visit to that particular location.

The following figure shows the results of the query:

	ENTRY	EXIT	DURATION (MINUTES)	LATITUDE	LONGITUDE	LOCATION UNCERTAINTY	DATA POINTS
1	2020-04-15 16:32:51	2020-04-16 23:06:51	1834.0	35.6593609837169	-78.8730660027371	32.8602404963937	7365
2	2020-04-17 19:35:14	2020-04-19 18:50:29	2835.25	35.6593609837169	-78.8730660027371	19.6819985540774	11438
3	2020-04-15 16:10:47	2020-04-15 16:20:19	9.5366063396136	35.6638133919877	-78.8479745012675	216.865382961763	39
4	2020-04-12 14:30:27	2020-04-15 16:03:04	4412.61572608352	35.6593609837169	-78.8730660027371	31.9387684448737	17726
5	2020-04-12 08:41:27	2020-04-12 13:55:27	314.0	35.6593609837169	-78.8730660027371	21.0690629834767	1257
6	2020-04-12 14:02:27	2020-04-12 14:19:27	17.0	35.6715623958704	-78.8770194584023	21.8376117000028	69

Figure 6.7 – The query results show details about significant location visits

As you can see from the query results, Significant Locations data can help the investigator identify locations where the user may have been at the time of an incident. It can also help identify common and frequently visited locations, such as *home* or *work*, which can help investigative leads.

A final note: this data can be deleted by the user. In the user interface, the **Clear History** option is present, and if the user selects this, significant location data will be deleted permanently.

Analyzing Wi-Fi locations

As we saw in the first part of the chapter, location-related data on iOS devices isn't limited to GPS coordinates, as the A-GPS technology uses multiple sources to figure out a location, such as radio signals from **Wi-Fi hotspots**.

When geocoordinates are requested from Location Services, the device will scan the surrounding area for any Wi-Fi signals and will log the details of these networks, if the RSSI is strong enough. It's important to note that iOS will use any wireless signal for geo-localization, including Wi-Fi networks that the device is not connected to. If the device has an internet connection, Apple's peer-based map will be used to resolve the radio signal to a physical location.

Details of Wi-Fi networks scanned by the device are stored in the `Cache.sqlite` database, in the `ZRTWIFIACCESSPOINTMO` table.

The following is a list of the most relevant columns:

- The ZMAC column indicates the **MAC address** (or hardware address), which is a unique identifier assigned to a network interface.

- The ZCHANNEL column stores the channel number used by the wireless interface.

- The ZRSSI column indicates the signal strength.

- The ZDATE column stores a timestamp of when the wireless interface was found.

Now that we know what data is stored, we can run the following SQL query to extract all the necessary data:

```
SELECT
        DATETIME(ZRTWIFIACCESSPOINTMO.ZDATE + 978307200,
'UNIXEPOCH') AS "DATE",
        ZRTWIFIACCESSPOINTMO.ZMAC AS "MAC ADDRESS",
        ZRTWIFIACCESSPOINTMO.ZCHANNEL AS "CHANNEL",
        ZRTWIFIACCESSPOINTMO.ZRSSI AS "RSSI"
        FROM ZRTWIFIACCESSPOINTMO
        ORDER BY "DATE" ASC;
```

The query will display the results in chronological order. The following figure shows what the results look like:

	DATE	MAC ADDRESS	CHANNEL	RSSI
1	2020-04-12 12:46:19	f8:bb:bf:1e:fa:ea	161	-57
2	2020-04-12 12:46:19	f8:bb:bf:1e:fa:e4	161	-57
3	2020-04-12 12:46:20	80:da:13:72:52:64	149	-90
4	2020-04-12 12:46:20	f8:bb:bf:1e:fa:eb	48	-51
5	2020-04-12 12:46:20	58:ef:68:25:35:34	48	-90
6	2020-04-12 12:46:20	d8:d7:75:b6:28:9	48	-89
7	2020-04-12 12:46:20	80:da:13:72:52:6a	149	-89
8	2020-04-12 12:46:20	f8:bb:bf:8d:b9:c2	48	-78
9	2020-04-12 12:46:20	f8:bb:bf:90:a8:f2	48	-70
10	2020-04-12 12:46:20	b8:66:85:53:d3:7	44	-85
11	2020-04-12 12:46:20	7c:db:98:c2:30:34	40	-89
12	2020-04-12 12:46:20	f8:bb:bf:1e:fa:e8	48	-50

Figure 6.8 – The results show details about wireless devices that were scanned by the device

Although this table does not store geocoordinates such as latitude and longitude, it still provides the investigator with details as to when and which wireless signals were captured by the device. By correlating this data to external data sources (such as a list of known network devices and their MAC addresses), it is possible to place the device at a certain location at a certain point in time.

Understanding Harvested Locations

At the start of the chapter, we introduced the A-GPS technology and learned how Apple maintains a peer-based map of locations that are downloaded back onto the device when geolocalization is requested from Location Services. This data comprises thousands of records related to cell towers and Wi-Fi networks that are located in close proximity to the device, along with their geographic coordinates. The device can use this data to resolve a radio signal into a physical location without needing a GPS signal.

The data downloaded onto the device from Apple is called **Harvested Locations** data and it can be found in the `cache_encryptedB.db` database.

Here, we can find several tables of interest:

- Cell tower data can be found in the following tables: `CdmaCellLocation`, `CellLocation`, and `LteCellLocation`.
- Wi-Fi device data is stored in the `WifiLocation` table.

Routined Locations versus Harvested Locations

Before we begin analyzing this data, it's important to understand the difference between locations that the device visited and locations provided by Apple: the data we looked at previously, also known as routined location data, is typically very accurate as it comes from the device's GPS and can show in detail where the device was located. Harvested Locations data, on the other hand, consists of locations provided by Apple as a way to augment the device's knowledge about the area. This data is not retrieved from the built-in GPS receiver, but rather represents cell towers and wireless devices that are located in close proximity to the device.

Analyzing harvested cell tower data

Cell tower data is stored in the `cache_encryptedB.db` database and is retained for about a week. The following is a list of the most relevant columns:

- MCC, or **Mobile Country Code**, indicates the country code of the cell tower.

- MNC, or **Mobile Network Code**, identifies the mobile operator.

- CI, or **Cell ID**, is a unique number used to represent each transceiver station of a cell tower.

- The `HorizontalAccuracy` value indicates how precise the device believes the coordinates are and is expressed in meters.

- The `Latitude` and `Longitude` columns store the geocoordinates.

We can extract all cell-related data by running a SQL query, such as the one shown in the following code block. On the device used for research, cell data was stored in the `LTECELLLOCATION` table; however, this is dependent on the device model and iOS version:

```
SELECT
        DATETIME(TIMESTAMP + 978307200,'UNIXEPOCH') AS
"TIMESTAMP",
        MCC AS "MCC",
        MNC AS "MNC",
        CI AS "CI",
        HORIZONTALACCURACY AS "HORIZONTAL ACCURACY",
        LATITUDE AS "LATITUDE",
        LONGITUDE AS "LONGITUDE"
    FROM LTECELLLOCATION;
```

The results of the query are shown in the following figure:

	TIMESTAMP	MCC	MNC	CI	HORIZONTAL ACCURACY	LATITUDE	LONGITUDE
1	2020-12-12 22:25:08	310	260	18005506	2142.0	35.6559143	-78.87465667
2	2020-12-12 22:25:08	310	260	256947784	1414.0	35.62225341	-78.87554168
3	2020-12-12 22:25:08	310	260	256769850	1414.0	35.66263961	-78.87255859
4	2020-12-12 22:25:08	311	480	39694094	2977.0	35.62737655	-78.84117126
5	2020-12-12 22:25:08	311	480	39694096	1414.0	35.62499618	-78.84272003
6	2020-12-12 22:25:08	310	410	196794049	2094.0	35.66758346	-78.87165069
7	2020-12-12 22:25:08	310	410	195403799	1414.0	35.64883804	-78.8419876
8	2020-12-12 22:25:08	311	480	116500503	1414.0	35.63685607	-78.86347198
9	2020-12-12 22:25:08	311	480	116500504	1414.0	35.63601303	-78.86531829
10	2020-12-12 22:25:08	310	410	195138569	1414.0	35.63536071	-78.86586761
11	2020-12-12 22:25:08	310	410	195001864	1414.0	35.66678237	-78.87182617
12	2020-12-12 22:25:08	311	480	39694114	13696.0	35.63697433	-78.86968231

Figure 6.9 – The query results show details about cell towers and geolocation

From research that has been carried out by comparing routined location data to cell tower data, it's clear that harvested data can be extremely inaccurate and should not be trusted without prior validation. Also, the `HorizontalAccuracy` value gives a good idea of how accurate (or inaccurate) the location data is. It's quite common for cell tower data to indicate a range of several kilometers and the device's position can fall anywhere within that range. Nevertheless, harvested data can still aid an investigation by providing an approximation of the device's location.

Analyzing harvested Wi-Fi data

In addition to cell tower data, the `cache_encryptedB.db` database also stores harvested wireless networking data. This data can be found in the `WifiLocation` table and is retained for about a week.

In addition to the `Timestamp`, `Latitude`, and `Longitude` values, the table contains the following columns:

- The `MAC` column contains the device's hardware address, stored as a base-10 number.

- The `Channel` column indicates the channel number used by the wireless device.

The following query will extract location data from the `WifiLocation` table:

```
SELECT
            DATETIME(TIMESTAMP + 978307200,'UNIXEPOCH') AS
"TIMESTAMP",
```

```
        MAC AS "MAC",
        CHANNEL AS "CHANNEL",
        SCORE AS "SCORE",
        REACH AS "REACH",
        HORIZONTALACCURACY AS "HORIZONTAL ACCURACY",
        LATITUDE AS "LATITUDE",
        LONGITUDE AS "LONGITUDE"
    FROM WIFILOCATION;
```

Keep in mind that the MAC address will have to be converted into a base-16 number. This data can be correlated to the Wi-Fi artifacts found in the `Cache.sqlite` database to gain a better understanding of where the device was located.

Advanced iOS location artifacts

So far, we've only just scratched the surface of the location-related data that can be found on iOS devices! There are many more sources of location data that should be kept in consideration during an investigation.

The following is a brief description of additional location-related artifacts:

- **GeoFences**: A GeoFence is a location, defined by latitude, longitude, and radius. The *fence*, defined by the radius, is constantly monitored for the device entering or exiting the area. As an example, some retail store applications create a GeoFence so that the user receives a push notification when they enter the store. GeoFences are stored in the `/private/var/root/Library/Caches/location/consolidated.db` database, within the `Fences` table.

- **Motion data**: Every iOS device contains an accelerometer that logs any kind of activity, such as the device moving. Motion data is also used for health purposes, such as to count steps. This data is stored in the `/private/var/root/Library/Caches/location/cache_encryptedC.db` database, in the `MotionStateHistory` table.

- **Multimedia files**: Media files such as photos and videos can contain metadata, including location data, although this can be edited by the user directly from the device, starting with iOS 15. Be sure to check out this data using an EXIF data viewer.

- **Third-party apps**: Applications such as Waze, Google Maps, or navigation-based third-party applications may contain additional location-related data. We'll look into these apps in *Chapter 10, Analyzing Third-Party Apps*.

So far, we have learned how to manually analyze location-related data by running SQL queries on databases. However, there are other options that automate the process, such as using forensic tools.

Analyzing location data using forensic tools

We will focus on two tools: a commercial tool, Cellebrite **Physical Analyzer**, and a free tool, **Apollo**.

Viewing location data with Physical Analyzer

Cellebrite Physical Analyzer automates the task of analyzing location data by displaying GPS, cellular, and Wi-Fi locations in a unified view. Keep in mind that, to access location data, you will need to perform a full filesystem acquisition, as the files of interest are not available in a logical or iTunes backup.

To view location data, from the menu on the left side, choose **Location Related | Device Locations | Native Locations**:

#	Origin	Timestamp	End time	Position	
22		19/02/2021 19:48:17(UTC-5)	19/02/2021 19:48:19(UTC-5)	(35.659316, -78.873008)	2
23		19/02/2021 19:48:16(UTC-5)	19/02/2021 19:48:16(UTC-5)	(35.659280, -78.872704)	
24		19/02/2021 19:48:05(UTC-5)	19/02/2021 19:48:15(UTC-5)	(35.659301, -78.873069)	3
25		19/02/2021 19:45:21(UTC-5)	19/02/2021 19:48:04(UTC-5)	(35.659478, -78.872969)	4
26		19/02/2021 19:44:35(UTC-5)	19/02/2021 19:44:35(UTC-5)	(35.659337, -78.872989)	
27		19/02/2021 19:43:45(UTC-5)	19/02/2021 19:44:31(UTC-5)	(35.659456, -78.872905)	4
28		19/02/2021 19:43:44(UTC-5)	19/02/2021 19:43:44(UTC-5)	(35.659482, -78.872730)	
29		19/02/2021 19:43:43(UTC-5)	19/02/2021 19:43:43(UTC-5)	(35.659476, -78.872523)	
30		19/02/2021 19:43:38(UTC-5)	19/02/2021 19:43:42(UTC-5)	(35.659695, -78.872598)	6
31		19/02/2021 19:43:26(UTC-5)	19/02/2021 19:43:28(UTC-5)	(35.659464, -78.872926)	4
32		19/02/2021 19:37:30(UTC-5)	19/02/2021 19:37:30(UTC-5)	(35.659345, -78.873005)	2
33		19/02/2021 19:23:56(UTC-5)	19/02/2021 19:28:29(UTC-5)	(35.659473, -78.872880)	1
34		19/02/2021 19:19:29(UTC-5)	19/02/2021 19:19:29(UTC-5)	(35.659334, -78.872951)	

(35.659476, -78.872523)

Figure 6.10 – Viewing location data in Physical Analyzer

The following figure shows the remaining columns in detail:

Map	Category	Type	Source	Account	Source file information	Extraction
		Visited	Native Locations		Local.sqlite-wal : 0x1BEC8	Legacy
		Visited	Native Locations		Local.sqlite-wal : 0x1BE44	Legacy
		Visited	Native Locations		Local.sqlite-wal : 0x1BD3F	Legacy
		Visited	Native Locations		Local.sqlite-wal : 0x1BCC0	Legacy
		Visited	Native Locations		Local.sqlite-wal : 0x1BC3F	Legacy
		Visited	Native Locations		Local.sqlite-wal : 0x1BBB7	Legacy
		Visited	Native Locations		Local.sqlite-wal : 0x1BB35	Legacy
		Visited	Native Locations		Local.sqlite-wal : 0x1BAB3	Legacy
		Visited	Native Locations		Local.sqlite-wal : 0x1BA34	Legacy
		Visited	Native Locations		Local.sqlite-wal : 0x1B9A8	Legacy
		Visited	Native Locations		Local.sqlite-wal : 0x1B92C	Legacy
		Visited	Native Locations		Local.sqlite-wal : 0x1B8A4	Legacy
		Visited	Native Locations		Local.sqlite-wal : 0x1B822	Legacy

Figure 6.11 – Physical Analyzer specifies the source file for the artifact

As you can see from the preceding figure, for each record, Physical Analyzer will specify the source file from which the record was parsed. Keep in mind that just because a location appears in the results, it doesn't necessarily mean that the device actually visited that location, as this tool will also display harvested data.

Analyzing location data with Apollo

Apollo, which we introduced in the previous chapter, is a Python script that correlates multiple sources of data into a unified **timeline**, simplifying the examiner's job of finding out what exactly was happening on the device. The tool consists of dozens of highly configurable modules that each query a specific iOS database to extract data and events. Apollo supports both routined location data and harvested data.

We'll now go over the steps required to download the tool, run it, and export location data into a KMZ file that can be imported into a map provider service:

1. To download Apollo, head over to its GitHub repository located at `https://github.com/mac4n6/APOLLO` and download the latest version as a ZIP archive or by cloning the repository by running the `git clone` command.

2. Next, run the tool by specifying the export format, the location of the module's directory, and the location of the data that should be analyzed, such as the folder that contains the SQLite databases or the full filesystem extraction. For example, running `python3 apollo.py extract -o sql -p apple -v 14 -k modules/ fs-extraction/` will run Apollo in SQL mode, analyzing the files in the `fs-extraction` folder and running all modules found in the `modules` folder. Make sure you use the `-k` option to output location files.

3. When the tool ends the process, the results will be stored in a file called `apollo.db` and in several KMZ files.

4. You can then proceed to import the KMZ files using your tool of choice, such as **Google Earth** or **Google Maps**.

The following figure shows one of the KMZ files outputted by Apollo imported into Google Maps:

Figure 6.12 – Google Maps displaying location data exported by Apollo

As you can see from the preceding figure, importing location-related data into a map service allows the investigator to instantly visualize the device's whereabouts and, possibly, the user's journey.

Summary

In this chapter, we learned all about location artifacts and how an investigator can benefit from analyzing such data.

First, we introduced the Location Services API. Then, we learned how A-GPS uses multiple technologies to figure out a device's position, such as satellite GPS, Wi-Fi, and cell towers. We learned how iOS manages Significant Locations and where this data is stored.

Later on in the chapter, we focused on the most popular location-related databases found on an iOS device. We learned which are the most data-rich tables and how the data is organized in different columns. Then, we learned how to extract location data by running SQL queries. We learned about the different accuracy levels that can be found in routined data versus harvested location data.

Finally, in the last section of this chapter, we went through the steps required to view location artifacts in Cellebrite Physical Analyzer and Apollo, an open source tool that greatly simplifies the process of analyzing location data by exporting it into KMZ files that can be imported into mapping providers, such as Google Maps.

In the next chapter, we will dive deep into connectivity forensics, including cellular usage and internet browsing.

7
Analyzing Connectivity Data

In the previous chapter, we introduced location-related artifacts and learned how an investigation can leverage such data to obtain a general geographical location of where the device may have been. In this chapter, we will focus on connectivity data.

The modern mobile phone has evolved from being a simple handheld device that's used to communicate via voice into a mobile computing device that communicates with the internet. Almost every interaction between a device and the external world is logged by the operating system, so it shouldn't come as a surprise that connectivity data has become the single most important source of evidence in virtually every type of investigation: artifacts such as call logs and internet navigation history are invaluable for the modern investigator.

We'll start this chapter by looking at cellular-related artifacts, contacts, and phone calls, including FaceTime videocalls. Then, we'll learn all about networking forensics, including how to analyze a device's favorite Wi-Fi networks and detailed network usage. We will also briefly look into Bluetooth forensics. Finally, we'll learn about internet-related artifacts and how to analyze Safari history.

In this chapter, we will cover the following topics:

- Introducing cellular forensics
- Analyzing networking data
- Introducing Bluetooth forensics
- Understanding Safari forensics

Introducing cellular forensics

In the first part of this chapter, we will focus on understanding what cellular-related artifacts can be found on an iOS device and what insights we can gain by analyzing such data.

But first, what exactly is cellular data? This term refers to all those artifacts that involve **telephony services** and **data connections**, and they allow the investigator to answer questions such as the following:

- Who has the user communicated with?
- When did the device register with the cellular network?
- What websites were browsed on the device?

The first step in our analysis involves extracting some meaningful data from the `com.apple.commcenter.plist` **property list (PLIST)**, which is located at `/private/var/wireless/Library/Preferences/`:

Figure 7.1 – The com.apple.commcenter PLIST

This PLIST contains several useful cellular-related values, such as its **Integrated Circuit Card Identifier (ICCID)**, **International Mobile Subscriber Identity (IMSI)**, **International Mobile Equipment Identity (IMEI)**, the device's phone number, and details of the last cell tower that the device connected to.

ICCID

The **ICCID** is the SIM card's serial number. This value uniquely identifies the physical SIM card and will change if the card is replaced, even if the phone number remains the same. This value can be extracted from the PLIST by looking at the `LastKnownICCID` key.

IMSI

The **IMSI** can be found by looking at the `lastGoodImsi` key. This value is typically 15 digits long and identifies a SIM card on its network. It's important to understand that this code is tied to the phone number, not the physical SIM card. The IMSI is used by mobile network operators to connect phone calls and communicate with the SIM card.

IMEI

The **IMEI** is a unique 15-digit code that identifies a particular mobile device. This code has no relationship with the subscriber and only identifies the mobile phone; however, when a mobile device registers on a GSM network, it also provides the device's IMEI, so operators can block devices that have been reported as stolen by adding their IMEI to a blocklist. This code can also be used by law enforcement and intelligence agencies to track mobile devices, which can be located by analyzing the cell tower the device connects to. The IMEI can be found in the PLIST by looking at the `kEntitlementsSelfRegistrationUpdateImei` key.

MCC and MNC

The **Mobile Country Code (MCC)** and **Mobile Network Code (MNC)** are a combination of values that uniquely identify a cell tower. Mobile iOS devices store the last known MCC and MNC values in the PLIST under the `LastKnownServingMcc` and `LastKnownServingMnc` keys. These values, together with a map of known cell towers, can be used to pinpoint the device's last position.

Phone number

Finally, the device's phone number is also stored in the PLIST, under the `NetworkPhoneNumber` key. It's important to keep in mind that iOS devices support not only physical SIM cards but also eSIM cards: these cards are embedded in a mobile device and can connect you to any operator offering eSIM services. The eSIM is configured directly on the device and works the same way as a traditional SIM card, but you don't need a physical SIM card to use it.

Analyzing the PowerLog

In the previous section, we learned how to extract cellular-related data, such as identifying the last cell tower that the device connected to. However, there are many more interesting artifacts, such as `CurrentPowerLog.PLSQL`, which can be found in `/private/var/containers/Shared/SystemGroup/<GUID>/Library/BatteryLife/`.

We introduced PowerLog in *Chapter 5, Pattern-of-Life Forensics*. We will now focus on the
PLBBAGENT_EVENTFORWARD_TELEPHONYREGISTRATION table, which logs events
such as when the device registers with the GSM network.

The following query will extract the relevant records:

```
SELECT
        DATETIME(TIMESTAMP , 'UNIXEPOCH') AS TIMESTAMP,
        DATAIND AS "SERVICE",
        OPERATOR AS "OPERATOR",
        STATUS AS "STATUS"
    FROM PLBBAGENT_EVENTFORWARD_TELEPHONYREGISTRATION;
```

As shown in the following screenshot, the STATUS column indicates what event occurred,
such as the device searching for or registering with the cellular network. The OPERATOR
column shows the name of the mobile network operator, while the SERVICE column
indicates whether the network provides **GSM**, **3G**, **4G**, or **5G** capabilities. Finally, the
TIMESTAMP column indicates when the event occurred:

	TIMESTAMP	SERVICE	OPERATOR	STATUS
3	2020-05-08 15:25:25	None	NULL	NotRegistered
4	2020-08-24 16:55:03	None	NULL	NotRegistered
5	2020-12-12 22:19:12	None	NULL	NotRegistered
6	2020-12-12 22:21:15	None	NULL	NotRegistered
7	2020-12-12 22:30:00	None	NULL	Searching
8	2020-12-12 22:30:11	None	NULL	Emergency Only
9	2020-12-12 22:30:49	None	NULL	Denied
10	2020-12-12 22:30:49	None	NULL	Emergency Only
11	2020-12-12 22:33:38	None	Google Fi	RegisteredHome
12	2020-12-12 22:33:38	4G	Google Fi	RegisteredHome
13	2020-12-12 22:33:43	None	Google Fi	RegisteredHome
14	2020-12-12 22:33:43	4G	Google Fi	RegisteredHome

Figure 7.2 – Records of cellular registration

Now that we've learned how to extract basic cellular-related data, we will learn about
analyzing communications. In this chapter, we will focus on phone calls; email and
messaging will be discussed in more depth in *Chapter 8, Email and Messaging Forensics*.

Analyzing the address book

Before we delve into the call history database, it's useful to introduce the `AddressBook.sqlite` database, which contains the names and details of the contacts stored on the device. The database is located at `/private/var/mobile/Library/AddressBook/` and contains two tables of interest – `ABPerson` and `ABMultiValue`. The first contains the contact's name and additional metadata that is used by the device, while the second table stores the actual data, such as phone numbers and email addresses. The two tables are connected through a one-to-many relationship.

Now that we know the address book's basic structure, we can extract the data by running the following query:

```sql
SELECT  p.First              AS "First Name",
        p.Last               AS "Last Name",
        GROUP_CONCAT(c.value) AS "Contacts"
FROM    ABPerson AS p
        LEFT JOIN ABMultiValue AS c
              ON c.record_id = p.rowid
GROUP   BY p.rowid,
           p.first;
```

First, we must select the columns that are relevant to the first name and last name; then, we must use the `GROUP_CONCAT` SQL function to aggregate all the contact data (phone numbers, emails, and so on) into one column, `Contacts`. Then, we must use a `JOIN` statement to establish a relationship between the `ABPerson` and `ABMultiValue` tables.

This query will extract a list of all the contacts that are stored in the address book, as shown in the following screenshot:

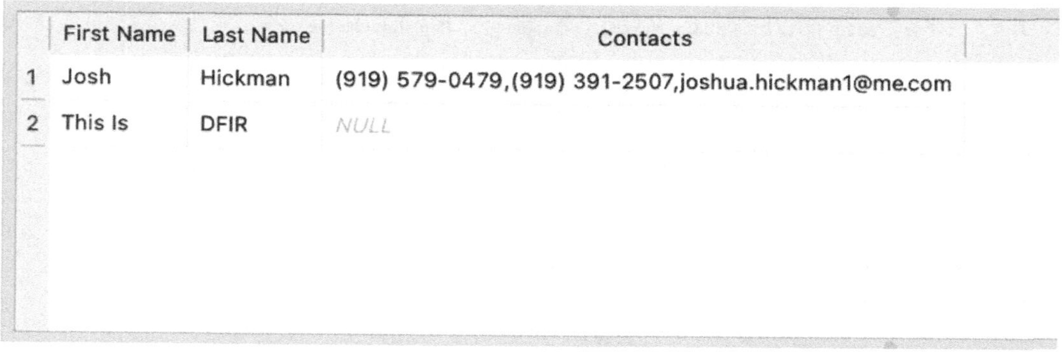

	First Name	Last Name	Contacts
1	Josh	Hickman	(919) 579-0479,(919) 391-2507,joshua.hickman1@me.com
2	This Is	DFIR	NULL

Figure 7.3 – Records extracted from the address book

Now that we've learned how to extract contact data, we can start analyzing the call log.

Analyzing the call log

All phone calls and FaceTime calls that have been placed, received, or missed are logged in the `CallHistory.storedata` database, which is located at `/private/var/mobile/Library/CallHistoryDB/`.

> **Tip**
>
> The `CallHistory.storedata` database was introduced in iOS 8. Previously, the call log was located in the `call_history.db` file. Also, keep in mind that the call history will only be available in an **After First Unlock (AFU)** state. Before the first unlock, the data is stored in a temporary file, called `CallHistoryTemp.storedata`.

The most important data, from a forensic perspective, is stored in the `ZCALLRECORD` table, where you will find the following columns:

- The `ZDATE` column contains the timestamp of when the call occurred, in Mac Absolute Time format.

- `ZADDRESS` indicates the phone number that was called or where the call originated from if it was an incoming call.

- The `ZLOCATION` column stores the location, which is calculated from the phone number.

- The `ZDURATION` column indicates the call duration, in seconds.

- The `ZORIGINATED` column indicates whether the call was incoming (0) or outgoing (1).

- The `ZANSWERED` column indicates whether an incoming call was answered (1) or not (0).

- The `ZSERVICE_PROVIDER` column shows the name of the service that generated the call. Typically, this will show `com.apple.Telephony` for traditional calls or `com.apple.FaceTime` for FaceTime calls.

The following SQL query will extract meaningful data from the `ZCALLRECORD` table:

```
SELECT
DATETIME(ZDATE + 978307200, 'unixepoch', 'localtime') AS "Date/
Time",
ZADDRESS AS "Phone Number",
```

```
ZLOCATION AS "Location",
ZDURATION AS "Call in Seconds",
CASE
WHEN ZORIGINATED = 0 THEN "Incoming"
    WHEN ZORIGINATED = 1 THEN "Outgoing"
END AS "Call Direction",
CASE
    WHEN ZANSWERED = 0 AND ZORIGINATED = 0 THEN "Call missed"
    WHEN ZANSWERED = 1 AND ZORIGINATED = 0 THEN "Call
answered"
END AS "Call Status",
ZSERVICE_PROVIDER AS "Service Provider"
FROM ZCALLRECORD;
```

The results of this query are shown in the following screenshot:

	Date/Time	Phone Number	Location	Call in Seconds	Call Direction	Call Status	Service Provider
26	2020-04-10 16:19:47	+14082560700	San Jose, CA	0.0	Incoming	Call missed	com.apple.Telephony
27	2020-04-10 16:32:21	+14082560700	San Jose, CA	0.0	Incoming	Call missed	com.apple.Telephony
28	2020-04-10 16:40:42	+14082560700	San Jose, CA	0.0	Incoming	Call missed	com.apple.Telephony
29	2020-04-12 03:13:23	+17042751134	Fairview, NC	0.0	Outgoing	NULL	com.apple.Telephony
30	2020-04-12 03:14:46	+17042751134	Fairview, NC	12.2448190450668	Incoming	Call answered	com.apple.Telephony
31	2020-04-12 16:04:06	9192853680	Fuquay-Varina, NC	64.6294050216675	Outgoing	NULL	com.apple.Telephony
32	2020-04-12 17:26:43	joshua.hickman1@me.com	<<RecentsNumberLocati...	98.0257830619812	Outgoing	NULL	com.apple.FaceTime
33	2020-04-13 20:41:27	+14082560700	San Jose, CA	0.0	Incoming	Call missed	com.apple.Telephony
34	2020-04-13 23:57:05	+14082560700	San Jose, CA	0.0	Incoming	Call missed	com.apple.Telephony
35	2020-04-14 14:43:26	+14082560700	San Jose, CA	0.0	Incoming	Call missed	com.apple.Telephony
36	2020-04-14 17:25:18	+14082560700	San Jose, CA	0.0	Incoming	Call missed	com.apple.Telephony
37	2020-04-14 17:56:12	+14082560700	San Jose, CA	0.0	Incoming	Call missed	com.apple.Telephony

Figure 7.4 – Data extracted from the call log

By now, you should have a general idea of how to parse through the contacts that are stored on a device and how to analyze the call log. Now, let's learn about networking forensics.

Analyzing networking data

Modern smartphones rely more than ever on a networking connection to perform their tasks and enrich the user's experience. At the beginning of this chapter, we discussed cellular-related artifacts; now, we will focus on **Wi-Fi connections** before discussing **network usage** in general.

Analyzing the networking data that's provided by an iOS device can give the investigator a precise idea of what services and applications are consuming bandwidth, and which networks the device is connected to.

We'll introduce the topic by learning how to extract some basic networking-related data from a full filesystem.

Airplane mode

To detect if the device was placed in airplane mode or not, you can examine the `com.apple.radios.plist` file, which is located at `/private/var/preferences/SystemConfiguration/`. The PLIST contains an `AirplaneMode` key with a value of `true` or `false`.

Wi-Fi MAC address

The MAC address of the wireless network interface within the device can be found by analyzing the `NetworkInterfaces.plist` file, which is located at `/private/var/preferences/SystemConfiguration/`. The `IOMACAddress` key indicates the desired value. Note that each iOS device has more than one networking interface and that each of those has a unique MAC address.

Known Wi-Fi networks

A list of known wireless networks is stored in the `/private/var/preferences/SystemConfiguration/com.apple.wifi.plist` file. This PLIST contains a key list of known networks, which is also an array of items:

- The `SSID_STR` key contains a user-readable SSID string that identifies the network.
- The `BSSID` key indicates the MAC address of the access point.

- The `lastJoined` key stores a timestamp of the last time the user manually accessed the network.

- The `lastAutoJoined` key indicates the last time the device automatically connected to the wireless access point:

```
⊗ ⊘  com.apple.wifi.plist                                        ⬆  Open with TextEdit

                    <key>SSID</key>
                    <data>
                    Q2Nvb2tpZXNEY2FzdGxlUjUgR3Vlc3Q=
                    </data>
                    <key>SSID_STR</key>
                    <string>CcookiesDcastleR5 Guest</string>
                    <key>SaveDataMode</key>
                    <integer>2</integer>
                    <key>ScaledRSSI</key>
                    <real>0.82863259315490723</real>
                    <key>ScaledRate</key>
                    <real>1</real>
                    <key>ShareableStatus</key>
                    <integer>1</integer>
                    <key>Strength</key>
                    <real>0.82863259315490723</real>
                    <key>VHT_CAPS_IE</key>
                    <dict>
                            <key>VHT_CAPS</key>
                            <integer>864041394</integer>
                            <key>VHT_SUPPORTED_MCS_SET</key>
                            <data>
                            +v8AAPr/AAA=
                            </data>
                    </dict>
                    <key>WiFiAutoInstantHotspotJoining</key>
                    <false/>
                    <key>WiFiInstantHotspotJoining</key>
                    <false/>
                    <key>WiFiManagerKnownNetworksEventType</key>
                    <integer>1</integer>
                    <key>WiFiNetworkAttributeIsKnown</key>
                    <true/>
                    <key>WiFiNetworkAttributeIsMoving</key>
                    <false/>
                    <key>WiFiNetworkAttributeIsPotentiallyMoving</key>
                    <true/>
                    <key>WiFiNetworkAttributeLowPopularity</key>
                    <true/>
                    <key>WiFiNetworkAttributePopularityScore</key>
                    <integer>0</integer>
                    <key>WiFiNetworkAttributeProminentDisplay</key>
                    <true/>
                    <key>WiFiNetworkAttributeSource</key>
                    <integer>2</integer>
                    <key>WiFiNetworkIsAutoJoined</key>
                    <true/>
                    <key>WiFiNetworkPasswordModificationDate</key>
                    <date>2020-03-22T19:00:00Z</date>
                    <key>addedAt</key>
                    <date>2020-03-22T19:00:00Z</date>
                    <key>enabled</key>
                    <true/>
```

Figure 7.5 – The com.apple.wifi.plist showing details of known networks

Now that we know how to analyze the basic networking data on the device, let's take a closer look at network usage artifacts.

Analyzing network usage

Dissecting which services or applications are using the network can help the investigator identify any abnormal processes, such as **malware** running on the device.

Data usage on iOS devices is stored in two different files:

- The `CurrentPowerLog.PLSQL` database, which can be found in `/private/var/containers/Shared/SystemGroup/<GUID>/Library/BatteryLife/`, contains several tables of interest. By correlating the data from different tables, the examiner can extract precise data usage for each process, both from the **Wi-Fi interface** and the **WAN interface**. The caveat here is that this database only stores process data for approximately 24 hours.

- The `DataUsage.db` database, which can be found in `/private/var/wireless/Library/Databases/DataUsage.sqlite`, contains two significant tables – `ZPROCESS` and `ZLIVEUSAGE`. The first stores the app's name, the app bundle, and the associated process, along with its timestamp; the second table stores the data that's coming in and out of the WAN interface for each process. Although this database will generally store several weeks' worth of data, keep in mind that, from research that has been carried out, it seems that data coming in and out of the Wi-Fi interface is not logged.

These databases can help the investigator determine not only which processes were using the network, but also whether a subject was using an application at a certain moment in time.

Process and network usage data can be extracted from the `DataUsage.db` database by running the following query:

```
SELECT
        DATETIME(ZPROCESS.ZTIMESTAMP+ 978307200,
'UNIXEPOCH') AS "PROCESS TIMESTAMP",
        ZPROCESS.ZPROCNAME AS "PROCESS NAME",
        ZPROCESS.ZBUNDLENAME AS "BUNDLE ID",
        ZLIVEUSAGE.ZWWANIN AS "WWAN IN",
        ZLIVEUSAGE.ZWWANOUT AS "WWAN OUT"
```

```
       FROM ZLIVEUSAGE
       LEFT JOIN ZPROCESS ON ZLIVEUSAGE.ZHASPROCESS = ZPROCESS.Z_
PK;
```

The following screenshot shows the output; it includes some valuable data for the investigator, especially if application usage is of interest in an investigation:

	PROCESS TIMESTAMP	PROCESS NAME	BUNDLE ID	WWAN IN	WWAN OUT
85	2020-03-22 15:14:45	com.apple.WebKit/imgurmobile	imgurmobile	3102060.0	275109.0
86	2020-03-22 15:16:40	mediaserverd/imgurmobile	imgurmobile	114007059.0	3366467.0
87	2020-03-22 15:10:24	nsurlsessiond/imgurmobile	imgurmobile	926878.0	45097.0
88	2020-03-22 18:02:57	nsurlsessiond/co.babypenguin.imo	co.babypenguin.imo	8978.0	6276.0
89	2020-03-22 18:59:22	mDNSResponder/com.burbn.instagram	com.burbn.instagram	5521.0	3440.0
90	2020-03-22 19:12:02	Instagram/com.burbn.instagram	com.burbn.instagram	15820543.0	662197.0
91	2020-03-22 18:48:48	InstagramNotific/com.burbn.instagram	com.burbn.instagram	28270.0	20203.0
92	2020-03-25 02:00:51	Threads/com.burbn.threads	com.burbn.threads	6336.0	23244.0
93	2020-03-27 19:02:30	appstored/com.kik.chat	com.kik.chat	14819.0	5875.0
94	2020-03-30 16:08:45	mDNSResponder/com.belkin.plugin	com.belkin.plugin	1452.0	1645.0
95	2020-03-30 16:07:06	WeMo_Universal/com.belkin.plugin	com.belkin.plugin	14913.0	8634.0
96	2020-04-04 16:16:50	mDNSResponder/com.facebook.talk	com.facebook.talk	367.0	485.0

Figure 7.6 – The query results showing the processes running on the device and their data usage

In the next section, we'll introduce Bluetooth forensics.

Introducing Bluetooth forensics

Using Bluetooth technology, users can transfer data between different devices and attach headphones, speakers, or any kind of wireless device to their smartphone. Typically, iOS devices operate as *Class 2* Bluetooth devices, which means they can operate at a range of approximately 10 meters (33 feet).

From a forensic viewpoint, iOS devices maintain the following:

- A list of *low-energy* Bluetooth devices that can connect to the user's device, also called **paired devices**. These are stored in the /private/var/containers/ Shared/SystemGroup/<GUID>/Library/Database/com.apple. MobileBluetooth.ledevices.paired.db database, under the PairedDevices table. This table maintains a list of devices, their names, their **Media Access Control (MAC)** addresses, and their last-seen timestamps.

- Other Bluetooth paired devices (*not just low-energy*), which are stored in the / private/var/containers/Shared/SystemGroup/<GUID>/Library/ Preferences/com.apple.MobileBluetooth.devices.plist file. This property list maintains a list of device names and last-detection times.

- A list of *seen* Bluetooth devices, which are other available Bluetooth-enabled devices that were close to the device but that did not connect. These devices can be found in the `/private/var/containers/Shared/SystemGroup/<GUID>/Library/Database/com.apple.MobileBluetooth.ledevices.other.db` database, under the `OtherDevices` table.

- A detailed log of Bluetooth-related events, such as **connection** and **disconnection** events. These are stored in the `knowledgeC.db` database.

As the first three files are trivial to query, we'll concentrate on extracting Bluetooth events from the `/private/var/mobile/Library/CoreDuet/Knowledge/knowledgeC.db` database, which we introduced in *Chapter 5, Pattern-of-Life Forensics*.

First, we must select the start and end dates for the events from the `ZOBJECT` table. Then, we must filter down the results by searching for the `/bluetooth/isConnected` stream. We must extract the event status and device details from the `ZSTRUCTUREDMETADATA` table. Finally, we must order the results chronologically.

The final query looks like this:

```
SELECT
DATETIME(ZOBJECT.ZSTARTDATE + 978307200, 'unixepoch',
'localtime') AS "Start",
DATETIME(ZOBJECT.ZENDDATE + 978307200, 'unixepoch',
'localtime') AS "End",
CASE
      WHEN ZOBJECT.ZVALUEINTEGER = 0 THEN "Disconnected"
      WHEN ZOBJECT.ZVALUEINTEGER = 1 THEN "Connected"
END AS "Status",
ZSTRUCTUREDMETADATA.Z_DKBLUETOOTHMETADATAKEY__ADDRESS AS
"Address",
ZSTRUCTUREDMETADATA.Z_DKBLUETOOTHMETADATAKEY__NAME AS "Device"
FROM ZSTRUCTUREDMETADATA
LEFT JOIN ZOBJECT ON ZSTRUCTUREDMETADATA.Z_PK = ZOBJECT.
ZSTRUCTUREDMETADATA
WHERE ZOBJECT.ZSTREAMNAME = "/bluetooth/isConnected"
ORDER BY "Start" ASC;
```

Once the query completes, the investigator can retrieve the list of events that were logged every time the device **connected** or **disconnected** from a Bluetooth-enabled device, along with the device's MAC address; the results are shown in the following screenshot:

	Start	End	Status	Address	Device
1	2020-03-27 19:32:42	2020-03-27 19:32:52	Connected	7C:04:D0:89:89:A0	Josh's AirPods
2	2020-03-27 19:32:52	2020-03-27 19:33:03	Disconnected	7C:04:D0:89:89:A0	Josh's AirPods
3	2020-03-27 19:33:03	2020-03-27 19:33:05	Connected	7C:04:D0:89:89:A0	Josh's AirPods
4	2020-03-27 19:33:05	2020-03-27 19:54:15	Disconnected	7C:04:D0:89:89:A0	Josh's AirPods
5	2020-03-27 19:54:16	2020-03-27 20:22:18	Connected	7C:04:D0:89:89:A0	Josh's AirPods
6	2020-03-27 20:22:18	2020-03-27 21:44:02	Disconnected	7C:04:D0:89:89:A0	Josh's AirPods
7	2020-03-27 21:44:04	2020-03-27 21:44:05	Connected	7C:04:D0:89:89:A0	Josh's AirPods
8	2020-03-27 21:44:05	2020-03-27 21:44:18	Disconnected	7C:04:D0:89:89:A0	Josh's AirPods
9	2020-03-27 21:44:20	2020-03-27 21:44:42	Connected	7C:04:D0:89:89:A0	Josh's AirPods
10	2020-03-27 21:44:42	2020-03-27 21:44:48	Disconnected	7C:04:D0:89:89:A0	Josh's AirPods
11	2020-03-27 21:44:49	2020-03-27 21:44:55	Connected	7C:04:D0:89:89:A0	Josh's AirPods

Figure 7.7 – The query displaying Bluetooth connection events

Bluetooth artifacts can be an essential part of an investigation. By leveraging data about paired or seen devices, the investigator can assess not only whether the device was in use and connected to a certain device, but also put the owner in an approximate location at a point in time, if the location of the Bluetooth device is known. In the next section, we'll introduce Safari forensics.

Understanding Safari forensics

Analyzing artifacts that have been left by internet browsing activity is typically a crucial aspect of mobile forensic investigations. Almost every activity a suspect performs while using a browser on a mobile device leaves a trace on the device itself, including, of course, searching for information and browsing through web pages.

In this section, we'll focus on the browser that is built into all iOS devices, **Safari**. Keep in mind that dozens of third-party browsers can be installed on a device, such as **Chrome**, **Firefox**, and **Opera**: it's important to review these applications and analyze their artifacts as they could potentially contain important data. We'll learn how to analyze third-party applications in *Chapter 10, Analyzing Third-Party Apps*.

Browsing history is likely the most commonly recovered item, but other files should be reviewed too. Typically, the following data can be recovered by analyzing Safari artifacts:

- Browsing history
- Open/private tabs

- Bookmarks/saved pages
- Cookies
- Cache files

Most of Safari's artifacts are stored in `/private/var/mobile/Library/Safari/`. Within this folder, you will find the following relevant files:

- The `Bookmarks.db` database, which contains the titles and URLs of pages that were added to Safari's bookmarks. The `bookmarks` table contains a `title` column, which identifies the title of the web page; a `url` column, which stores the URL; and several columns that relate to iCloud's syncing technology. Web pages that are added to the **Reading List** are also stored in this file.

- `BrowserState.db`, which contains two tables – `tabs`, which describes the current state of open tabs within Safari, and `tab_sessions`, which contains a record for each open tab and a corresponding binary BLOB that contains session data, such as previously browsed pages within that tab. The `tabs` table contains columns such as `title`, `url`, and `last_viewed_time`, which describe the open tab. Keep in mind that private tabs will also be stored in this table; these can be identified by checking the flag value of the `private_browsing` column.

- The `CloudTabs.db` file, which stores open tabs across all iCloud synced devices.

- The `History.db` database, which stores Safari browsing history. We'll take an in-depth look at this in the next section.

So far, we have seen the most common sources of evidence for Safari browsing. However, other Safari-related artifacts could contain traces related to user activity, such as **session cookies** and the **cache**:

- `/private/var/mobile/Containers/Data/Application/GUID/Library/Caches/com.apple.mobilesafari/`

    This folder contains any data that was cached by Safari. The `cache.db` database should always be analyzed since it could contain traces of user navigation, even if the browsing history was deleted. Cached data is typically stored within the database as a **BPLIST** and should be exported and converted into an XML-encoded PLIST to be manually analyzed.

- `/private/var/mobile/Containers/Data/Application/GUID/Library/Cookies/Cookies.binarycookies`

  Safari cookies are stored in this file, in binary format. To understand the format specification, please refer to the following link: `https://github.com/libyal/dtformats/blob/main/documentation/Safari%20Cookies.asciidoc`. Cookies can also be extracted using **automated scripts**, such as the `Safari-Binary-Cookie-Parser` Python script by Mari DeGrazia. It can be downloaded from `https://github.com/mdegrazia/Safari-Binary-Cookie-Parser`.

- `/private/var/mobile/Containers/Data/Application/GUID/Library/Safari/`

  This folder should be analyzed as it contains several useful files, such as Safari **thumbnails**, **preferences, auto-fill data**, and a **downloads** list.

Finally, let's cover two different ways of analyzing Safari browsing history.

Analyzing Safari history

As we learned earlier, Safari stores browsing history in the `/private/var/mobile/Library/Safari/History.db` database. It's important to understand that this file doesn't just store browsing history from the local device – it also contains data that's been **synced from iCloud**, such as the browsing history from other devices. It's the examiner's job, when analyzing this data, to dissect which websites were visited on the device that is being examined and what data has been synced from different devices.

The following screenshot shows a query example that extracts all the relevant data and the resulting records:

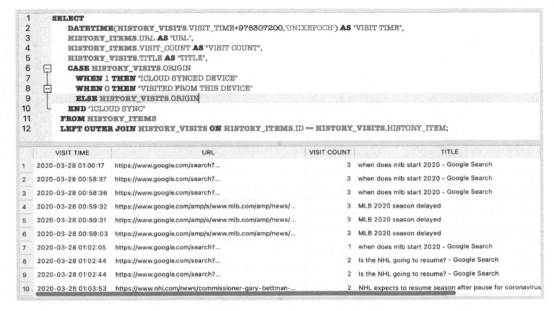

Figure 7.8 – Analyzing the browsing history of History.db

Note that the `history_visits` table has an `origin` column, which indicates whether the website was synced from iCloud (1) or not (0).

This database is not the only location where browsing history is stored; essential data can also be found in the `knowledgeC.db` database. Although it only stores about 1 months' worth of data, `knowledgeC.db` will still contain details about visited web pages, even if the user chooses to delete the browsing history.

The following query will extract Safari events from the `ZOBJECT` table within the `knowledgeC.db` database:

```
SELECT
        DATETIME(ZOBJECT.ZSTARTDATE+978307200,'UNIXEPOCH') AS
"DATE",
        ZSTRUCTUREDMETADATA.Z_DKSAFARIHISTORYMETADATAKEY__TITLE
AS "TITLE",
        ZOBJECT.ZVALUESTRING AS "URL",
        ZOBJECT.ZSECONDSFROMGMT/3600 AS "GMT OFFSET"
    FROM ZOBJECT
            LEFT JOIN
        ZSTRUCTUREDMETADATA
        ON ZOBJECT.ZSTRUCTUREDMETADATA =
```

```
ZSTRUCTUREDMETADATA.Z_PK
        LEFT JOIN
            ZSOURCE
            ON ZOBJECT.ZSOURCE = ZSOURCE.Z_PK
        WHERE
            ZSTREAMNAME IS "/safari/history"
ORDER BY DATE ASC;
```

First, we must select the timestamp of when the browser event occurred and transform it into a readable string by using the DATETIME function. Then, we must perform a JOIN on the ZSTRUCTUREDMETADATA table to extract the title of the web page. After that, we must select the URL and calculate the GMT offset. Finally, we must order the results chronologically.

The following screenshot shows the results of this query:

	DATE	TITLE	URL	GMT OFFSET
1	2020-03-28 00:58:40	when does mlb start 2020 - Google Search	https://www.google.com/search?...	-4
2	2020-03-28 01:02:50	Is the NHL going to resume? - Google Search	https://www.google.com/search?...	-4
3	2020-03-28 01:04:05	NHL expects to resume season after pause for ...	https://www.nhl.com/news/commissioner-gary-bettman-...	-4
4	2020-03-28 01:05:45	Is the NHL going to resume? - Google Search	https://www.google.com/search?...	-4
5	2020-03-28 01:06:35	Apple	https://www.apple.com/	-4
6	2020-03-28 01:07:45	iPad Pro - Apple	https://www.apple.com/ipad-pro/	-4
7	2020-03-28 01:37:10	iPad Pro - Apple	https://www.apple.com/ipad-pro/	-4
8	2020-03-28 01:38:55	Cult of Mac	Tech and culture through an Apple lens	https://www.cultofmac.com/	-4
9	2020-03-28 01:43:45	Apple	https://www.apple.com/	-4
10	2020-03-28 01:43:55	DFIR Review	https://dfir.pubpub.org/	-4

Figure 7.9 – Analyzing the browsing history of KnowledgeC.db

When analyzing the user's browsing history, the investigator should always examine both databases since one of them could potentially contain unique data.

Introducing private browsing

To finish this chapter, we will introduce **private browsing**, a feature that Apple introduced in iOS 5. When this feature is active, the details of the user's browsing history are not stored and the websites that have been visited are not synced to iCloud.

As stated in Apple's official documentation, *"Safari won't remember the pages you visited, your search history, or your AutoFill information AFTER you close a tab in private browsing mode."*

Theoretically, this poses a problem from a forensic perspective as both `History.db` and `KnowledgeC.db` do not store this data. There are, however, other options:

- You can analyze the cookies that are stored on the device. Safari's web cache could also reveal traces of websites that were browsed with private browsing active.

- The `BrowserState.db` database stores details of active tabs, **including private tabs**. For each tab, there is an entry in the `tab_sessions` table that contains a binary PLIST. Converting this BPLIST into XML format will allow the investigator to parse through the file, which contains the history of the pages that were browsed within that tab. This will only work if the private tab is still open in Safari.

- As we learned in the previous chapters, deleted data is not permanently removed from a SQLite database – it is merely marked as deleted. By using **forensic tools**, it is possible to recover deleted records from the `BrowserState.db` database, which may include details of tabs that have been opened in private mode. To learn how to attempt data recovery from SQLite databases, please refer to *Chapter 4, Working with Common iOS Artifacts*.

Internet browsing artifacts are an important part of any mobile forensics investigation. Analyzing the browsing history may provide some insight, but accessing the data that's relevant to private internet browsing can be far more enlightening, revealing any activity that the user wanted to keep hidden.

Summary

In this chapter, we learned about connectivity data and how iOS devices communicate through cellular, Wi-Fi, and Bluetooth technologies.

First, we introduced cellular forensics and learned how to extract cellular-related data from an iOS extraction, such as the device's IMSI and IMEI codes. Then, we analyzed the PowerLog to view the relevant events, such as the device registering with the cellular network.

After that, we focused on phone calls and learned how to extract contact data from the address book, as well as how to access the call log, which contains details of all incoming and outgoing communications, including FaceTime videocalls. Then, we introduced the topic of network usage and learned which queries allow an investigator to see which processes were running on a device, as well as how much networking data they were consuming.

Finally, we learned about Safari forensics. We took an in-depth look at where common Safari artifacts are located and how to analyze browsing history through the `History.db` and `KnowledgeC.db` databases. We also briefly discussed some options for recovering data in terms of private browsing.

In the next chapter, we will learn about email and messaging forensics.

8
Email and Messaging Forensics

In the previous chapter, we discussed artifacts related to connectivity and learned how an investigator can leverage such data to understand who a user has been in contact with, how and when network data was used, and what websites the user visited. In this chapter, we will focus on email and messaging forensics.

Any investigation of a mobile device usually includes the search and analysis of messaging artifacts, as they can contain invaluable evidence: emails, text messages, and instant messaging can be used to transmit and receive all kinds of data, such as passwords, notes, confessions, threats, intellectual property, and multimedia files. In this chapter, we will learn where this evidence is stored, what an investigator can expect to find, and how to parse through the artifacts.

We'll begin the chapter with an introduction to email forensics with a focus on the Apple Mail app. We will learn where emails are stored and how to analyze them. Then, we will learn all about messaging forensics, starting with the analysis of SMS messages and iMessage. We will also understand how to investigate third-party messaging apps, such as WhatsApp, Telegram, and Signal. Finally, in the last part of the chapter, we'll look into recovering deleted messages.

In this chapter, we will cover the following topics:

- Introducing email forensics
- Understanding messaging forensics
- Introducing third-party messaging apps
- Recovering deleted messages

Introducing email forensics

In the first part of this chapter, we will introduce email forensics and we will focus on the **Apple Mail** application. It's safe to say that Apple Mail is certainly the most popular email client on iOS devices; however, investigators should keep in mind that there are many more third-party email apps available, such as **Outlook**, **Spark**, **Gmail**, and **Airmail**. Analyzing third-party apps is covered in *Chapter 10, Analyzing Third-Party Apps*. A comprehensive forensic analysis of email artifacts should entail analyzing Apple Mail and any third-party clients that have been installed on the device.

The first step in investigating Apple Mail data is locating the artifacts: these can be found in the folder located at `/private/var/mobile/Library/Mail`. Please note that a full filesystem extraction is required. The following is a list of the most relevant files and their description:

- For each email account configured on the device, there will be a corresponding folder within the `Mail` folder; the folder's name refers to the account's unique identifier. Each of these contains additional subfolders, such as `Inbox`, `Sent`, `Spam`, and `Drafts`, which contain the actual emails, stored as **Electronic Mail (EML)** files.
- The `Envelope Index` file is a SQLite database that contains a number of tables that store **metadata** related to each email account that was configured on the device.
- The `Protected Index` database contains the actual data related to emails, such as a **summary** of the email's body, **subjects**, and **addresses**.
- `MailboxCollections.plist` stores user preferences related to every account.
- The `metadata.plist` file stores a timestamp of when each mailbox was last synced to the device.

Now that we know where email artifacts are located, we're going to jump right into these SQLite databases to parse through email metadata and its content.

Extracting email metadata

We're going to start by examining the Envelope Index database. The first table of interest is mailboxes. As the name suggests, this table stores a list of all mailboxes configured on the device. This includes different folders for a single account, such as Important, Spam, Drafts, and Trash.

The following screenshot shows some sample data from the mailboxes table:

	ROWID	url
	Filter	Filter
1	1	imap://4FD35256-CE13-47FE-9840-EBEB5B9FD9C1/INBOX
2	2	imap://4FD35256-CE13-47FE-9840-EBEB5B9FD9C1/%5BGmail%5D/%5CImportant
3	3	imap://4FD35256-CE13-47FE-9840-EBEB5B9FD9C1/%5BGmail%5D/%5CAllMail
4	4	imap://4FD35256-CE13-47FE-9840-EBEB5B9FD9C1/%5BGmail%5D/%5CSpam
5	5	imap://4FD35256-CE13-47FE-9840-EBEB5B9FD9C1/%5BGmail%5D/%5CSent
6	6	local://LocalAccountId/x-apple-transient-drafts
7	7	local://LocalAccountId/Outbox
8	8	imap://4FD35256-CE13-47FE-9840-EBEB5B9FD9C1/%5BGmail%5D/%5CTrash
9	9	imap://4FD35256-CE13-47FE-9840-EBEB5B9FD9C1/%5BGmail%5D/%5CStarred
10	10	imap://4FD35256-CE13-47FE-9840-EBEB5B9FD9C1/%5BGmail%5D/%5CDrafts

Figure 8.1 – The mailboxes table displayed in DB Browser

As you can see from the screenshot, each account is identified by a **Universally Unique Identifier** (**UUID**) (*in this example, 4FD35256-CE13-47FE-9840-EBEB5B9FD9C1*) while each folder is identified by a unique **ROWID**. By analyzing this table, the examiner can gain a rough idea of how many, and which, email accounts are configured on the device.

The next step involves extracting and analyzing email metadata, which is stored in the messages table. It's important to note that some of the data stored in this table will have to be correlated to other records to make sense; in fact, the relationships between data span not only between tables but also between the Envelope Index and Protected Index databases.

The following is a list of columns of interest from a forensic viewpoint:

- The external_id column indicates the name of the EML file that contains the actual email content.

- The `sender` column indicates the email address of the sender; this value needs to be correlated to the records stored in the `Addresses` table, in the `Protected Index` database.

- The `subject` column also needs to be correlated to the `Subjects` table in `Protected Index`.

- The `summary` column, which is correlated to the `Summaries` table, stores the first 500 bytes of the email's content.

- The `date_sent` column stores a timestamp of when the email was sent.

- The `mailbox` column shows which account and folder contain the email.

- The `read` column will have a value of `1` if the email was read, or `0` if it was not.

The following query extracts all relevant metadata from the table:

```
SELECT
DATETIME(messages.date_sent, 'UNIXEPOCH', 'localtime') AS "DATE
/ TIME",
messages.sender AS SENDER,
messages.subject AS SUBJECT,
messages.summary AS SUMMARY,
messages.read AS READ,
mailboxes.url AS MAILBOX,
messages.external_id AS "EML FILENAME"
FROM messages
LEFT JOIN mailboxes ON messages.mailbox = mailboxes.ROWID
ORDER BY "DATE / TIME" ASC;
```

The result is shown in the following screenshot:

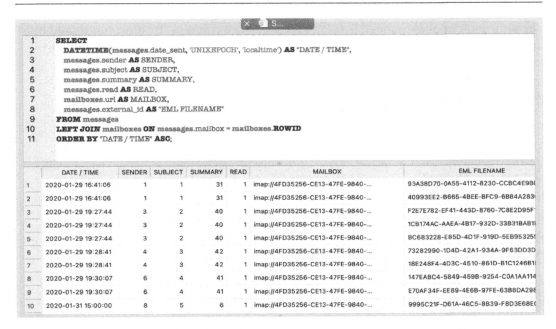

Figure 8.2 – The SQL query extracts email metadata from the messages table

As you can see from the screenshot, the SENDER, SUBJECT, and SUMMARY columns show a numerical value, which is the row ID for the relevant record in the Protected Index database.

For example, the first record has a value of 1 in the SENDER column. If we view the addresses table in DB Browser and filter the results based on ROWID, we can see that in this sample data, the email sender refers to Google, so that particular email was sent from no-reply@accounts.google.com.

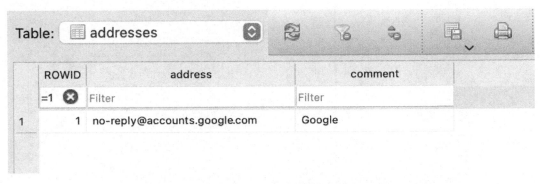

Figure 8.3 – The addresses table filtered by ROWID

The same logic applies to the SUBJECT and SUMMARY columns. By now, you should have a general understanding of how to extract email metadata. In the following section, we'll learn how to analyze email content.

Analyzing email content

Identifying a specific email is a straightforward task as Apple Mail stores every email as a separate file. When we previously extracted email metadata, we learned that the messages table stores an external_id record for each email, which is the name of an EML file. These files are stored in /private/var/mobile/Library/Mail/MAILBOX-UUID/.

EML files can be opened on a macOS system using the Apple Mail desktop application, and on Windows using **Microsoft Outlook**. It's also possible to view the email content in any **web browser**, by renaming the file extension as .html.

To get the full content, including the email's **headers**, the EML file can be opened using a **text editor** or it can be viewed through the **terminal**, as shown in the following screenshot:

Figure 8.4 – An EML file viewed through the terminal showing the email's content

Keep in mind that the content of an email is often split up between multiple EML files; in such cases, the partial files must be merged into a single file in order to view the entire email.

Now that we have learned where to look for email artifacts and how to analyze them, we will focus on messaging forensics in the next part of the chapter.

Understanding messaging forensics

Short Message Service (SMS) messages and **Instant Messaging (IM)** chat applications, such as **WhatsApp** or **Telegram**, may contain very important information that can aid any kind of investigation.

Before we dive into the details of how to analyze this data, we'll briefly introduce the different messaging solutions available on an iOS device:

- **SMS** is the traditional form of messaging, which uses the GSM/LTE cellular network to deliver messages. The service allows the user to send and receive messages of up to 160 characters, although messages can be concatenated to support longer text. In SMS messaging, the message is sent from one phone number to another.

- **iMessage** was introduced in iOS 5 and allows users to exchange instant messages along with likes, emojis, reactions, and attachments. As iMessage is preinstalled on every iOS device, it has a huge user base of more than 1.6 billion active users worldwide. An iMessage account is not tied to a particular phone number, but it is associated with an Apple ID; users can then send/receive messages through their email address and phone number.

- **Third-party IM applications** have become the de facto platform for messaging. These include apps such as **WhatsApp**, **Telegram**, **Line**, **Viber,** and **Signal**. From a forensic viewpoint, these present a set of additional challenges, as these apps should be regarded as **cloud applications**, so data can be stored both on the device and in the cloud.

We'll start our analysis of messaging artifacts by looking at SMS and iMessage forensics.

Analyzing SMS and iMessage artifacts

Analyzing artifacts pertaining to SMS and iMessage chats is a straightforward task, as these types of messages are both stored in the same SQLite database. In fact, these messages are essentially the same from the user's perspective, and iOS stores them both in the `sms.db` database, indicating whetherthe message is a regular SMS or an iMessage in one of the table's columns.

The following is a list of artifacts related to SMS or iMessage messaging:

- The `/private/var/mobile/Library/Preferences/com.apple.madrid.plist` property list contains a set of properties and user preferences related to SMS, iMessage, and FaceTime. In particular, the plist contains a dictionary under the `allAliases` key that indicates all the aliases connected to the iMessage account, such as phone numbers and email addresses.

- `/private/var/mobile/Library/Preferences/com.apple.MobileSMS.plist` stores preferences related to SMS and iMessage, including the `KeepMessageForDays` key, which indicates the retention period. By default, this is set to `Forever`.

- The `/private/var/mobile/Library/SMS/Attachments/` folder, as the name implies, contains attachments that were sent through MMS or iMessage, such as photos, videos, and audio recordings.

- The `/private/var/mobile/Library/SMS/Drafts/` folder stores draft messages and pending messages (messages that the user sent but that iOS did not send due to, for example, the absence of connectivity).

- The `/private/var/mobile/Library/SMS/sms.db` database stores all metadata and content of all messages, SMS and iMessage.

- Messages received **Before First Unlock (BFU)** are stored in a temporary database, which is located at `/private/var/mobile/Library/SMS/sms-temp.db`.

We're going to focus on the `sms.db` file to learn how to extract all messages and their metadata from the `message`, `chat_message_join`, `chat`, and `attachment` tables. The following SQL query will do the job:

```
SELECT
CASE when LENGTH(chat_message_join.message_date)=18 THEN
    datetime(chat_message_join.message_date/1000000000 +
978307200,'unixepoch','localtime')
    when LENGTH(chat_message_join.message_date)=9 THEN
    datetime(chat_message_join.message_date +
```

```
978307200,'unixepoch','localtime')
    else 'NA'
END as "Message Date",
message.text,
message.service,
message.account,
chat.account_login,
chat.chat_identifier,
CASE when LENGTH(message.date_read)=18 THEN
    datetime(message.date_read/1000000000 +
978307200,'unixepoch','localtime')
    when LENGTH(message.date_read)=9 THEN
    datetime(message.date_
read+978307200,'unixepoch','localtime')
    else 'NA'
END as "Date Read",
CASE when message.is_read=1
    THEN 'Incoming'
    when message.is_read=0
    THEN 'Outgoing'
END AS "Message Direction",
CASE when LENGTH(chat.last_read_message_timestamp)=18 THEN
    datetime(chat.last_read_message_
timestamp/1000000000+978307200,'unixepoch','localtime')
    when LENGTH(chat.last_read_message_timestamp)=9 THEN
    datetime(chat.last_read_message_timestamp +
978307200,'unixepoch','localtime')
    else 'NA'
END as "Last Read"
FROM message
left join chat_message_join on chat_message_join.message_
id=message.ROWID
left join chat on chat.ROWID=chat_message_join.chat_id
left join attachment on attachment.ROWID=chat_message_join.
chat_id
order by "Message Date" ASC;
```

Although that query may seem complicated, it's actually a lot easier if we break it down into logical steps. Before we analyze the query, it may be useful to look at the result.

The following screenshot shows all the data spread across two rows, for better readability:

	Message Date	text	service	account	account_login
1	2020-03-22 02:10:59	G-773293 is your Google verification code....	SMS	p:+19195794674	P:+19195794674
2	2020-03-22 16:16:16	imo code: 258465...	SMS	p:+19195794674	P:+19195794674
3	2020-03-22 20:21:40	Please enter 737950 into LINE within the next 30 mins....	SMS	p:+19195794674	P:+19195794674
4	2020-03-23 02:06:38	Please enter this code in the app to reset your MeWe ...	SMS	p:+19195794674	P:+19195794674
5	2020-03-23 02:38:03	Your Signal verification code: 903-394...	SMS	p:+19195794674	P:+19195794674
6	2020-03-23 18:41:36	🔔 ThisIs,you have 2 new notifications on Facebook: ...	SMS	p:+19195794674	P:+19198887386
7	2020-03-24 02:21:34	Telegram code: 95037...	SMS	p:+19195794674	P:+19195794674
8	2020-03-24 02:27:40	[TikTok] 8494 is your verification code,valid for 5 minutes.	SMS	p:+19195794674	P:+19195794674
9	2020-03-24 02:52:23	Your WhatsApp code: 203-591...	SMS	p:+19195794674	P:+19195794674
10	2020-03-25 01:47:38	Your Skout verification code is 3079....	SMS	p:+19195794674	P:+19195794674

	account	account_login	chat_identifier	Date Read	Message Direction	Last Read
1	p:+19195794674	P:+19195794674	22000	2020-03-22 02:11:03	Incoming	2020-04-07 03:05:23
2	p:+19195794674	P:+19195794674	+18634205597	2020-03-22 16:16:19	Incoming	2020-03-22 16:16:19
3	p:+19195794674	P:+19195794674	+13176444906	2020-03-22 20:21:53	Incoming	2020-03-22 20:21:53
4	p:+19195794674	P:+19195794674	85760	2020-03-23 02:06:44	Incoming	2020-03-23 02:06:44
5	p:+19195794674	P:+19195794674	+17026604496	2020-03-23 02:38:05	Incoming	2020-03-23 02:38:05
6	p:+19195794674	P:+19198887386	32665	2020-03-24 02:00:59	Incoming	2020-04-16 00:14:06
7	p:+19195794674	P:+19195794674	+12074242620	2020-03-24 02:21:36	Incoming	2020-03-24 02:21:36
8	p:+19195794674	P:+19195794674	+13233208923	2020-03-24 02:27:42	Incoming	2020-03-24 02:27:42
9	p:+19195794674	P:+19195794674	47543	2020-03-24 02:52:25	Incoming	2020-03-24 02:52:25
10	p:+19195794674	P:+19195794674	+12349008110	2020-03-25 01:47:41	Incoming	2020-03-25 01:47:41

Figure 8.5 – Extracting message data from sms.db

The first thing to keep in mind is that since **iOS 11**, Apple started storing timestamps as 18-digit numbers, while previously, message timestamps were only nine digits long. This means that the sms.db database will most likely contain both nine-digit and 18-digit timestamps. Our query begins by verifying the length of the timestamp and displaying the date and time of when the message was sent accordingly. Then, we extract the text column and the service column, which indicates whether the message is a traditional SMS, or an iMessage. The account and account_login columns show the phone number or email address that the user was using to send or receive the message. The chat_identifier column stores the phone number or email address of the person the user was communicating with. Finally, the Date Read, Message Direction, and Last Read columns are self-explanatory.

During an investigation that involves SMS and iMessage forensics, the `Drafts` and `Attachments` folders should not be overlooked, as these may contain evidence that is not tracked by the `sms.db` database; in fact, multimedia attachments shared through a message may contain additional metadata, such as the location where a photo was taken. We'll learn how to analyze multimedia files in *Chapter 9, Photo, Video, and Audio Forensics*.

In the next section, we'll learn how to analyze chats from third-party messaging applications.

Introducing third-party messaging apps

Third-party messaging applications allow users to keep in touch with their contacts, and share photos, videos, and audio messages. Many of these apps also allow users to send likes, emojis, animations, and any kind of attachment.

Most forensic tools do an excellent job at analyzing and parsing through these apps; however, the examiner should have a basic understanding of how these applications work, how they store their data, where they store it, and how to extract it. In this section, we'll focus on three of the most popular messaging apps: **WhatsApp**, **Telegram,** and **Signal**:

- With over 2 billion worldwide users, **WhatsApp** is definitely one of the most popular IM apps. From a forensic perspective, the app stores its data on the device, in unencrypted form. Chats and messages are not stored on WhatsApp's servers; however, if this feature is enabled, an encrypted backup can be stored on iCloud. Artifacts related to WhatsApp can be found in `/private/var/mobile/Containers/Data/Application/<APP_GUID>/` and in `/private/var/mobile/Containers/Shared/AppGroup/<APP_GUID>/`. The investigator can expect to extract chats, messages, media files, blocked contacts, call logs, and application logs. The main databases of interest are `ChatStorage.sqlite`, which contains the actual chats in the `ZWAMESSAGE` table, and `CallHistory.sqlite`, which stores data pertaining to WhatsApp voice calls and video calls. These databases are also included in a local (iTunes) backup.

- **Telegram** is a multi-platform IM application that is compatible with a huge list of devices, including desktop computers. Chats and messages are stored both on the local device and on Telegram's servers. There is also the option of creating secret chats, where data is never stored on the application's servers. Telegram artifacts are not included in local or iCloud backups but are only available in a full filesystem acquisition. Artifacts and logs can be found in `/private/var/mobile/Containers/Data/Application/<APP_GUID>/` and `/private/var/mobile/Containers/Shared/AppGroup/<APP_GUID>/`. Chats and messages, including secret chats, can be found in the `db_sqlite` database.

- **Signal** is a secure, encrypted messaging app available for mobile devices and desktop computers, including Linux. All communications on Signal, such as messages, group chats, photos, and file transfers, are end-to-end encrypted. Signal conversations are not stored on their servers, they're not available in a local backup, and it's not possible to back up the data to iCloud. Signal's database is stored on the local device in encrypted form. The only way to access these artifacts is by performing a full filesystem acquisition and decrypting the keychain to access the encryption key, which will in turn decrypt the database. Log files and user preferences are stored in `/private/var/mobile/Containers/Data/Application/<APP_GUID>/`. The encrypted database, `signal.sqlite`, can be found in `/private/var/mobile/Containers/Shared/AppGroup/<APP_GUID>/`.

In this section, we briefly discussed third-party messaging applications and learned how and where these apps store conversation data. In the final part of this chapter, we'll learn how to attempt the recovery of deleted messages.

Recovering deleted messages

One of the most common tasks in a mobile device investigation is to attempt the recovery of data that was deleted by the user, such as chats and messages, as these may contain invaluable evidence.

In this chapter, we learned that SMS messages and chats from third-party applications are all stored in SQLite databases; this means that the ability to recover deleted chats effectively depends on the possibility of recovering any records from the SQLite database.

In *Chapter 4, Working with Common iOS Artifacts*, we discussed several options for the recovery of deleted records, such as the following:

- Parsing through the database using a hex viewer
- String carving

- Analyzing the **Write Ahead Log (WAL)** files
- Using forensic tools such as FQLite to recover data from free blocks and unallocated space

All of these solutions can be effective in recovering deleted messages, but only if the database was not vacuumed after the records were purged from the database.

> **Tip**
> It's important to note that to attempt data recovery, the database should be extracted through a full filesystem acquisition and not a logical acquisition, as the latter will contain a vacuumed copy of the database, which is rebuilt from scratch during the backup process. Research has also shown that since iOS 11, the sms.db database is regularly vacuumed, so SMS messages and iMessages may be purged before the examiner has the possibility of acquiring the device.

In the following section, we'll introduce an open source tool that can be used to recover deleted messages.

Detecting deleted messages using Mirf

There are some occasions where recovering deleted messages is simply not possible; however, in such circumstances, it may still be possible to detect the fact that the user deleted a message, even if its content cannot be recovered.

Chats and messages are stored in SQLite tables as individual records; each record is identified through a unique, progressive identifier called a **primary key**. For example, in the following screenshot, which contains an extract of data from the WhatsApp ChatStorage.sqlite database, individual messages are referenced using an identifier stored in the Z_PK column:

	Z_PK	DATE	ZTEXT
1	1	2020-03-26 19:42:57	NULL
2	2	2020-03-26 19:42:57	What's up?!
3	3	2020-03-26 19:43:48	Not much. Just waiting to hop on a conference call. You?
4	4	2020-03-26 19:44:44	A little busy. Finished one report this morning and going to…
5	6	2020-03-26 19:47:12	Not yet but the effects of this will be felt later I'm sure.
6	7	2020-03-27 01:35:26	NULL
7	8	2020-03-27 01:36:36	Lol!!
8	9	2020-03-27 01:37:02	My turn.
9	10	2020-03-27 01:38:00	NULL
10	11	2020-04-11 20:23:43	NULL

Figure 8.6 – The Z_PK column stores a unique identifier for each message

By analyzing the values in the Z_PK column, the examiner can look out for any missing records: in the previous example, the record associated with value 5 is missing. This is sufficient to state that a message has been deleted. Even if it is not possible to recover the actual message, it may be possible to deduce the timeframe of when the message was sent or received, by looking at the timestamps of the previous and next records. Thankfully, this process can be automated by using an open source Python script called **Missing Record Finder for SQLite Databases** (**Mirf**), which can help detect if any rows of data were deleted by discovering gaps.

The following steps illustrate the process of downloading Mirf and running the tool to detect the deleted message from the previous example:

1. To download Mirf, head over to its GitHub repository located at `https://github.com/sheran/mirf` and download the latest version as a ZIP archive or by cloning the repository by running the `git clone` command.

2. Install the required packages by running the following command from a terminal:

    ```
    pip install -r requirements.txt
    ```

3. Next, run Mirf by running the `./mirf.py` command followed by the path to the database that should be analyzed.

4. The tool will prompt you to specify the name of the table that contains the messages. In our example, this is the ZWAMESSAGE table that stores WhatsApp chats.

5. When the tool finishes the process, it will display a list of missing records from the table of choice.

If Mirf is used to analyze artifacts pertaining to **SMS messages** or **iMessages**, the tool will also automatically calculate the timeframe of when the deleted message was sent or received.

The following screenshot shows the tool's output when run on the `sms.db` database:

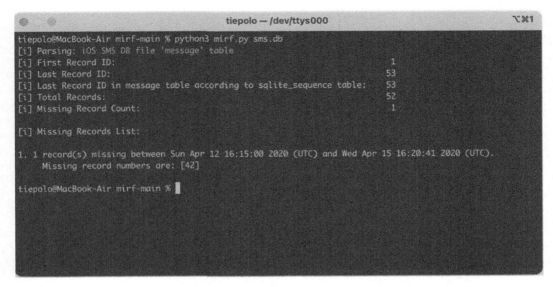

Figure 8.7 – Running Mirf to detect deleted messages

In this case, one missing record is identified, including date ranges in the UTC time zone and the missing record number.

Summary

In this chapter, we learned all about how iOS stores emails and messages on the device and what artifacts an investigator can expect to find.

First, we introduced the Apple Mail application and discovered where emails are stored. We analyzed the relevant SQLite databases to extract email metadata and learned how to parse through EML files to view the email's body.

Later in the chapter, we focused on messaging forensics by looking at how iOS stores SMS and iMessage data on the sms.db database and how a SQL query can be used to extract all messages and their metadata. Then, we introduced the topic of third-party messaging applications and focused on three of them: WhatsApp, Telegram, and Signal. We learned what data can be extracted from these apps and which are the most relevant SQL databases.

Finally, in the last section of this chapter, we discussed different options to attempt the recovery of deleted messages, such as using an open source tool called Mirf, which can detect gaps between records in a SQL table.

In the next chapter, we will learn all about photo, video, and music forensics.

9
Photo, Video, and Audio Forensics

In the first few chapters of the book, we focused on the identification and analysis of mobile evidence stored in system-generated artifacts such as databases, PLISTs, and log files. However, any type of investigation will also typically involve analyzing user-generated content found on a device, such as media files.

A modern iOS device can contain tens of thousands of media files, and each of these files is associated with unique metadata that can be critical to an investigation. In this chapter, we will learn how to identify and analyze multimedia content such as photos, videos, and audio files.

We will start the chapter with an introduction to media forensics and discuss where photos, videos, and audio recordings are stored on an iOS device. Then, we'll learn all about analyzing media metadata to gain meaningful insights, both from the file itself and from the corresponding databases. In the last part of the chapter, we will learn how to analyze user behavior to find out what media the user has accessed or watched through Apple apps such as Music and Safari, and third-party apps such as Spotify or Netflix.

In this chapter, we will cover the following topics:

- Introducing media forensics
- Analyzing photos and videos
- Introducing EXIF metadata
- Analyzing user viewing activity

Introducing media forensics

Media forensics can be defined as the process of locating, analyzing, and extracting meaningful metadata from any kind of multimedia object, such as an **image** or a **video**. Modern iOS devices such as the iPhone 13 have huge storage capacities (*the base model has 128 GB of storage*), and this allows them to potentially store tens of thousands of media files. Each of these is linked to particular **metadata** that may give an investigator a lot more information than the file itself.

Although it may be tempting to think of multimedia assets merely as photos or videos, iOS devices, in reality, handle a lot more than that; the following is a list of common media assets that can be found on an iOS device:

- Camera roll photos, videos, and live photos
- Saved photos and videos
- Screenshots
- Audio recordings and music
- Media files received from third-party apps (such as WhatsApp and Telegram)
- Streamed content

It's important to understand that when an examiner is tasked with analyzing any kind of media file from a mobile device, the focus shouldn't be solely on *where* the file was located but rather on *how* the media object got there.

By analyzing media files, their metadata, and iOS-related artifacts, the investigator will be able to answer questions such as the following:

- Was a particular photo taken from the device's camera?
- What was the location where the photo was taken?
- Was a video file received from a messaging app?

- When was a media file last modified?

- What does a media file say about the user?

We're going to start by highlighting some of the most common locations where media-related artifacts are located:

- `/private/var/mobile/Media/DCIM/1**APPLE/`: This folder stores photos and videos that were created by the user or saved to the device. Typically, images will be stored in **JPG**, **PNG**, or **HEIC** format, and videos will be stored as **MP4** or **MOV** files.

- `/private/var/mobile/Media/PhotoData/`: The `PhotoData` folder stores several artifacts related to the media metadata, such as the `Photos.sqlite` database, **thumbnails** (which are stored in `/private/var/mobile/Media/PhotoData/Thumbnails/V2/DCIM/1**APPLE/IMG_****.JPG/****.JPG`), and **photo album** data. Generally, this folder will be the primary source of evidence for any kind of media file stored on the device. We'll take an in-depth look at this folder in the next section.

- `/private/var/mobile/Media/PhotoData/PhotoCloudSharingData/`: The `PhotoCloudSharingData` folder contains artifacts pertaining to Shared Albums, an iOS feature that allows users to easily share photo collections. Each shared album will have a subfolder that contains an `Info.plist` file, which contains album metadata (the name, the owner, and more), and `DCIM_CLOUD.plist`, which stores the number of photos in the album.

- `/private/var/mobile/Media/Recordings/*`: This folder contains user-recorded **voice memos**.

The following screenshot shows which files and folders can be found in the `PhotoData` folder:

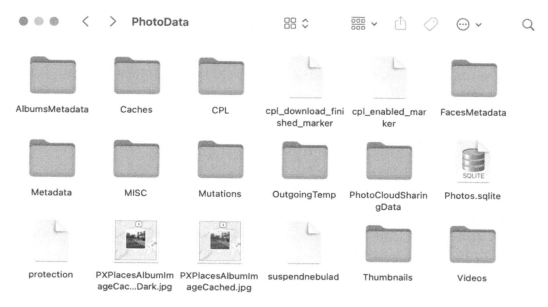

Figure 9.1 – The PhotoData folder contains media metadata

Each media asset has two different kinds of metadata associated with it – **EXIF metadata**, which contains details such as the device that generated the image or the location, is stored within the file itself, while iOS-generated metadata is stored in the `Photos.sqlite` database.

In the following section, we'll analyze the database to learn how to extract meaningful information for each image or video that is stored on the device.

Analyzing photos and videos

Every time a photo or video is taken through a device's camera or saved onto a device, iOS analyzes it and generates a multitude of metadata, which is stored in the `Photos.sqlite` database.

The following is a list of events that occur during the process:

1. First, the newly created photo or video is saved in `/private/var/mobile/Media/DCIM/1**APPLE/` as a JPG, HEIC, MP4, or MOV file. The folder name will iterate upward (`100APPLE`, `101APPLE`, `102APPLE`, and so on) as more photos or videos are stored on the device.

2. Additionally, the `PreviewWellImage.tiff` image is created and stored in `/private/var/mobile/Media/PhotoData/MISC/`. This image is the thumbnail that is displayed in the **Photos** app where the most recent image is displayed.

3. As the new media is stored, a new entry is created in the `Photos.sqlite` database, in the `ZGENERICASSET` table. Since iOS 14, this table is now called `ZASSET`. The new record will contain metadata such as the date and time when the content was saved, the date and time of when it was last edited, the filename, and the color space.

4. In the background, iOS starts processing the newly created media by running several algorithms, such as facial and object recognition. If a name has been associated with a face that iOS recognizes in the media file, the photo or video will also be displayed in the **People** album, in the **Photos** app. The results of the analysis are then stored in the `Photos.sqlite` database and in `mediaanalysis.db`, which can be found in `/private/var/mobile/Media/MediaAnalysis/`.

As you can see, there's a lot going on! Now that we know where the artifacts are located, we will focus on analyzing photos and videos.

Understanding Photos.sqlite

With over 60 tables packed full of data, the `Photos.sqlite` database is one of the largest datasets that can be found in an iOS acquisition. A detailed analysis of this database is beyond the scope of this book, so we'll focus on extracting the most important pieces of metadata from the `ZGENERICASSET` (`ZASSET` in iOS 14 and 15) table.

Once you've opened the file with your tool of choice, such as *DB Browser for SQLite*, run the following query:

```
SELECT
Z_PK,
DATETIME(ZDATECREATED + 978307200, 'UNIXEPOCH') AS "Created
date",
DATETIME(ZMODIFICATIONDATE + 978307200, 'UNIXEPOCH') AS
"Modified date",
DATETIME(ZTRASHEDDATE + 978307200, 'UNIXEPOCH') AS "Deleted
date",
ZFILENAME AS "File name",
ZDIRECTORY AS "Directory",
ZWIDTH AS "Width",
```

```
ZHEIGHT AS "Height",
ZHIDDEN AS "Hidden"
FROM ZGENERICASSET
ORDER BY Z_PK ASC;
```

The following screenshot shows the result of the query by running it on our example dataset:

	Z_PK	Created date	Modified date	Deleted date	File name	Directory	Width	Height	Hidden
1	1	2020-03-22 13:05:24	2020-04-06 15:02:38	NULL	IMG_0001.JPG	DCIM/100APPLE	1125	1137	0
2	2	2020-03-22 13:05:39	2020-04-06 15:02:38	NULL	IMG_0002.JPG	DCIM/100APPLE	3550	3150	0
3	3	2020-03-22 13:10:50	2020-04-13 19:32:52	NULL	IMG_0003.JPG	DCIM/100APPLE	1668	860	0
4	4	2020-03-22 13:25:02	2020-04-06 15:02:38	NULL	IMG_0004.JPG	DCIM/100APPLE	1117	886	0
5	5	2020-03-22 13:25:02	2020-04-06 15:02:38	NULL	IMG_0005.JPG	DCIM/100APPLE	1522	1775	0
6	6	2020-03-22 13:25:02	2020-04-06 15:02:38	NULL	IMG_0006.JPG	DCIM/100APPLE	1170	1175	0
7	7	2020-03-22 13:25:02	2020-04-19 18:25:57	NULL	IMG_0007.JPG	DCIM/100APPLE	1178	781	0
8	8	2020-03-22 13:25:02	2020-04-13 19:32:52	NULL	IMG_0008.JPG	DCIM/100APPLE	1125	1156	0
9	9	2020-03-22 13:31:03	2020-04-06 15:02:38	NULL	IMG_0009.JPG	DCIM/100APPLE	828	637	0
10	10	2020-03-22 13:40:14	2020-04-19 18:25:58	NULL	IMG_0010.JPG	DCIM/100APPLE	620	553	0

Figure 9.2 – The results of the query from the Photos.sqlite database

As you can see, the query extracts the list of all media stored on the device, including metadata such as when the media object was created, when it was last modified, if and when it was deleted, if the user chose to hide it, the width and the height, and of course, the directory and the filename.

So far, we've only scratched the surface of `Photos.sqlite`, as this database has a lot more to offer. By going deeper into the evidence and correlating data between different tables, the examiner can leverage the metadata provided by iOS to gain insights such as the following:

- Was the media asset shared? If so, when?

- Was a particular photo adjusted/corrected on the device?

- Was the photo taken on the device or did the user receive it?

- Which application received and stored the photo?

- How many times did the user view a media asset?

- Was the media asset added to a specific album?

To extract all this data from the database, we're going to use a more complex SQL query that was written by *Scott Koenig* (`@Scott_Kjr`). The query can be found on his blog: `theforensicscooter.com`.

> **Tip**
>
> To gain a full understanding of how `Photos.sqlite` works and what data can be found by delving into the database, you can refer to this article: *Using Photos.sqlite to Show the Relationships Between Photos and the Application they were Created with?*, *DFIR Review, Koenig, S., 2021* (retrieved from `https://dfir.pubpub.org/pub/v19rksyf`).

The following screenshot shows the query executed through DB Browser:

	GenericAsset_zpk	AddAttributes_Key	DetectedFaceAsset	Kind	DateCreated	EXIFtimestamp	SceneAnalysisTim
45	33	33	*NULL*	Photo	2020-04-11 17:56:09	2020:04:11 13:56:09	2020-04-11 17:56:
46	34	34	*NULL*	Photo	2020-04-11 17:56:55	2020:04:11 13:56:56	2020-04-11 17:56:
47	35	35	*NULL*	Photo	2020-04-12 00:45:00	*NULL*	2020-04-12 00:45
48	36	36	*NULL*	Photo	2020-04-12 01:29:12	*NULL*	2020-04-12 01:29:
49	37	37	*NULL*	Video	2020-04-12 01:57:09	2020:04:11 21:57:09	2020-04-12 01:57:
50	38	38	38	Photo	2020-04-12 12:58:25	*NULL*	2020-04-12 12:58:
51	39	39	*NULL*	Photo	2020-04-12 13:25:00	2020:04:12 09:25:00	2020-04-12 13:25:
52	40	40	*NULL*	Photo	2020-04-12 13:25:26	2020:04:12 09:25:26	2020-04-12 13:25:
53	41	41	*NULL*	Photo	2020-04-12 13:26:13	2020:04:12 09:26:13	2020-04-12 13:26:
54	42	42	*NULL*	Photo	2020-04-12 13:26:30	2020:04:12 09:26:30	2020-04-12 13:26:

Figure 9.3 – The results of the query from the Photos.sqlite database

As you can see, this query provides a lot more data. The following is a list of the most relevant columns and their descriptions:

- The query provides us with a `Kind` column, which indicates whether the media asset is a photo or a video.

- The `AlbumTitle` column shows whether the asset belongs to a specific album, such as the **WhatsApp** album.

- By looking at `CreatorBundleID`, the investigator can learn which application on the device created the media asset – for instance, the `com.facebook.Messenger` value is a clear indication that the media was received through the Facebook app.

- `EditorBundleID` indicates which application edited the asset last – for example, in the following screenshot, the `com.apple.ScreenshotServicesService` value shows that a screenshot was taken on the device and that the screenshot utility was used to edit the image:

e		AlbumTitle	CreatorBundleID	EditorBundleID	Directory	Uniforml
22	720D5959.jpg	Imgur	NULL	NULL	DCIM/100APPLE	public.jpeg
23	720D5959.jpg	Imgur	NULL	NULL	DCIM/100APPLE	public.jpeg
24		NULL	NULL	com.apple.ScreenshotServicesService	DCIM/100APPLE	public.jpeg
25	A30D6460.jpg	NULL	NULL	NULL	DCIM/100APPLE	public.jpeg
26	0460310D.jpg	NULL	NULL	NULL	DCIM/100APPLE	public.jpeg
27	I-13D1A552AFDF.jpg	NULL	NULL	NULL	DCIM/100APPLE	public.jpeg
28		NULL	com.reddit.Reddit	NULL	DCIM/100APPLE	public.jpeg
29		NULL	org.whispersystems.signal	NULL	DCIM/100APPLE	public.png
30		NULL	NULL	NULL	DCIM/100APPLE	public.jpeg
31		NULL	NULL	com.apple.ScreenshotServicesService	DCIM/100APPLE	public.jpeg

Figure 9.4 – CreatorBundleID and EditorBundleID indicate where the asset originates from

- The `SavedAssetType` column indicates whether the asset was created on the device or whether it was synced from another source.

- `Favorite`, `Hidden_File`, and `TrashState` indicate whether the media asset was included in the *Favorites* album, whether the user opted to hide it, or whether it was marked for deletion.

- The `ShareCount` and `LastSharedDate` columns indicate how many times a particular media asset was shared and the timestamp of the last time it occurred:

	rashDate	ViewCount	PlayCount	ShareCount	LastSharedDate	FileModificationDate	Has_Adjustments	AdjustmentsTimeS
31		2	0	0	NULL	2020-04-06 15:02:38	Yes	2020-03-25 01:53:
32		1	0	0	NULL	2020-04-06 15:02:38	No	NULL
33		2	0	0	NULL	2020-04-19 18:25:57	No	NULL
34		1	0	0	NULL	2020-04-06 15:02:38	No	NULL
35		1	0	1	2020-04-05 19:13:52	2020-04-19 18:25:57	No	NULL
36		1	0	1	2020-04-05 19:13:52	2020-04-19 18:25:57	No	NULL
37		1	0	1	2020-03-27 01:17:03	2020-04-19 18:25:58	No	NULL
38		1	0	1	2020-03-27 01:17:03	2020-04-19 18:25:58	No	NULL
39		1	0	1	2020-03-27 01:17:03	2020-04-19 18:25:58	No	NULL
40		0	0	0	NULL	2020-03-27 00:38:01	No	NULL

Figure 9.5 – The ShareCount column indicates whether a media asset was shared with other devices

- By checking the `Has_Adjustments` column, the investigator can understand whether the media asset was adjusted, edited, or cropped on the device.

- If location services were enabled, the `Latitude` and `Longitude` columns store the coordinates of the location where a photo or video was taken.

- Finally, the `UUID` column indicates the asset's unique identifier.

As we can see from the result of this query, there is a significant amount of metadata stored within the database; however, this is not the only source of media metadata. In the following section, we'll focus on extracting information from the media file itself.

Introducing EXIF metadata

The `Photos.sqlite` database can be a huge source of metadata, but there may be some occasions in which the database is not available, and the investigator only has access to the media file. Thankfully, images and videos often contain embedded metadata, which is known as **Exchangeable Image File Format (EXIF)**.

EXIF metadata can provide a wealth of information to investigators, such as the following:

- The device model
- Camera settings
- Exposure and lens specifications
- Timestamps
- Location data
- Altitude and bearing
- Speed reference

When a photo or video is captured through an iOS device's built-in camera, EXIF metadata is automatically added to the media asset. The following screenshot shows the amount of metadata that can be extracted from a photo that was taken on an iPhone SE:

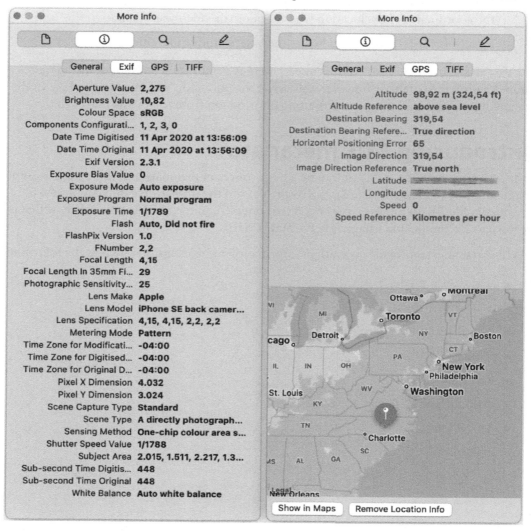

Figure 9.6 – EXIF metadata extracted from a photo that was captured on an iPhone

As you can see, by analyzing the EXIF metadata, we can learn that the photo was taken on an iPhone SE, using the back camera. The camera's flash was set to **Auto**, but it didn't fire, the shutter speed was automatically set to **1/1788**, while the exposure time was **1/1789**. The timestamp indicates when the photo was taken, based on the device's time zone, which is also indicated.

Metadata related to **GPS** is possibly even more useful; the iPhone automatically stored the device's **coordinates**, **altitude**, **bearing**, and **speed** when the photo was captured. Of course, this is dependent on **Location Services** being enabled on the device.

> **Tip**
>
> The investigator should always attempt to validate EXIF metadata: with iOS 15, Apple introduced the possibility of editing the file's location and capturing the timestamp directly from within the **Photos** application. However, from research that has been carried out, it seems that editing the metadata from the **Photos** app only affects the data stored in the `Photos.sqlite` database, while the EXIF metadata remains unchanged.

Although EXIF metadata can be extremely valuable for media assets created on a device, it won't be as useful when dealing with photos or videos received through a third-party application; most instant messaging apps, such as **WhatsApp** or **Telegram**, compress images before transferring them, resulting in the EXIF data being stripped from the file.

Now that we know what EXIF metadata is, we'll learn which tools can be used to view it.

Viewing EXIF metadata

There are a number of free tools available to view a media asset's EXIF, although most operating systems allow the user to view the data without installing any third-party tool.

On Windows, you can view a file's metadata by right-clicking on the media and selecting **Properties**. Then, click on the **Details** tab and scroll down to view the EXIF data. The `exiftool` free tool can also be used for the same purpose. It can be downloaded from `http://exiftool.org` and is compatible with both Windows and macOS.

On macOS, you can view EXIF simply by opening the file using **Preview**. Once open, click on **Tools** and select **Show Inspector**. Then, click on the **Exif** tab.

On most Linux distributions, the `exif` command-line tool can be used for this purpose.

By now, you should have a general understanding of what EXIF metadata is, how it can be beneficial to an investigation, and how to analyze it.

Analyzing user viewing activity

So far, we have focused on analyzing photo and video media assets; however, the investigator may want to understand not only what media was stored on a device but also what media the user viewed.

This may include any of the following:

- Audio/video streamed through Safari or other browsers
- Music played through Apple Music or third-party apps such as Spotify
- Videos played through third-party apps such as YouTube and Netflix

The KnowledgeC.db database, which we discussed in *Chapter 5, Pattern-of-Life Forensics*, tracks most of the user's day-to-day activity, including events related to audio or video playback.

The table of interest is the ZOBJECT table, which stores device events, organizing them by *stream name*. Every time iOS detects that the user has initiated media playback, a /media/nowPlaying event is triggered.

The following screenshot shows some example data from the KnowledgeC.db database, analyzed using DB Browser:

	ZUUID	ZSTREAMNAME	ZVALUESTRING
		/media/nowPlaying ⊗	Filter
74	4698C-793C-46F2-93C0-4C3C5C6A4F2E	/media/nowPlaying	com.apple.podcasts
75	97505-A71C-494E-9CC6-59291287024C	/media/nowPlaying	com.apple.podcasts
76	9B7F4-FEFD-4E8E-931B-359E2EEECC3C	/media/nowPlaying	com.apple.podcasts
77	22CEE-4834-42B3-9531-E2BDB3F3D1C4	/media/nowPlaying	com.apple.podcasts
78	5BFD9-C420-43F4-B6F2-DB1ADA37DB44	/media/nowPlaying	com.apple.podcasts
79	F2219-190C-4AAF-86C4-5CE72450F13C	/media/nowPlaying	com.apple.podcasts
80	8C843-9905-41D2-9E91-86F9EE1F0399	/media/nowPlaying	com.apple.podcasts
81	3F5AE-9168-4A64-A425-BD6E9A819D53	/media/nowPlaying	com.apple.podcasts
82	38C00-B90C-4B93-80E3-3206D399F163	/media/nowPlaying	com.apple.podcasts
83	ACB47-489B-4563-A46B-EA117D67F931	/media/nowPlaying	com.apple.podcasts
84	004A8-5501-4C06-94C9-7A7CDEAD6708	/media/nowPlaying	com.apple.podcasts
85	014E4-3F63-4A0B-9F98-1DF287575D2B	/media/nowPlaying	com.apple.podcasts
86	E3A15-CC82-4BBD-896A-AEA0C9C93BBF	/media/nowPlaying	com.apple.podcasts

|◀ ◀ 74 - 86 of 281 ▶ ▶| Go to: 1

Figure 9.7 – Media events extracted from the KnowledgeC.db database

By correlating the data from the ZOBJECT table with the metadata stored in ZSTRUCTUREDMETADATA, the examiner can gain many useful insights, such as what song the user was listening to, what video was streaming through Safari, or what show they were binge-watching on Netflix.

The following query will extract all the relevant data from KnowledgeC.db:

```
SELECT
datetime(ZOBJECT.ZSTARTDATE+978307200,'UNIXEPOCH', 'LOCALTIME')
as "START",
```

```
datetime(ZOBJECT.ZENDDATE+978307200,'UNIXEPOCH', 'LOCALTIME')
as "END",
(ZOBJECT.ZENDDATE-ZOBJECT.ZSTARTDATE) as "USAGE IN SECONDS",
ZOBJECT.ZVALUESTRING,
ZSTRUCTUREDMETADATA.Z_DKNOWPLAYINGMETADATAKEY__ALBUM as "NOW
PLAYING ALBUM",
ZSTRUCTUREDMETADATA.Z_DKNOWPLAYINGMETADATAKEY__ARTIST as "NOW
PLAYING ARTIST",
ZSTRUCTUREDMETADATA.Z_DKNOWPLAYINGMETADATAKEY__GENRE as "NOW
PLAYING GENRE",
ZSTRUCTUREDMETADATA.Z_DKNOWPLAYINGMETADATAKEY__TITLE as "NOW
PLAYING TITLE",
ZSTRUCTUREDMETADATA.Z_DKNOWPLAYINGMETADATAKEY__DURATION as "NOW
PLAYING DURATION"
FROM ZOBJECT
left join ZSTRUCTUREDMETADATA on ZOBJECT.ZSTRUCTUREDMETADATA =
ZSTRUCTUREDMETADATA.Z_PK
left join ZSOURCE on ZOBJECT.ZSOURCE = ZSOURCE.Z_PK
WHERE ZSTREAMNAME like "/media%"
ORDER BY "START";
```

As you can see from the following screenshot, the query provides us with a wealth of information, such as which app the user was using to view the media, the **duration**, and the **name** of the song or video:

	ZVALUESTRING	NOW PLAYING ALBUM	NOW PLAYING ARTIST	NOW PLAYING GENRE
87	com.apple.Music	B.o.B Presents: The Adventures of Bobby Ray (Deluxe)	B.o.B	Hip-Hop/Rap
88	com.apple.Music	Mother's Milk	Red Hot Chili Peppers	Alternative
89	com.apple.Music	Faster Kill Pussycat (feat.Brittany Murphy)	Oakenfold	Dance
90	com.apple.Music	Mayday	Boys Noize	Breakbeat
91	com.apple.Music	Until Now	Swedish House Mafia	Dance
92	com.apple.Music	Until Now	Swedish House Mafia	Dance
93	com.apple.Music	Until Now	Swedish House Mafia	Dance
94	com.apple.Music	Until Now	Swedish House Mafia	Dance
95	com.apple.Music	Until Now	Swedish House Mafia	Dance
96	com.apple.Music	Until Now	Swedish House Mafia	Dance

Figure 9.8 – Extracting media viewing data from KnowledgeC.db

It is worth noting here that `KnowledgeC.db` doesn't just store playback events pertaining to media applications such as **Apple Music** or **Spotify**; it also logs any viewing activity that occurs through the **Safari** browser, including content that was viewed in **private browsing** mode.

Finally, if more context is required for an investigation, the `CurrentPowerlog.PLSQL` database can be queried to extract insights on any app that is utilizing the device's audio functions. In particular, the `PLAUDIOAGENT_EVENTPOINT_AUDIOAPP` table will provide the app, service name, or bundle ID for the process that is using the audio function.

By now, you should have a general understanding of what kind of media assets can be found on a typical iOS acquisition, what metadata can be extracted from iOS and EXIF artifacts, and how to analyze user viewing activity.

Summary

In this chapter, we learned all about photo, video, and audio forensics. First, we introduced the concept of media forensics to learn which artifacts an investigator should expect to find on an iOS device and where they are located.

Later on in the chapter, we focused on analyzing metadata from photos and videos. We introduced the `Photos.sqlite` database and discussed different options to extract data pertaining to the media files stored on the device. Then, we learned all about EXIF metadata, how an investigation can benefit from such data, and how to extract it using Windows, macOS, and Linux.

Finally, in the last section of this chapter, we discussed how to detect user viewing activity by using the events logged in the `KnowledgeC.db` database.

In the next chapter, we will learn how to analyze third-party applications.

10
Analyzing Third-Party Apps

The App Store, which was released in 2008, allows users to download third-party apps on their iOS devices. As of 2021, there were more than 4.5 million apps available for download. Once an app is available on the store, developers can publish updates containing bug fixes or new features that will automatically be installed on the device. This poses a problem from a forensic viewpoint, as many forensic tools aren't able to keep up with the speed at which apps are updated, while some applications are simply not supported altogether.

When a third-party application needs to be analyzed for an investigation, the examiner will most likely have to resort to manually researching, validating, and analyzing the artifacts, and this is exactly what we'll be discussing in this chapter.

We will start by learning how to understand which apps are installed on a device, where they are located, and where the investigator should be looking for any artifacts. Then, we will introduce dynamic application analysis and discuss several tools that can be used for researching and validating purposes. Finally, we'll take an in-depth look at some of the most popular third-party apps, such as Facebook, Twitter, Instagram, YouTube, and others.

In this chapter, we will cover the following topics:

- Introducing iOS applications

- Dynamic application analysis

- Practical third-party applications forensics

Introducing iOS applications

In *Chapter 1*, *Introducing iOS Forensics*, we learned where iOS applications are stored and how their data is structured into **containers**. We're going to build on that knowledge to learn how to get a list of all the apps that are stored on a device and how to locate the data container, which is where most of the artifacts are stored.

Every time an application is installed on a device, iOS generates a **global unique identifier (GUID)** that uniquely represents the application. This GUID is also used in the path to the application's containers:

- The application bundle container, which stores the app itself, is located at `/private/var/containers/Bundle/Application/<app-GUID>/`.

- The application data container is located at `/private/var/mobile/Containers/Data/Application/<app-GUID>/`.

In this chapter, we're going to focus on data containers, which typically have the following directory structure:

Figure 10.1 – The data container's directory structure

The `Documents` folder contains user-created artifacts, the `Library` folder is used by the application to store its data, settings, and preferences, the `tmp` folder stores any temporary files, and the `SystemData` folder is typically empty.

As shown in the previous screenshot, the `Applications` folder contains a subfolder for each app that is installed on the device; however, since the folders are named by the application's GUID, it's impossible to understand which app is which simply by looking at the directory's structure.

In the following sections, we'll learn how to associate an application with its GUID to understand what apps are installed on a device.

Identifying installed applications

The `applicationState.db` database, which is located at `/private/var/mobile/Library/FrontBoard/`, keeps track of Bundle IDs for any application that is installed on the device, including deleted ones. By querying this database, the examiner can understand not only what apps are currently installed on a device, but also where their artifacts are located.

The database contains three tables of interest: `application_identifier_tab`, `key_tab`, and `kvs`. The first table contains a list of applications that, at some point in time, were installed on the device, identified by their **Bundle ID**, also called their **application identifier**.

The following screenshot shows the table's content, based on our example dataset:

id	application_identifier
Filt...	Filter
1	1 com.apple.MobileSMS
2	2 com.apple.Diagnostics
3	3 com.apple.Health
4	4 com.apple.datadetectors.DDActionsService
5	5 com.apple.TVRemoteUIService
6	6 com.apple.Preferences
7	7 com.apple.CarPlaySettings
8	8 com.apple.Home.HomeUIService
9	9 com.apple.Magnifier
10	10 com.apple.BarcodeScanner
11	11 com.apple.Passbook
12	12 com.apple.siri

Figure 10.2 – The application_identifier table from applicationState.db

The `kvs` table contains two columns of interest: `application_identifier`, which maps the record to the Bundle ID in the previous table, and a column named `value`, which contains a binary BLOB.

The `key_tab` table is a *guide* that describes the content of the BLOB. Delving deep into this table is beyond the scope of this section, but keep in mind that a `key_tab` value of 1 indicates that the corresponding application is still installed on the device.

Based on this logic, the following SQL query will extract the Bundle IDs of all the applications that are currently installed on the device:

```
SELECT
application_identifier_tab.[application_identifier],
kvs.[value]
FROM kvs, key_tab,application_identifier_tab
WHERE key_tab.[id] = '1'
AND kvs.[key] = key_tab.[id]
AND application_identifier_tab.[id] = kvs.[application_identifier]
ORDER BY application_identifier_tab.[id];
```

The result of this query is shown in the following screenshot:

	application_identifier	value
1	com.apple.MobileSMS	BLOB
2	com.apple.Diagnostics	BLOB
3	com.apple.Health	BLOB
4	com.apple.datadetectors.DDActionsService	BLOB
5	com.apple.TVRemoteUIService	BLOB
6	com.apple.Preferences	BLOB
7	com.apple.CarPlaySettings	BLOB
8	com.apple.Home.HomeUIService	BLOB
9	com.apple.Magnifier	BLOB
10	com.apple.BarcodeScanner	BLOB

Figure 10.3 – The query prints bundle IDs for all the installed applications

As you can see, the query prints the Bundle IDs for all the installed apps, including those developed by Apple that come pre-installed on the device.

The `value` column contains a BLOB that we will use in the next section to find where an application stores its data.

Tracking application GUIDs

At the beginning of this chapter, we pointed out that application artifacts are stored in the data container, which can be located if the app's GUID is known; now, we'll learn how to associate an application with its GUID.

The `applicationState.db` database, which we covered in the previous section, contains a `kvs` table that stores a binary BLOB under the `value` column. We're going to start by looking at the result of the query from the previous example, which prints Bundle IDs for each app that is installed, as well as their associated BLOB values.

Here, we're going to analyze the binary BLOB from the `com.burbn.instagram` Bundle ID to find where the Instagram application stores its data:

	application_identifier	value
54	com.facebook.Messenger	BLOB
55	org.mozilla.ios.Focus	BLOB
56	imgurmobile	BLOB
57	co.babypenguin.imo	BLOB
58	com.burbn.instagram	BLOB
59	com.kik.chat	BLOB
60	jp.naver.line	BLOB
61	com.mewe	BLOB
62	com.reddit.Reddit	BLOB
63	org.whispersystems.signal	BLOB

Figure 10.4 – Each Bundle ID has an associated binary BLOB

By looking at the BLOB through a hex viewer, such as DB Browser's built-in viewer, we can see that the data is a binary PLIST. If we extract the BLOB cell, convert it into an XML-based PLIST, and then analyze it, we'll be able to view its contents.

The following screenshot shows the binary BLOB displayed through a hex viewer:

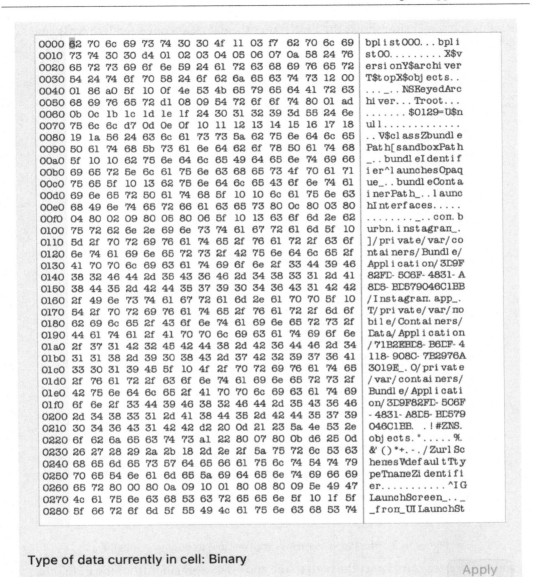

```
0000  62 70 6c 69 73 74 30 30 4f 11 03 f7 62 70 6c 69    bplist000...bpli
0010  73 74 30 30 d4 01 02 03 04 05 06 07 0a 58 24 76    st00.........X$v
0020  65 72 73 69 6f 6e 59 24 61 72 63 68 69 76 65 72    ersionY$archiver
0030  54 24 74 6f 70 58 24 6f 62 6a 65 63 74 73 12 00    T$topX$objects..
0040  01 86 a0 5f 10 0f 4e 53 4b 65 79 65 64 41 72 63    ..._..NSKeyedArc
0050  68 69 76 65 72 d1 08 09 54 72 6f 6f 74 80 01 ad    hiver...Troot...
0060  0b 0c 1b 1c 1d 1e 1f 24 30 31 32 39 3d 55 24 6e    .......$0129=U$n
0070  75 6c 6c d7 0d 0e 0f 10 11 12 13 14 15 16 17 18    ull.............
0080  19 1a 56 24 63 6c 61 73 73 5a 62 75 6e 64 6c 65    ..V$classZbundle
0090  50 61 74 68 5b 73 61 6e 64 62 6f 78 50 61 74 68    Path[sandboxPath
00a0  5f 10 10 62 75 6e 64 6c 65 49 64 65 6e 74 69 66    _..bundleIdentif
00b0  69 65 72 5e 6c 61 75 6e 63 68 65 73 4f 70 61 71    ier^launchesOpaq
00c0  75 65 5f 10 13 62 75 6e 64 6c 65 43 6f 6e 74 61    ue_..bundleConta
00d0  69 6e 65 72 50 61 74 68 5f 10 10 6c 75 6e 63 63    inerPath_..lunce
00e0  68 49 6e 74 65 72 66 61 63 65 73 80 0c 80 03 80    hInterfaces.....
00f0  04 80 02 09 80 05 80 06 5f 10 13 63 6f 6d 2e 62    ........_..com.b
0100  75 72 62 6e 2e 69 6e 73 74 61 67 72 61 6d 5f 10    urbn.instagram_.
0110  5d 2f 70 72 69 76 61 74 65 2f 76 61 72 2f 63 6f    ]/private/var/co
0120  6e 74 61 69 6e 65 72 73 2f 42 75 6e 64 6c 65 2f    ntainers/Bundle/
0130  41 70 70 6c 69 63 61 74 69 6f 6e 2f 33 44 39 46    Application/3D9F
0140  38 32 46 44 2d 35 43 36 46 2d 34 38 33 31 2d 41    82FD-5C6F-4831-A
0150  38 44 35 2d 42 44 35 37 39 30 34 36 43 31 42 42    8D5-BD579046C1BB
0160  2f 49 6e 73 74 61 67 72 61 6d 2e 61 70 70 5f 10    /Instagram.app_.
0170  54 2f 70 72 69 76 61 74 65 2f 76 61 72 2f 6d 6f    T/private/var/mo
0180  62 69 6c 65 2f 43 6f 6e 74 61 69 6e 65 72 73 2f    bile/Containers/
0190  44 61 74 61 2f 41 70 70 6c 69 63 61 74 69 6f 6e    Data/Application
01a0  2f 37 31 42 32 45 42 44 38 2d 42 36 44 46 2d 34    /71B2EBD8-B6DF-4
01b0  31 31 38 2d 39 30 38 43 2d 37 42 32 39 37 36 41    118-908C-7B2976A
01c0  33 30 31 39 45 5f 10 4f 2f 70 72 69 76 61 74 65    3019E_.O/private
01d0  2f 76 61 72 2f 63 6f 6e 74 61 69 6e 65 72 73 2f    /var/containers/
01e0  42 75 6e 64 6c 65 2f 41 70 70 6c 69 63 61 74 69    Bundle/Applicati
01f0  6f 6e 2f 33 44 39 46 38 32 46 44 2d 35 43 36 46    on/3D9F82FD-5C6F
0200  2d 34 38 33 31 2d 41 38 44 35 2d 42 44 35 37 39    -4831-A8D5-BD579
0210  30 34 36 43 31 42 42 d2 20 0d 21 23 5a 4e 53 2e    046C1BB. .!#ZNS.
0220  6f 62 6a 65 63 74 73 a1 22 80 07 80 0b d6 25 0d    objects.".....%.
0230  26 27 28 29 2a 2b 18 2d 2e 2f 5a 75 72 6c 53 63    &'()*+.-./ZurlSc
0240  68 65 6d 65 73 57 64 65 66 61 75 6c 74 54 74 79    hemesWdefaultTty
0250  70 65 54 6e 61 6d 65 5a 69 64 65 6e 74 69 66 69    peTnameZidentifi
0260  65 72 80 00 80 0a 09 10 01 80 08 80 09 5e 49 47    er...........^IG
0270  4c 61 75 6e 63 68 53 63 72 65 65 6e 5f 10 1f 5f    LaunchScreen_.._
0280  5f 66 72 6f 6d 5f 55 49 4c 61 75 6e 63 68 53 74    _from_UILaunchSt
```

Type of data currently in cell: Binary

1061 byte(s)

Apply

Figure 10.5 – The BLOB contains a binary PLIST

By looking at the data, it's possible to make out some strings, such as paths and locations.

Now, let's extract the BLOB and view the resulting PLIST. Please refer to *Chapter 4, Working with Common iOS Artifacts*, to learn how to convert a BPLIST into an XML-based PLIST.

The following screenshot shows the PLIST after the data was converted into XML and then base-64 decoded:

```
❌ ⊘ instagram.plist                                                          ⬆  Open with TextEdit
<?xml version="1.0" encoding="UTF-8"?>
<!DOCTYPE plist PUBLIC "-//Apple//DTD PLIST 1.0//EN" "http://www.apple.com/DTDs/PropertyList-1.0.dtd">
<plist version="1.0">
<dict>
        <key>$archiver</key>
        <string>NSKeyedArchiver</string>
        <key>$objects</key>
        <array>
                <string>$null</string>
                <dict>
                        <key>$class</key>
                        <dict>
                                <key>CF$UID</key>
                                <integer>12</integer>
                        </dict>
                        <key>bundleContainerPath</key>
                        <dict>
                                <key>CF$UID</key>
                                <integer>5</integer>
                        </dict>
                        <key>bundleIdentifier</key>
                        <dict>
                                <key>CF$UID</key>
                                <integer>2</integer>
                        </dict>
                        <key>bundlePath</key>
                        <dict>
                                <key>CF$UID</key>
                                <integer>3</integer>
                        </dict>
                        <key>launchInterfaces</key>
                        <dict>
                                <key>CF$UID</key>
                                <integer>6</integer>
                        </dict>
                        <key>launchesOpaque</key>
                        <true/>
                        <key>sandboxPath</key>
                        <dict>
                                <key>CF$UID</key>
                                <integer>4</integer>
                        </dict>
                </dict>
                <string>com.burbn.instagram</string>
                <string>/private/var/containers/Bundle/Application/3D9F82FD-5C6F-4831-A8D5-BD579046C1BB/Instagram.app</
string>
                <string>/private/var/mobile/Containers/Data/Application/71B2EBD8-B6DF-4118-908C-7B2976A3019E</string>
                <string>/private/var/containers/Bundle/Application/3D9F82FD-5C6F-4831-A8D5-BD579046C1BB</string>
                <dict>
                        <key>$class</key>
                        <dict>
                                <key>CF$UID</key>
```

Figure 10.6 – The PLIST contains details related to the app's containers

As you can see, we can extract the path to the app's data container from the PLIST. In our example dataset, if we locate the `/private/var/mobile/Containers/Data/Application/71B2EBD8-B6DF-4118-908C-7B2976A3019E` folder, we will find Instagram's artifacts.

So far, we have learned how to identify what apps are installed on an iOS device and where the data is stored. In the following sections, we'll dive deep into analyzing third-party applications.

Dynamic application analysis

Third-party applications can be a huge source of evidential artifacts since most apps collect, store, and process a tremendous amount of data from their users. Unfortunately, investigators will most likely have to resort to manually analyzing these applications, as forensic tools cannot possibly support each update of every app. Even if a tool *does* support a certain application, a manual examination should still be carried out to validate the tool's results and to ensure that all the data was parsed correctly.

Often, before the examination can be performed, the examiner will have to do some research on the application of interest to understand how it works, what data it stores, and where it stores it. This entails using a research device to install the app and analyze it.

When analyzing mobile applications, there is no standard process that an investigator should take to examine the data since each application performs differently; in this chapter, we will learn about one of the possible methodologies we can use, known as **dynamic analysis**.

Generally speaking, there are two approaches to application analysis:

- **Static analysis** involves taking an in-depth look at an application's code to identify known functions and API calls that can help determine exactly how the app works.

- **Dynamic analysis** entails running the application in a controlled environment and analyzing the app's behavior to understand how it works.

Static analysis is not a viable option for analyzing third-party apps as the examiner doesn't usually have access to the application's source code. However, by performing dynamic analysis, the investigator can monitor the application's **inputs**, **outputs**, and **connectivity** while the app is running.

From a more practical perspective, most iOS applications will store their data either in SQLite databases or in PLISTs, so the analysis process will entail running the application on a test device, locating the relevant artifacts, and analyzing them to understand how the app works.

The examiner can also choose to monitor how the application interfaces with the network by using a proxy interceptor such as **Burp Suite** or **mitmproxy**. We will learn how to accomplish this in the next section.

Tip

It is recommended to research and analyze third-party applications using a test device that is specifically for that purpose. Note that, since dynamic application analysis requires direct access to the device and its filesystem, the test device should be jailbroken. This could mean using older devices to perform testing, such as those vulnerable to the checkm8 exploit, as these can easily be jailbroken using Checkra1n. For further details, please refer to *Chapter 2, Data Acquisition from iOS Devices.*

The following steps summarize the process of performing dynamic application analysis:

1. Download the application and install it on the test device.

2. Run the application, register it (if applicable) using unique details, and use the app and its features normally.

3. Take notes of any user-provided input, such as usernames, passwords, and emails.

4. Monitor how the application writes data to disk by using a filesystem monitor.

5. Monitor the app's network activity by using a proxy monitoring tool.

6. Locate the application's artifacts on the filesystem and analyze them by searching for strings or manually parsing through the data.

In the next section, we'll introduce some of the tools that can be used to perform dynamic analysis on a third-party iOS application.

Connecting to the test device

The first step in the dynamic analysis process is establishing a connection between the examiner's workstation and the iOS device. This will allow us to install some tools by copying the executables to the device.

We're going to connect to the device through an SSH connection, but first, we need to install the `libimobiledevice` library.

The following steps describe the process:

1. Plug a USB cable into the iOS test device so that it's connected to the forensic workstation. Make sure that the device has been successfully jailbroken by using `checkra1n` or `unc0ver`.

2. Download and install the `libimobiledevice` library from `https://libimobiledevice.org`. If you're using a Mac, you can install the library by running the `brew install libimobiledevice` command from a Terminal.

3. Then, run the `iproxy 4242 44` command to start a proxy running on port 4242 that connects to the device's port 44 via the USB cable. If the device was jailbroken using `unc0ver`, you may need to use port 22 instead of port 44.

4. Now, connect to the device by running `ssh root@127.0.0.1 -p 4242`. You will be prompted for the device's password. The default password is `alpine`.

If all the commands were successful, you should see a root command prompt. Once a connection to the device has been established, we can use a simple tool that simplifies the task of locating an application's containers.

Using cda to locate an application's containers

In the first part of this chapter, we learned how to query the `applicationState.db` database to locate where an iOS application stores its data; however, if the examiner has direct access to the device, the `cda` tool can be used to quickly identify an app's containers.

This tool, which can be downloaded from `https://github.com/ay-kay/cda`, is written in Objective-C; the source files can be compiled by following the instructions on the project's page.

To make this process easier, the binary executable that's been compiled for 64-bit ARM devices can be downloaded from `https://github.com/tiepologian/iOS-Tools`.

The next step involves copying the `cda` binary to the device. This can be done by using the `scp` command, which performs file transfers through an **SSH connection**. Assuming you downloaded the binaries and decompressed the ZIP file, follow these steps:

1. Open a Terminal shell on your local workstation and navigate to the `iOS_tools` folder by using the `cd` command.

2. Run the `scp -P 4242 cda root@127.0.0.1:/usr/bin/` command and press *Return*. You will be prompted to enter the device's password, which is `alpine`. Enter it and press *Return*.

3. If the command succeeds, the `cda` binary will be copied to the `/usr/bin/` folder on the iOS device. By placing the executable in that folder, the tool can be called from any location within the device.

4. To ensure that it worked, from the terminal shell that is connected to the device, run the `ls -la /usr/bin/` command. You should see a long list of files, including `cda`.

Once the tool has been copied to the device, we can use it to quickly locate any application that has been installed. Simply run `cda`, followed by the name (or partial name) of the app.

For example, on a test device that has the **Instagram** app installed, we can find where the application stores its data by running the following command:

```
iPhone:~ root# cda instagram
[1] Instagram (com.burbn.instagram)
Bundle: /private/var/containers/Bundle/Application/D054F8DC-
95A4-4489-BBBD-68F3E457A575
Data: /private/var/mobile/Containers/Data/Application/2A2FEE52-
B59D-42F1-A810-333364E12525
```

As you can see, the tool provides the examiner with the list of containers associated with the application. This includes the **data container**, which is where the app stores user data and preferences, and the **group container**, which contains data that is shared between applications of the same group.

Locating an application's containers is often the very first step in dynamic analysis as this will narrow down the scope of the examination, allowing the examiner to focus on just one or two folders. In the next section, we'll learn how to monitor these folders to understand how and where the application stores its data.

Using fsmon to monitor filesystem events

Previously, we introduced dynamic application analysis and learned that one of the steps of this process involves running the app and live monitoring its behavior. One aspect worth monitoring is how the application interacts with the filesystem; this includes detecting any files that are written, edited, or deleted by the application.

By using a filesystem monitor, the examiner can run the application, perform a task such as entering some data (user authentication, forms, and so on), and visualize how the application reacts to user input. This can help them understand which files store what data.

One of the most popular filesystem monitoring tools is `fsmon`, an open source tool developed by *Sergi Àlvarez* that supports many operating systems, including **Linux**, **macOS**, **Android**, and, of course, **iOS**. The tool can be downloaded from GitHub at `https://github.com/nowsecure/fsmon`.

Pre-built binaries for 64-bit ARM devices can also be downloaded from `https://github.com/tiepologian/iOS-Tools`.

The first step involves copying `fsmon` to the device, as we did with the `cda` tool:

1. Open a terminal shell on your local workstation and, if you're using the pre-built binaries, navigate to the `iOS_tools` folder by using the `cd` command.

2. Run the `scp -P 4242 fsmon root@127.0.0.1:/usr/bin/` command and press *Return*. Enter the device's password and press *Return*.

3. If the command succeeds, the `fsmon` binary will be copied to the `/usr/bin/` folder on the iOS device.

To run the tool, type `fsmon`, followed by the path to the location that should be monitored. For example, to run `fsmon` and monitor all events over the entire filesystem, type `fsmon /`. The following screenshot shows the tool's output:

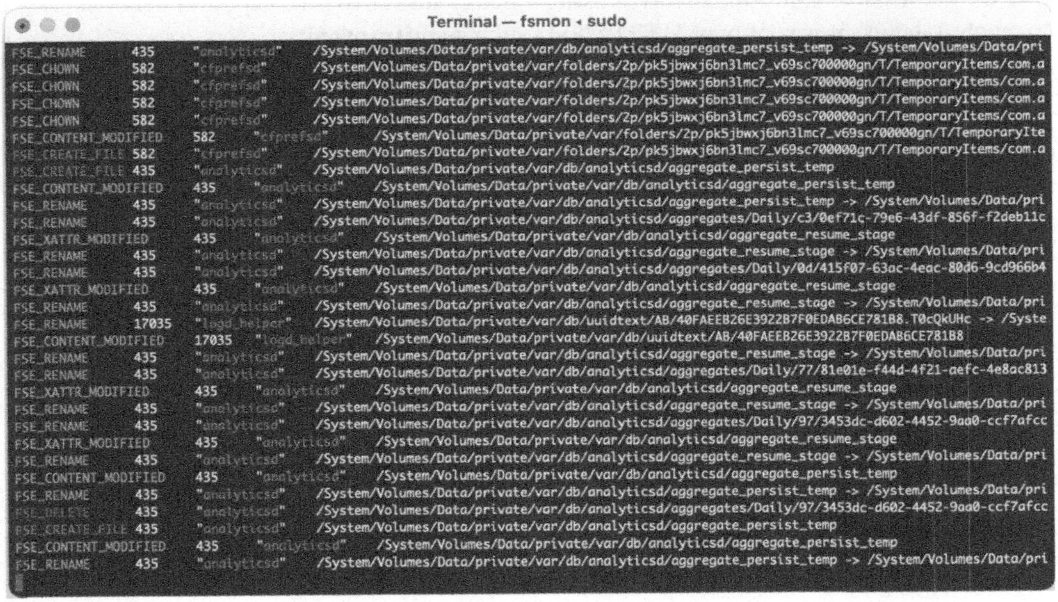

Figure 10.7 – The fsmon tool prints any filesystem events

As you can see, `fsmon` shows any events that occur on the filesystem in different colors, depending on the type of event. Events displayed in yellow indicate that a file was *edited* or its attributes were *modified*, a red event shows that a file was *deleted*, and a purple event indicates a newly *created* file.

To understand how an application works under the hood, use `cda` to find where the app's data container is located. Then, use `fsmon` to monitor that location and run the app normally, performing typical user activity. Monitor the tool's output to understand what files are created or edited following a specific action being performed in the application.

Finally, in the next section of this chapter, we'll take a brief look at how to monitor networking activity.

Using mitmproxy to monitor network activity

When you're performing a dynamic application analysis, you may come across a situation in which you want to look at what **API calls** an application is making, what servers it connects to, and, more generally, what data is sent or received over the network.

One of the possible solutions involves using a **proxy server** to intercept and decode encrypted data that is sent over HTTPS/SSL, such as **mitmproxy**.

mitmproxy is an open source interactive **HTTPS proxy** that sits in the middle between the client (iOS application) and the server. **Man-in-the-middle** (**MITM**) is the name of the technique that's used by the proxy server to intercept the traffic: the idea is that `mitmproxy` pretends to be the server to the client, and pretends to be the client to the server, all while decoding traffic from both sides. Decrypting traffic is made possible by installing a digital certificate on the device, which registers `mitmproxy` as a trusted **Certificate Authority** (**CA**).

To use `mitmproxy`, you must install the certificate manually onto the iOS device, then configure the device to send traffic to the proxy server. Finally, you must run the proxy server on your workstation so that you can monitor and analyze networking activity.

To install `mitmproxy`, go to `https://mitmproxy.org` and download the installer. If your workstation has `brew` installed, you can install the proxy by running the following command from your terminal:

```
brew install mitmproxy
```

Once the server has been installed, start it by running `mitmproxy` from your terminal.

When the server is up and running, the CA certificate needs to be installed on the iOS device. You can accomplish this by going to `http://mitm.it` from the device's browser; however, before you install the certificate, its networking settings need to be configured to allow traffic to be sent from the device to the proxy. Follow these steps:

1. On the device, open **Settings** | **Wi-Fi** and click on the wireless network to open **Advanced settings**.

2. Scroll down to **HTTP Proxy** and tap **Configure Proxy**.

3. Select **Manual** and, in the **Server** field, enter the IP address of the workstation that is running mitmproxy. In the **Port** field, enter 8080.

4. From the device, browse to `mitm.it` and follow the instructions to install the CA certificate.

5. Navigate to **Settings | General | About | Certificate Trust Settings**. Find the certificate and enable it by turning the toggle on.

If everything has been set up correctly, open any application on the device and monitor the terminal on your workstation: you should see the network traffic flowing in and out of the device.

The following screenshot shows `mitmproxy` intercepting network traffic:

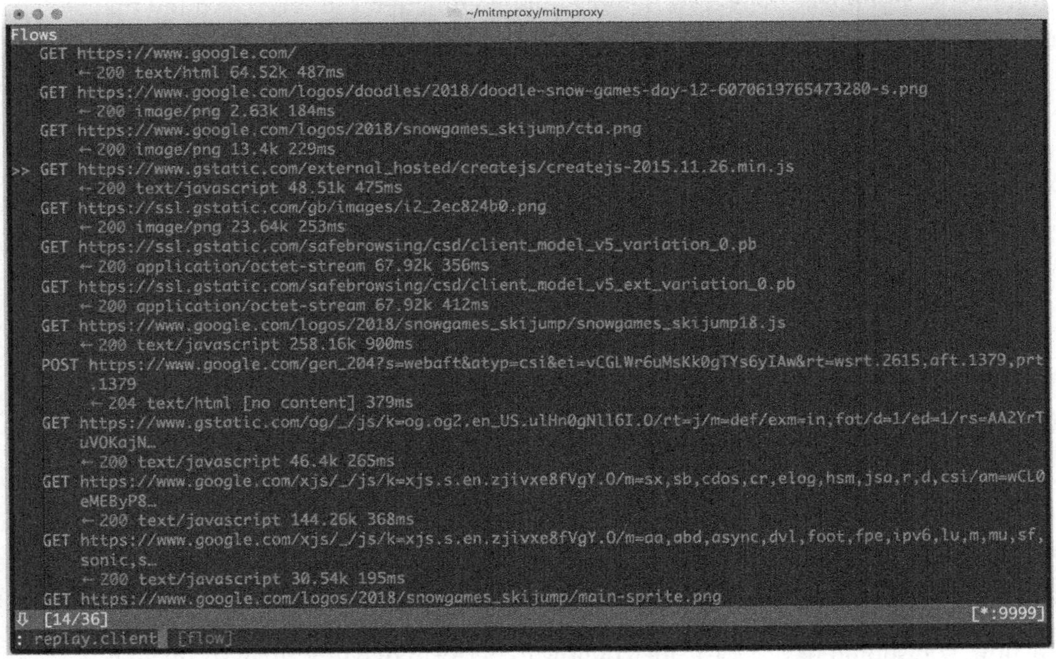

Figure 10.8 – Intercepting network traffic using mitmproxy

Generally, a proxy server is a great option to understand exactly how an iOS application interacts with the network. However, there are some occasions where this approach may not work. We'll discuss more advanced options in the next section.

Advanced application analysis

Performing dynamic application analysis is generally a straightforward task; however, there are some apps, especially popular third-party social networks such as **Instagram** or **Twitter**, that have some built-in mechanisms that prevent MITM attacks.

One of these is Certificate Pinning, which essentially means that mitmproxy's certificate will not be accepted by the application. On such occasions, monitoring the application's network traffic will simply not work. This is because the digital certificate will not be trusted and the app won't be able to connect to its servers.

The only workaround is to inject custom code into the application to change the way it works. One of the most popular code instrumentation toolkits is **Frida**, an open source tool that allows you to inject JavaScript code into any iOS application. Frida allows examiners to trace what functions an application is calling, print or modify a function's arguments, and **inject their code** before or after a function call. Keep in mind that running this tool requires the device to be jailbroken.

A complete tour of all Frida's features is beyond the scope of this book; you can get started with the tool by following the tutorials at `https://frida.re/docs/home/` or by reading *Alexander Fadeev's* blog articles; for example, `https://fadeevab.com/quick-start-with-frida-to-reverse-engineer-any-ios-application/`.

From a forensic viewpoint, Frida can be used together with other tools, such as **Meduza**, to bypass Certificate Pinning and allow the examiner to analyze any kind of iOS app. Meduza is an open source tool developed by *Dima Kovalenko* that works in two steps: first, it analyzes an application and collects the certificates that are used by the app to connect to its servers; then, the tool automatically generates a Frida JavaScript script that unpins the certificates that were collected. Running the application by injecting this JavaScript code will allow the examiner to catch all network traffic by using `mitmproxy` or any other proxy server.

To learn about Meduza and download the tool, visit the project's page at `https://opensourcelibs.com/lib/meduza`.

By now, you should have a basic idea of how to perform dynamic analysis on an iOS application, understand what artifacts are generated, and know where they're stored.

In the last section of this chapter, we'll take a more practical approach by looking at some of the most popular third-party applications and their artifacts.

Practical third-party applications forensics

In this section, we're going to look at some of the most popular iOS third-party applications and their artifacts. The purpose of this section is not to take an in-depth look at each application, but rather to give you a practical reference of what artifacts can be expected for each app, as well as where they're located.

It's important to understand that the names and paths of artifacts are subject to change, and each update may change the way an application interfaces with iOS.

Applications are grouped into four categories: social networking, messaging, productivity, and multimedia.

For each application, the path to the artifact is provided, along with a description. Keep in mind that all the paths are relative to the application's data container or group container.

Social networking applications

In this section, we will focus on the three primary social networking applications, **Facebook**, **Instagram**, and **Twitter**. The **Reddit** app is also included in this category.

Facebook

The following table shows the most common artifacts for Facebook:

Artifact	Description
Library/Preferences/com.facebook.Facebook.plist	User preferences and details of logged-in users (email and Facebook ID).
Library/Caches/com.facebook.Facebook.*/	Cached files and images, such as media, are stored while browsing through posts and pages.

Table 10.1 – Common Facebook artifacts

Instagram

The following table shows the most common artifacts for Instagram:

Artifact	Description
Library/Preferences/com.burbn.instagram.plist	User preferences and details of logged-in users (email and Instagram ID)
Library/Application Support/DirectSQLiteDatabase/*.db	SQLite database containing user data
Library/Application Support/<User_ID>/pending-requests.plist	Property List containing pending friend and message requests
Library/Caches/com.burbn.instagram.IGImageCache/*	Cached images
Library/Caches/com.burbn.instagram.IGSparseVideoCache/*	Cached videos

Table 10.2 – Common Instagram artifacts

Twitter

The following table shows the most common artifacts for Twitter:

Artifact	Description
Library/Preferences/com.atebits.Tweetie2.plist	User preferences and details of logged-in users
Library/Caches/com.twitter.api.cache/Cache.db	SQLite database containing cached API requests, such as visited profiles
Library/SplashBoard/Snapshots/*	App-generated screenshots
Library/Caches/TIPImagePipeline/*	Cached images
Library/Caches/com.atebits.Tweetie2/fsCachedData/*	Cached data

Table 10.3 – Common Twitter artifacts

Reddit

The following table shows the most common artifacts for Reddit:

Artifact	Description
Library/Preferences/com.reddit.Reddit.plist	User preferences and details of logged-in users
Documents/release2/accountData/*	Binary Property Lists containing user data
Library/SplashBoard/Snapshots/*	App-generated screenshots
Library/Caches/com.reddit.Reddit/Cache.db	SQLite database containing cached API requests
Library/Caches/com.reddit.Reddit/imagedownload/*	SQLite database containing cached images

Table 10.4 – Common Reddit artifacts

Now, let's look at a few messaging apps.

Messaging applications

Although messaging applications were discussed in detail in *Chapter 8, Email and Messaging Forensics*, this section will provide a reference for some of the most commonly used instant messaging apps, such as **WhatsApp**, **Telegram**, **Facebook Messenger**, and **Signal**.

WhatsApp

The following table shows the most common artifacts for WhatsApp:

Artifact	Description
Documents/CallHistory.sqlite	Audio and video call history
Documents/blockedcontacts.dat	Contacts blocked by user
Library/2fa.plist	Propery List indicating if multi-factor authentication is enabled
Library/Caches/*	Cached media and API requests
Library/Preferences/net.whatsapp.WhatsApp.plist	User preferences
Library/SplashBoard/Snapshots/*	App-generated screenshots
Shared/AppGroup/*/ChatStorage.sqlite	SQLite database storing messages
Shared/AppGroup/*/ContactsV2.sqlite	SQLite database storing contact details
Shared/AppGroup/*/Library/Preferences/*	Property Lists storing preferences

Table 10.5 – Common WhatsApp artifacts

Telegram

The following table shows the most common artifacts for Telegram:

Artifact	Description
Library/Preferences/ph.telegra.Telegraph.plist	Property List containing user preferences
Library/Caches/ph.telegra.Telegraph/fsCachedData/*	Cached media and API requests
Shared/AppGroup/telegram-data/account-<Account_ID>/postbox/db/db_sqlite	SQLite database containing chats and messages
Shared/AppGroup/telegram-data/account-<Account_ID>/postbox/media/*	Chat media files

Table 10.6 – Common Telegram artifacts

Facebook Messenger

The following table shows the most common artifacts for Facebook Messenger:

Artifact	Description
Documents/com.facebook.Messenger.preferences/*	Property List containing user preferences
Library/Preferences/com.facebook.Messenger.plist	Application settings
Shared/AppGroup/shared_messenger_contacts/*.db	SQLite database containing contacts
Shared/AppGroup/shared_messenger_messages/*.db	SQLite database that stores chats and messages
Shared/AppGroup/lightspeed-imageCache/*	Cache

Table 10.7 – Common Facebook Messenger artifacts

Signal

The following table shows the most common artifacts for Signal:

Artifact	Description
Library/Preferences/org.whispersystems.signal.plist	Application settings
Library/Caches/*	Cached media and API requests
Shared/AppGroup/Attachments/*	Media files
Shared/AppGroup/grdb/signal.sqlite	SQLite database containing chats and messages

Table 10.8 – Common Signal artifacts

Next, we'll discuss artifacts related to productivity applications.

Productivity applications

The following tables describe artifacts concerning work and productivity applications, such as **Microsoft Teams, Zoom, Dropbox, Microsoft OneDrive**, and **Gmail**.

Microsoft Teams

The following table shows the most common artifacts for Microsoft Teams:

Artifact	Description
Library/Preferences/com.microsoft.skype.teams.plist	User preferences and application settings
SplashBoard/Snapshots/*	App-generated screenshots
Shared/AppGroup/Library/Preferences/*	Property Lists containing user data

Table 10.9 – Common Microsoft Teams artifacts

Zoom

The following table shows the most common artifacts for Zoom:

Artifact	Description
Library/Preferences/us.zoom.videomeetings.plist	User preferences and application settings
Documents/Data/zoommeeting.db	SQLite database containing data related to Zoom meetings and messages exchanged during a meeting
Documents/Data/zoomus.db	SQLite database that stores user data

Table 10.10 – Common Zoom Artifacts

Dropbox

The following table shows the most common artifacts for Dropbox:

Artifact	Description
Library/Preferences/com.getdropbox.Dropbox.plist	User preferences and application settings
Documents/Users/<id>/Dropbox.sqlite	SQLite database containing user data and file information
Documents/Users/<id>/metadata.sqlite	SQLite database that stores the metadata of files stored on Dropbox

Table 10.11 – Common Dropbox artifacts

Microsoft OneDrive

The following table shows the most common artifacts for Microsoft OneDrive:

Artifact	Description
Library/Preferences/com.microsoft.skydrive.plist	User preferences and application settings
Library/Database/moddatabase.db	SQLite database containing user data
Shared/AppGroup/OneDrive/StramCacheQT/*	Cached files

Table 10.12 – Common OneDrive artifacts

Gmail

The following table shows the most common artifacts for Gmail:

Artifact	Description
Library/Preferences/com.google.Gmail.plist	User preferences, application settings, and logged-in user data
Library/ApplicationSupport/data/<email>/*	SQLite database containing user data
Library/Caches/*	Cached files

Table 10.13 – Common Gmail artifacts

Next, we'll look at a few multimedia apps.

Multimedia applications

This section includes applications that allow you to view or share media files, such as **Netflix**, **YouTube**, **Spotify**, **Snapchat**, and **TikTok**.

Netflix

The following table shows the most common artifacts for Netflix:

Artifact	Description
Library/Preferences/com.netflix.Netflix.plist	User preferences and application settings
Documents/store.sqlite	SQLite database containing information on the logged-in user
Library/Caches/*	Cached video streams and API requests

Table 10.14 – Common Netflix artifacts

YouTube

The following table shows the most common artifacts for YouTube:

Artifact	Description
Library/Preferences/com.google.ios.youtube.plist	User preferences and application settings
Library/Caches/*	Video and API requests caches

Table 10.15 – Common YouTube artifacts

Spotify

The following table shows the most common artifacts for Spotify:

Artifact	Description
Library/Preferences/com.spotify.client.plist	User preferences and application settings
Documents/InstrumentsModel.sqlite	SQLite database that stores app events
Library/ApplicationSupport/PersistentCache/mercury.db	Playback history cached media
Library/ApplicationSupport/Users/<id>/recently_played	Recently played history in binary format
SplashBoard/Snapshots/*	App-generated screenshots

Table 10.16 – Common Spotify artifacts

Snapchat

The following table shows the most common artifacts for Snapchat:

Artifact	Description
Library/Preferences/com.toyopagroup.picaboo.plist	User preferences and application settings
Documents/user.plist	Property List that stores details regarding the logged-in user
Documents/chatConversationStore.plist	Property List containing chats
Documents/stories.plist	Property List that stores story data
Library/Caches/*	Cached media and API requests

Table 10.17 – Common Snapchat artifacts

TikTok

The following table shows the most common artifacts for TikTok:

Artifact	Description
Library/Preferences/com.zhiliaoapp.musically.plist	User preferences and application settings
Documents/AwemeIM.db	SQLite database that stores TikTok contacts
Documents/Aweme.db	SQLite database that contains published TikTok videos
Library/ApplicationSupport/ChatFiles/<id>/db.sqlite	SQLite database that stores chats and messages
Library/Caches/*	Cached media and API requests

Table 10.18 – Common TikTok artifacts

When analyzing third-party apps, the examiner should keep in mind that researching and validating is always required since apps are constantly being updated, and each update may change the way an application stores its data.

Summary

In this chapter, we learned about third-party iOS applications. First, we learned where an application stores its data, how to identify installed applications, and how to associate an app with its GUID. Then, we focused on analyzing third-party apps. We introduced the concept of dynamic analysis and learned about the step-by-step process of analyzing an application. We also learned how to identify data containers using the cda tool, how to monitor filesystem changes, and how to visualize an application's network traffic.

Finally, we provided a practical cheat sheet with paths and descriptions of the most common artifacts that can be found in popular third-party iOS applications.

In the next chapter, we will discuss more advanced topics in iOS forensics.

11
Locked Devices, iTunes Backups, and iCloud Forensics

Up to this point in the book, we have learned how to perform an iOS acquisition using different methods and how to analyze the extracted data to gain meaningful insights, such as interpreting location artifacts, parsing through media files, or analyzing pattern-of-life data. Everything we have covered so far relies on the fact that the iOS device that is being examined is unlocked, or the passcode is known; however, this is not always the case. There are some occasions in which the investigator may have to deal with locked devices, and that will be the focus of this chapter.

We will start the chapter by learning how to deal with locked devices, what options the examiner has, and how to attempt passcode cracking. Then, we will discuss **Before First Unlock (BFU)** acquisitions and learn what kind of data we can expect to find in such extractions. Later on in the chapter, we will introduce iTunes backups and we will learn how to extract and analyze them. In the final part of the chapter, we'll discuss iCloud forensics and learn how to extract backups, the keychain, and data synced to iCloud.

In this chapter, we will cover the following topics:

- Acquiring locked devices
- BFU acquisition of locked devices
- Introducing iTunes backups
- Introducing iCloud forensics

Acquiring locked devices

At the start of this book, in *Chapter 1, Introducing iOS Forensics*, we discussed the iOS operating system and learned how Apple achieves **data protection** by encrypting files stored on the device.

The device's passcode is an essential aspect of the encryption process, as it is used to generate the **encryption key**, which, in turn, is used to decrypt the data. Until the user enters the screen lock passcode, almost every piece of data remains inaccessible. Of course, there are some exceptions, as some files are required for the operating system to work and they need to be always accessible, even when the device is locked.

For these reasons, acquiring and analyzing a locked device is no easy task but there are a few options. When an investigator is tackling a locked device, the first step requires **identifying** the device and its current state, as the options available to attempt data acquisition will vary depending on a number of factors, such as the model and iOS version.

The initial identification phase should allow the examiner to answer the following questions:

- Is the locked device in a BFU or **After First Unlock (AFU)** state?
- What's the device's hardware model?
- Is the device vulnerable to Checkm8?
- What iOS version is the device running?
- Has the device ever been paired to a desktop or laptop computer?

By answering these questions, the examiner will be able to assess what the best course of action might be to gain access to the locked device. Before we go further, it's important to understand the differences between the BFU and AFU states:

- **BFU**: Devices in a BFU state are those that have been powered off or rebooted and have not been unlocked, not even once, since the device was powered on.

- **AFU**: When a device is powered on and the correct passcode is entered, the device ends up in AFU mode.

The point here is that when a device is found in an AFU state, a lot more data can be extracted and analyzed, as some encryption keys are actually retained in memory.

Once the device has been successfully identified, the following options should be considered:

- Locating and using **lockdown pairing records**
- Passcode cracking
- Performing a **BFU acquisition**
- Sending the device to third-party labs or premium services, such as **Cellebrite Advanced Services** or **Grayshift's GrayKey**
- Locating and analyzing **iTunes backups**
- Downloading and analyzing **iCloud backups**
- Downloading and analyzing iCloud synced data

In the following sections of this chapter, we'll discuss the pros and cons of each of these options, starting with using lockdown pairing records.

Using lockdown pairing records to access the device

Lockdown records, also called **pairing records**, are essentially files stored on a host computer that contain cryptographic keys that are used to allow iOS devices to communicate with paired computers.

The first time an iOS device is connected to a PC or macOS computer that has iTunes installed, the user will be prompted to *trust* the device by entering the device's passcode. This will create a lockdown record on the host, which means that the user will not have to unlock the device every time it is connected to the computer.

If the investigator has physical and legal access to a host computer that was paired with the device, the lockdown file can be used to access the locked device and successfully perform a logical acquisition.

There are, however, some caveats. First of all, accessing a locked device using a pairing record will only work if the device is in an **AFU state**; secondarily, lockdown records **expire** after some time. Although there is no definite answer as to when exactly these records expire, research that has been carried out seems to suggest that lockdown records expire anytime between 7 and 30 days after they were created.

On Windows machines, lockdown records are typically stored in `\%ProgramData%\Apple\Lockdown\`.

On macOS computers, they can be found in `/var/db/lockdown/`.

Once the investigator has located the lockdown record, a logical acquisition can be performed using tools such as the **Elcomsoft iOS Forensic Toolkit** or **MOBILedit Forensic Express**.

The following steps describe the process using the Elcomsoft iOS Forensic Toolkit:

1. First, launch the Toolkit.

2. Connect the device to the workstation using a USB-A cable.

3. Select the **B – Backup** option.

4. When prompted, enter the path to the lockdown record.

If the pairing record is accepted, a logical backup will be created. The following screenshot shows the Toolkit's main menu:

Figure 11.1 – Elcomsoft iOS Forensic Toolkit can acquire locked devices using pairing records

If the device is configured to produce unencrypted backups, the tool will automatically set a temporary password to ensure that all data is acquired during the backup process.

In the next section, we'll discuss passcode cracking.

Passcode cracking

In the past, there were several methods for attempting to crack a device's passcode, such as *black boxes* that could be connected to the device that would brute force every possible combination. Unfortunately, these methods only support legacy devices.

With the iPhone 5s, Apple introduced the **Secure Enclave**, which effectively slows down passcode attempts, rendering brute force attacks impossible.

There are still some software tools that can be used for the purpose, such as Elcomsoft's iOS Forensic Toolkit, which can brute force the passcode for iPhones 4, 5, and 5c running iOS 4 up to iOS 10.

If the examiner is fortunate enough to run into one of these devices, a full physical acquisition can be performed, cracking the passcode, and effectively accessing the locked device. To perform a brute force attack, the device will have to be booted in **DFU mode** and exploited through the **Checkm8** vulnerability. A full brute force attack of a **six-digit passcode** takes approximately 21 hours to complete on an iPhone 5, and up to 40 hours on an iPhone 4.

If passcode cracking is not an option and a lockdown record is not found, performing a BFU acquisition may be the only option. We'll discuss these acquisitions in the next section.

BFU acquisition of locked devices

In *Chapter 2, Data Acquisition from iOS Devices*, we introduced the **Checkm8** vulnerability and the **checkra1n** jailbreak, which allows the examiner to gain full access to the filesystem of devices ranging from the **iPhone 5s** to the **iPhone X**. This vulnerability can be exploited to perform an acquisition from *locked* or *disabled* devices, even if the passcode is unknown. This kind of acquisition is called a **BFU acquisition**.

It's important to understand that a BFU acquisition only allows a *partial* extraction of the device's data, as most files remain encrypted until the passcode is entered. Still, a partial extraction, including data from the keychain, is definitely better than nothing, as this could include notable evidence.

The following table lists some of the most popular artifacts that can be extracted through a BFU acquisition:

Artifacts
`/private/var/mobile/Library/Preferences/*`
`/private/var/preferences/SystemConfiguration/*`
`/private/var/root/Library/Preferences/*`
`/private/var/mobile/Library/Accounts/Accounts3.sqlite`
`/private/var/mobile/Library/DataAccess/*`
`/private/installd/Library/Logs/MobileInstallation/*`
`/private/var/mobile/Library/SpringBoard/*`
`/private/var/mobile/Library/CallHistoryDB/CallHistoryTemp.storedata`
`/private/var/mobile/Library/Preferences/com.apple.*`
`/private/var/mobile/Library/SMS/sms-temp.db`
`/private/var/mobile/Library/Preferences/com.apple.preferences.network.plist`
`/private/var/wireless/Library/Databases/CellularUsage.db`
`/private/var/root/Library/Caches/locationd/consolidated.db`

Table 11.1 – Common artifacts found in BFU acquisition

As you can see from the table, some key artifacts can be extracted from a locked device through a BFU acquisition, provided the device is vulnerable to Checkm8.

To perform a BFU acquisition, the device is initially jailbroken using checkra1n, which doesn't require it to be unlocked. Then, the **keychain** is partially extracted, and a filesystem acquisition is performed using a tool such as the Elcomsoft iOS Forensic Toolkit. Some forensic tools, such as the **Cellebrite UFED**, don't require the device to be jailbroken, as the Checkm8 exploit is performed directly within the tool.

Performing a BFU acquisition using the Elcomsoft iOS Forensic Toolkit

The following steps describe the process of performing a BFU acquisition using the Elcomsoft iOS Forensic Toolkit:

1. First, put the device in recovery mode and start checkra1n.

2. Follow the instructions to put the device in DFU mode and apply the temporary jailbreak. Make sure that the device is connected using a USB-A cable, as using a USB-C cable will not work.

3. Launch the Elcomsoft iOS Forensic Toolkit and choose the **K – Keychain** option.

4. When the tool prompts you for the passcode, skip this step by pressing *Enter*.

5. When the process completes, choose the **F – File System** option from the main menu to acquire the device's filesystem.

6. When the tool prompts you for the passcode, press *Enter* and wait for the process to finish.

The following screenshot illustrates the process:

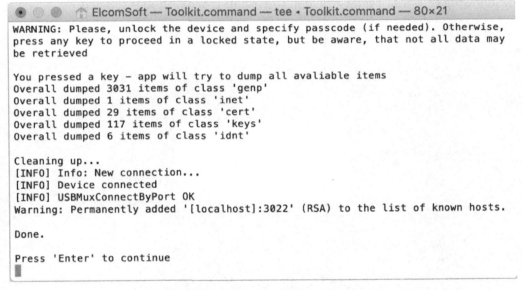

Figure 11.2 – Elcomsoft iOS Forensic Toolkit performing a BFU acquisition

Next, we will repeat the process using a different tool.

Performing a BFU acquisition using the Cellebrite UFED

Performing a BFU acquisition using Cellebrite UFED is also straightforward, and it doesn't require the device to be jailbroken through checkra1n:

1. Launch Cellebrite UFED.

2. Select **Advanced Logical** and choose the **Full File System (checkm8)** option.

3. Connect the device using a USB-A cable and click **Continue**.

4. When the tool prompts you for the device's password, click **Cancel**.

5. Click **YES** to perform a BFU acquisition.

The following screenshot shows the step where a BFU acquisition is selected:

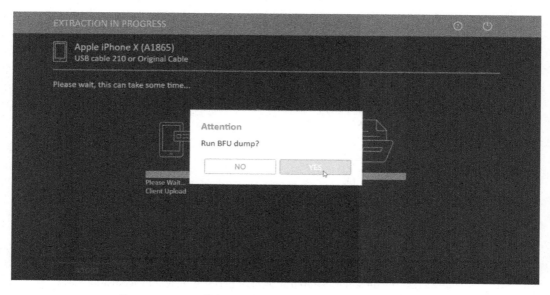

Figure 11.3 – Cellebrite UFED performing a BFU acquisition

Once the acquisition process completes, the keychain and filesystem dumps can be analyzed as usual, manually, or using forensic software, such as **Cellebrite Physical Analyzer**.

> **Tip**
>
> It's worth mentioning that performing a BFU acquisition completely bypasses USB Restricted Mode; with iOS 11, Apple introduced a security feature that prevents USB accessories from making any data connection if the device wasn't unlocked at least once within the past hour. Theoretically, this should limit the attack surface against physically connected *hacking tools*; however, exploiting the device through Checkm8 bypasses this security feature.

Although a BFU acquisition is the best option to extract data from a locked device, it's clear that newer devices – which are not vulnerable to Checkm8 – cannot be acquired with this method. Investigators attempting to access these devices will have to resort to sending the phone to a third-party lab that offers forensic services, such as Cellebrite Advanced Services.

If a device cannot be acquired *directly*, it may still be possible to extract its data *indirectly*, by locating and analyzing the device's **backup**, which may be stored on a host computer or in the **cloud**.

In the next section of this chapter, we'll introduce iTunes backups, and we'll learn how to extract and analyze them.

Introducing iTunes backups

Investigating a device that is locked by an unknown passcode can quickly bring an investigation to a halt if the iPhone in question is one of the newer models, such as the **iPhone 13** or the **iPhone 12**; however, if the suspect has backed up their device to their desktop or laptop and the investigator has access to this machine, the backup can easily be recovered, extracted, and analyzed.

Another reason why examining backups may be beneficial is that the user may have deleted some data from their mobile device, but that doesn't delete the data that resides within the backup: it's quite common, in fact, that backup files contain data that the user believes no longer exists.

Local backups, also called **iTunes backups**, are essentially a logical acquisition of the device and typically contain contacts, SMS messages, media files, logs, databases, keychains, preferences, configurations, browsing artifacts, and location data, for example. A backup can be created manually by the user using **iTunes**, or the device can be configured to automatically create a new backup when it is plugged into a machine. On macOS computers, iTunes is no longer required, and the backup process can be started directly from **Finder**.

When an iTunes backup is created, iOS allows the user to enhance security by encrypting the backup with a password. Once the user sets the password, all subsequent backups will be encrypted, and the files will only be accessible to the examiner if the password is known. However, password cracking can be attempted, and this will be covered in detail later on in the chapter.

It's important to understand that since iOS 13, iTunes backups will not contain user-sensitive data (such as call logs, keychain, and Safari history) if encryption is not enabled.

Locating backup files

An iTunes backup is essentially a folder named with a **GUID** that contains numerous subfolders and files. The following screenshot should give you an idea of what it looks like:

Name	Date Modified	Size	Kind
> ea	Today at 14:59	--	Folder
> ee	Today at 14:59	--	Folder
> ef	Today at 14:59	--	Folder
> f0	Today at 14:59	--	Folder
> f1	Today at 14:59	--	Folder
> f2	Today at 14:59	--	Folder
> f3	Today at 14:59	--	Folder
> f4	Today at 14:59	--	Folder
> f5	Today at 14:59	--	Folder
> f6	Today at 14:59	--	Folder
> f7	Today at 14:59	--	Folder
> f8	Today at 14:59	--	Folder
> f9	Today at 14:59	--	Folder
> fa	Today at 14:59	--	Folder
> fb	Today at 14:59	--	Folder
> fc	Today at 14:59	--	Folder
> fd	Today at 14:59	--	Folder
> fe	Today at 14:59	--	Folder
> ff	Today at 14:59	--	Folder
Info.plist	Today at 15:00	676 KB	property list
Manifest.db	Today at 14:59	40,4 MB	Document
Manifest.plist	Today at 14:59	104 KB	property list
Status.plist	Today at 14:59	189 bytes	property list

Figure 11.4 – File structure of an iTunes backup

On Windows machines, iOS backups are typically stored at `C:\Users\<user>\AppData\Roaming\Apple Computer\MobileSync\Backup`. If, however, the Windows app version of iTunes is installed, local backups will be stored at `C:\Users\<user>\Apple\MobileSync\Backup`.

On machines running macOS, local backups will be stored at `/Users/<user>/Library/Application Support/MobileSync/Backup/`.

By examining these locations, the investigator may find multiple backups of the same device, or backups for different devices.

In the root folder of each backup, there are four files of interest:

- `Info.plist`: This property list contains details from the device such as the **IMEI**, **ICCID**, model number, the list of all installed applications, and the timestamp of when the backup was created.

- `Manifest.db`: The `Manifest` database is a normal SQLite database, but it will be encrypted if a password was specified for the backup. The main table of interest, `Files`, contains a list of all files included in a backup and their properties, such as `fileID`, `domain`, and `path`.

- `Manifest.plist`: The `Manifest` property list stores information for every application that is installed on the device, such as the path to the app's containers. This file also contains the `IsEncrypted` key, which indicates whether the backup was encrypted or not, and the `WasPasscodeSet` key, which tells us whether the device had a passcode.

- `Status.plist`: This property list contains generic metadata, such as the backup's unique identifier and the timestamp of when it was completed.

Since we now have all the information from a backup, we can start putting the filesystem back together using our forensic tools.

Analyzing iTunes backups

Once the investigator has located an iTunes backup, the filesystem has to be rebuilt and the files will need to be decrypted. Although this can also be done manually, the easiest solution is to import the backup into any mobile forensic software, such as Cellebrite Physical Analyzer or **Elcomsoft Phone Viewer**, and analyze the data as usual.

To import an iOS backup into Cellebrite Physical Analyzer, follow these steps:

1. Launch the tool and from the main menu, choose **File | Open case**.
2. Then, in **Case wizard**, click on **Add**.
3. Choose **Common source | Backup | iTunes backup**.
4. Select the folder that contains the backup and click **Continue**.

Once Cellebrite Physical Analyzer has finished parsing the files, the artifacts can be examined as if they were a normal logical acquisition. The following screenshot shows the correct option within **Case wizard**:

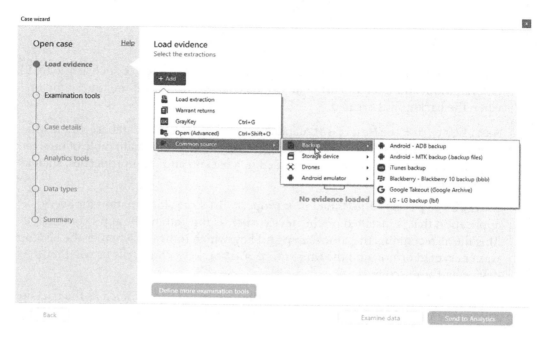

Figure 11.5 – Loading an iTunes backup into Cellebrite Physical Analyzer

Previously, we learned that iTunes backups can be encrypted by setting a custom password. On such occasions, if the password is not known, the only available option is to attempt password cracking. We'll learn how to do this in the following section.

Cracking iTunes backup passwords

If the password to an iTunes backup is not known, password cracking can be attempted by performing a **dictionary attack** or by **brute-forcing** the password. In a dictionary attack, a long list of common passwords is used to attempt to break into the iTunes backup; a brute force attack, on the other hand, is a trial-and-error method that tries every possible combination of characters for a password until it succeeds.

The possibility of successfully cracking the password greatly depends on its complexity. Since iOS 10, the encryption process has been strengthened and most tools can only test around 200 passwords per second, even on a high-end workstation. This makes long and complex passwords virtually unbreakable.

One of the most popular tools for iTunes password cracking is **Elcomsoft Phone Breaker**, which works on both Windows and macOS machines.

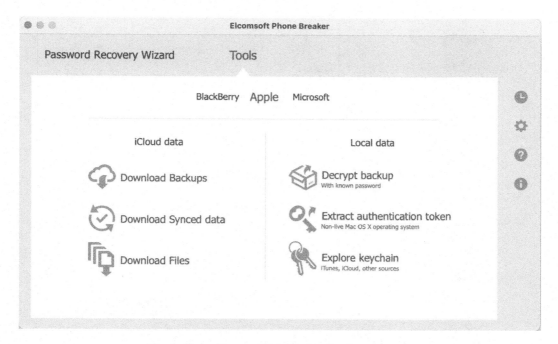

Figure 11.6 – Elcomsoft Phone Breaker home screen

To attempt password cracking of an iTunes backup, follow these steps:

1. Launch **Elcomsoft Phone Breaker** and click on **Password Recovery Wizard**.

2. Select **Choose source** and navigate to the folder that contains the iTunes backup you want to crack.

3. Next, set up the recovery pipeline by choosing **Dictionary Attack, Brute-Force Attack,** or both.

Figure 11.7 – Set up a dictionary attack or a brute-force attack

4. You can set additional parameters, such as the password length, common character sets, or custom character sets. Then, click **Done**.

5. Click on **Start recovery** to begin the process.

From the research that has been carried out, it's recommended to attempt brute-forcing a four-digit password first, followed by a six-digit password and a dictionary attack, as these are the most common and easily crackable.

Unfortunately, there are some cases in which recovering the password to an iTunes backup is simply not possible, or there may even be no local backup available. In these situations, one of the possible courses of action is to attempt to download and extract backups or data synced to iCloud.

The final section of this chapter will discuss iCloud forensics.

Introducing iCloud forensics

In October 2011, Apple introduced **iCloud**, a cloud-based platform that allows users to store and share files between their devices, and backup their data. iCloud is integrated directly into iOS and is accessible from Windows machines, macOS computers, or directly from the web by browsing to `https://www.icloud.com`.

From a forensic viewpoint, cloud forensics is arguably the future of mobile forensics as it allows investigators to access data that may not even be stored on the device itself. As the majority of new devices do not (yet) support jailbreaks and full filesystem acquisitions, performing a cloud acquisition is a great alternative.

Before we dive deep into the technical details of extracting data from iCloud, it's important to understand exactly what kind of data we can expect to find, starting with **iCloud backups**.

iCloud backups

Since the release of iOS 5 in 2011, Apple allows users to back up their devices automatically to their iCloud accounts. These backups are similar to the iTunes backups we discussed in the previous section and include most of the data that is stored on a device, such as application data, device settings, call logs, messages, notes, and Safari history.

The user can elect to include or exclude certain elements from the backup directly from the device by navigating to **Settings | [User] | iCloud | Manage storage | Backups**.

To perform an iCloud backup, there is no need to connect the device to a computer, as the backup process happens automatically during the night when the device is charging and connected to a Wi-Fi network. The process can also be started manually from the device.

Cloud backups are made incrementally to save space and time, and typically, at least two or three backups are retained in the cloud. All data is securely encrypted both in transit and in storage, and the encryption key is stored by Apple in the user's iCloud account. More sensitive data, such as Apple Card transactions and health data, is secured with a stronger form of protection known as **end-to-end encryption**; this data is encrypted using keys derived from information unique to the device, so nobody – not even Apple – has access to this data.

> **Tip**
>
> When an investigation involves a locked device that cannot be acquired using any of the methods described in previous chapters, one of the possible workarounds is to take advantage of iCloud's automatic backup capabilities. Putting the device close to a known Wi-Fi network and charging it for a few hours will trigger the creation of a new backup that can then be downloaded and analyzed, revealing the data stored on the device.

Backups are not the only thing that is stored in iCloud, as iOS also provides automatic syncing capabilities for certain data categories.

iCloud synced data

Syncing data between iOS devices has become a seamless experience for the user thanks to iCloud. The following is a list of the most common categories that are synced to the cloud:

- Account information
- User settings
- Mail
- Call history
- Messages
- Contacts, notes, and calendars
- Safari history, tabs, and bookmarks
- iCloud Keychain
- Apple Health

The user has a certain degree of control over what data is synchronized to iCloud, as syncing can be enabled on a per-app setting directly from the device. The following screenshot shows iCloud syncing settings, which can be accessed by going to **Settings | [User] | iCloud** and toggling individual apps in the **Apps using iCloud** section:

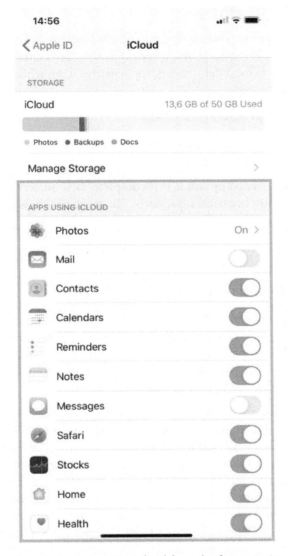

Figure 11.8 – Apps using iCloud from the device settings

iCloud synced data can be downloaded using forensic tools, provided the investigator has legal access to cloud data. Downloading synced data can be extremely valuable for an investigation as it gives examiners quick access to specific artifacts, removing the need to download an entire backup.

Accessing iCloud data

Access to iCloud backups and synced data can be provided to law enforcement by Apple through the course of legal requests. As Apple holds the user's **encryption keys**, they can decrypt most of a user's iCloud data, except for sensitive data, which is encrypted with end-to-end encryption.

This solution, however, has several drawbacks:

- Processing law enforcement and government requests is a very slow process due to the large volumes of data requested.

- The data that is returned by Apple is incomplete, as it doesn't include sensitive artifacts, such as Apple card transactions, the keychain, messages, and Safari history.

There are other options that allow the investigator to pull the data directly from iCloud, but these requests will have to be authorized by Apple servers by providing some sort of **authentication credentials**.

Currently, iCloud credentials can be supplied in three different formats:

- **Apple ID and password**: If the investigator has legal access to the user's Apple ID (*email address*) and password, these credentials can be used to access iCloud data, download backups, and synced data, decrypt them, and convert the data to an iTunes backup. If **two-factor authentication (2FA)** is enabled for the account, access to the device or SIM card is required.

- **Authentication token**: A token is a small portion of binary data that works like a browser cookie to log in to a website. Authentication tokens are used as a replacement for user credentials and allow devices to authenticate with iCloud without requesting an Apple ID and password for every request. If a user logged into their iCloud account from a Windows or macOS machine, and the investigator has access to the computer, the token can be used to access iCloud data without the need for the Apple ID and password. Although Apple frequently changes iCloud authentication protocols, at present, tokens only work for a limited period of time and can only be used from the machine that generated them. Finally, using a token will only provide access to some of the data stored in iCloud, such as photos, iCloud Drive files, emails, call logs, and Safari history. At the time of writing, authentication tokens cannot be used to access iCloud backups. Tokens can be extracted by using Elcomsoft Phone Breaker.

- **Trusted device**: If the Apple ID and password are not available but the investigator has access to a user's device, it may still be possible to access all of the user's iCloud data. The device must be logged into the iCloud profile and the device's passcode must be known. To gain access to iCloud, connect the device to the workstation and run Elcomsoft Phone Breaker. Once a trust relationship has been established, the tool will sideload an extraction agent onto the device and the examiner will be presented with a list of iCloud backups and data that can be extracted. Currently, this solution works with devices running iOS 9 through 14.3, or jailbroken devices.

By supplying the user's credentials to Apple servers, the investigator will be able to pull backups and synced data from iCloud, potentially revealing critical evidence that may no longer be present on the device itself. Next, we'll discuss **iCloud Keychain**.

Introducing iCloud Keychain

The **keychain** is a system-wide storage mechanism designed to store a user's most sensitive data, such as passwords, authentication tokens, encryption keys, and credit card details. A *local* keychain is stored on each of a user's devices and any changes are pushed to iCloud, where iCloud Keychain is securely stored.

Users can choose to save passwords and login details to the keychain, while iOS applications typically use it behind the scenes to store encryption keys and tokens. The keychain has been designed with security in mind, so each application can only access its own data and cannot access system records or any other app's data.

When an application creates a new record in the keychain, different security classes can be selected depending on the circumstances in which the data should be accessed (*BFU*, *AFU*, and always accessible, for example). There is also a `kSecAttrSynchronizable` attribute that indicates whether the record should be synced to iCloud Keychain or not.

The following screenshot shows what the keychain looks like:

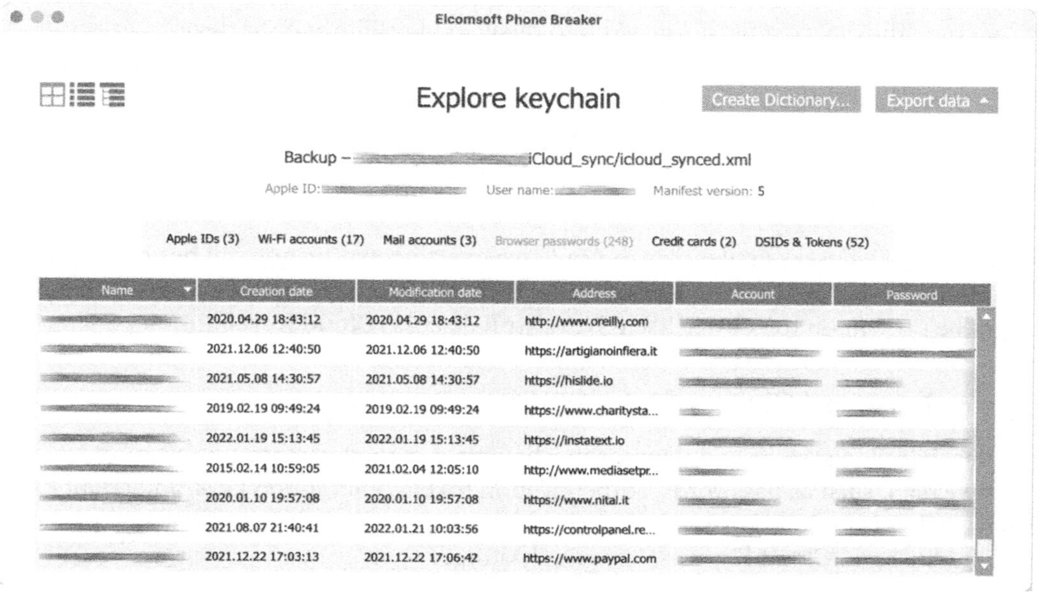

Figure 11.9 – Analyzing iCloud Keychain in Elcomsoft Phone Breaker

Since iCloud Keychain stores a user's most sensitive data, this data will most likely be of interest for an investigation. To access iCloud Keychain, an investigator will require all of the following:

- Apple ID and password
- 2FA code (push notification and SMS code)
- Device passcode

In the following section, we'll learn how to extract iCloud Keychain and iCloud synced data.

Extracting iCloud Keychain and synced data

If the investigator has access to iCloud credentials, the keychain and synced data can be downloaded using Elcomsoft Phone Breaker. The following steps describe the process:

1. Launch the tool, select the **Apple** tab, and from the **iCloud Data** section, click on **Download Synced data**.

2. Choose the authentication method depending on the type of credentials you have access to (*Apple ID, authentication token, or trusted device*) and click the **Sign in** button.

3. Select what data should be downloaded by ticking the checkbox, then click **Download**.

4. Once the tool finishes downloading the data, the keychain can be analyzed by clicking on the **Explore Keychain** button from the tool's home screen.

The following screenshot shows what kind of data can be extracted from iCloud:

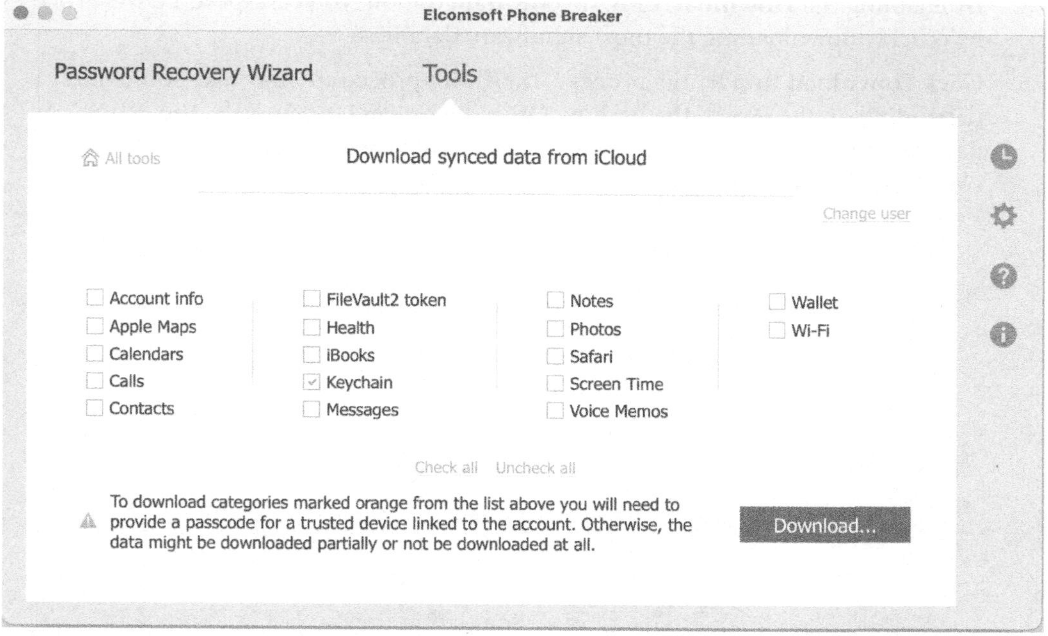

Figure 11.10 – Downloading iCloud synced data with Elcomsoft Phone Breaker

In the final part of this chapter, we'll go through the procedure of extracting an iCloud backup.

Extracting iCloud backups

Forensic tools, such as Elcomsoft Phone Breaker or **Belkasoft X**, not only allow examiners to download cloud-synced data, but also provide a simple solution to extract and decrypt a full **iCloud backup**. Keep in mind that authentication tokens will provide access to synced data, but not to iCloud backups: the **Apple ID** and **password** are required.

Before attempting the extraction of iCloud backups, make sure you have the legal authority and consent to access this data.

To download an iCloud backup, launch Elcomsoft Phone Breaker and follow these steps:

1. From the **Tools** menu, select the **Apple** tab and click on **Download backups**.
2. Provide authentication credentials and press **Sign in**.
3. Once the tool signs into the iCloud account, a list of available devices and backups will be displayed. Select the device whose backups you would like to download by ticking the checkboxes.
4. By enabling the **Download only specific data** option, you can speed up the process by quickly downloading the most significant data first.
5. Click **Download** to start the process. The entire procedure may take some time, depending on the size of the backup. Once the process is complete, the extracted data can be examined using forensic software, such as Elcomsoft Phone Viewer or Cellebrite Physical Analyzer.

The following screenshot shows what the process looks like:

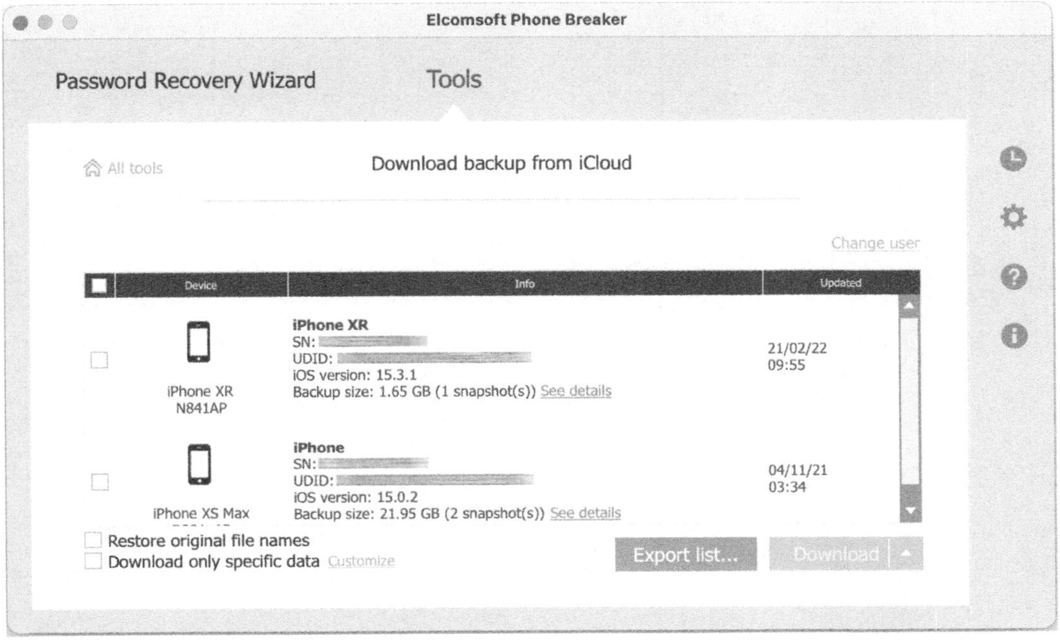

Figure 11.11 – Downloading iCloud backups using Elcomsoft Phone Breaker

The power of cloud forensics resides in the fact that, under some circumstances, it is even possible to acquire iOS backups without having physical access to that particular device. The wealth of user data stored in iCloud can be crucial for any kind of mobile forensic investigation or incident response case.

Summary

In this chapter, we introduced the topic of locked devices and learned all about different investigative approaches that can lead to the acquisition of a device that has an unknown passcode. First, we learned where to locate lockdown records and how to use them to perform a logical acquisition of a locked device. Then, we briefly discussed passcode cracking, before moving on to BFU acquisitions. Next, we learned where iTunes backups are stored and how to analyze their metadata. Finally, in the last section of the chapter, we introduced iCloud forensics by learning what data is synced to the cloud, how to gain access to it, and how to extract it using forensic tools.

In the final chapter of this book, we will learn how to write a mobile forensics report and how to export a device's artifacts to a timeline.

Section 3 – Reporting

In this part, you will understand the importance of structuring data correctly in a report and how to present it using a timeline.

This part of the book comprises the following chapters:

- *Chapter 12, Writing a Forensic Report and Building a Timeline*

12

Writing a Forensic Report and Building a Timeline

So far, it has been a journey of testing, acquiring, analyzing, and researching artifacts from iOS devices. We have worked on different methodologies and techniques for extracting data from a device, and we have learned how to analyze this data to highlight the evidence. In this final chapter, we will talk about the best practices and industry standards for writing a mobile forensic report.

We will start the chapter by learning how a report should be structured, what should be included, and how evidence should be reported in an impartial manner. Then, we will learn how to automatically generate a report using forensic software. In the final part of this chapter, we will discuss timelines, which have become the backbone of digital forensic analysis in both the public and private sectors, as they help explain what was happening on a given device during an incident or a crime. We will learn how to generate a timeline using forensic tools.

In this chapter, we will cover the following topics:

- Mobile forensics reporting
- Creating reports using Cellebrite Physical Analyzer
- Introducing timelines
- Building a timeline with Magnet AXIOM

Mobile forensics reporting

Presenting the findings of an investigation through a **technical report** is arguably one of the most important aspects of the mobile forensics process. Much of what was learned by analyzing the data will be lost if the data is not presented in a clear and concise manner. An effective forensic report should explain not only *what* data was found, but also *how* that data arrived at that location, how it was generated, and what it means for the investigation.

One of the first issues that arises is determining *what* should be included in the report. If too much information is included, the most important details may be overlooked. If there is too little information, the report may seem incomplete or incomprehensible.

The exact structure of the report will vary depending on what kind of knowledge the reader has. Presenting the results of an investigation to a court of law, a corporation's top management, or any kind of non-technical audience will require technical concepts to be explained even more clearly and in detail. It's important that all actions performed during the investigation are accounted for and described in a way that is understandable to the audience.

Generally speaking, the following information should be included in any kind of forensic report:

- Executive summary
- Roles and tasks assigned (that is, *Who conducted the acquisition process? Who examined the data?*)
- Description and identification of the devices that were examined
- Description of how evidence integrity was preserved and how the chain of custody was maintained

- Explanation of the acquisition process
- Description of how the analysis process was performed and what tools were used
- Information that supports the repeatability or reproducibility of the process
- Findings and sources for each piece of evidence
- Comments and conclusions

Forensic tools have built-in **reporting features** that document and summarize all the interactions that have been carried out on a device and during the analysis process; however, relying on reports generated by a tool is not enough, since an examiner will most likely have used a variety of tools and performed manual tasks during the process. This means that an investigator must be able to describe the entire process so that it is understandable to a non-technical audience.

Most tools' reporting systems will output reports in **Microsoft Word**, **PDF**, or **CSV** documents. The output of these tools will be used to supplement the main document, which may be created in a word processor, such as Microsoft Word or Apple Pages, and then exported as a PDF file.

Presenting the findings and evidence in a clear and understandable manner is the ultimate goal of an investigation.

Writing a forensic report

Presenting a forensic report professionally and in a visually appealing format will make the complex and unstructured data available in an easily understandable way. Diagrams, charts, and timelines can also be used to present the data visually.

The objective of a forensic report is simply to tell the story of what a digital artifact indicates. The following diagram illustrates the logical questions that a report should answer:

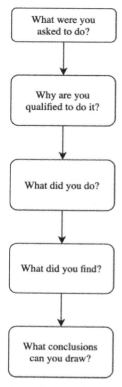

Figure 12.1 – The logical steps of a forensic report

Building on the points described on the previous page, the following sections will give the reader a better understanding of how a report should be written and what information should be included.

Cover/title page/roles assigned

The first page in a forensic report will be the title page, which at a minimum should include a title, the name of the case, the case number, and the name of the investigator. Additionally, roles and assignments should also be part of this page. This includes the names and titles of those responsible for the acquisition process, who analyzed the data, and who prepared the report.

A table of contents may also be included to provide a quick reference, especially if the report is long.

Abstract or executive summary

The executive summary gives the reader an overview of the investigation and includes a summary of the activities completed and the final result. This section will vary in length, but typically this would be a one-paragraph summary of the entire report. By reading the executive summary, the reader should be able to understand *what* the examiner was asked to do and *why* they were asked to do it. Furthermore, the executive summary should also describe what this particular task has to do with the overall investigation.

Device identification

This section should contain a descriptive analysis of the physical evidence items that were examined. This often starts with information documenting the device, such as the model, serial number, condition, configuration information, and pictures of the device. The pictures may be of the device in the place where it was seized, and drawings of the location may also be included.

Details describing the legality of the examination should also be included. If the device was seized, what right did the examiner have to collect, acquire, and analyze the device? If a search warrant was required and obtained, this should also be reported.

Chain of custody

A well-documented **chain of custody** is what holds the forensics process together and supports the integrity of the evidence so that it can be presented as evidence in court. The inability to document any phase of the chain of custody could potentially compromise the authenticity and integrity of the evidence, rendering it useless in court. The person writing the report should also describe how the device was isolated from the cellular and data networks.

Device acquisition

The entire acquisition process should be described in detail, starting with the names of the tools that were used for the purpose. This data can also be reported in a table and should include the name of the software, the manufacturer, the exact version number, and the task that the tool was used for. If an invasive technique was performed, such as jailbreaking the device to obtain a full filesystem acquisition, the examiner must document the reasons why such actions were necessary. Typically, jailbreaking a device or performing an agent-based acquisition is necessary when specific data is required that is not present in a logical acquisition. On such occasions, it's important that the examiner provides a detailed technical explanation of any data changes that may have occurred during the acquisition process.

Analysis process

Typically, an examiner will use multiple tools during the examination process: one tool is used to perform the acquisition, a different tool for the analysis, and additional tools to manually parse through the data, such as SQLite viewers. The report should distinctly outline these tools, specifying if and when a manual examination was performed and the reasons why this was necessary. If multiple tools were used and there were any discrepancies in the data, this should be included in the report. This is extremely common, due to the fact that a single tool cannot possibly support every third-party iOS application.

Evidence

The findings of an examination should be listed in detail in this section of the report. Depending on the scope of the investigation, there may potentially be thousands of artifacts; for this reason, the evidence should be arranged logically within the report and broken into categories, such as phone log, browsing history, and WhatsApp messages, for example. For each artifact, the source file and hash should be indicated.

Another way of describing the artifacts is through a **timeline**, which we'll look at in more detail in the next section. Using a timeline, a list of events is represented in a particular order – usually in chronological order – and this is a great technique to determine what kind of activity occurred on a device at a certain time.

Some examiners like to add comments to this section to explain the data or draw conclusions based on the evidence. Personally, I believe that no conclusions should be written in this part of the report, as this section should simply describe the evidence in an objective manner. The digital forensic examiner's job is to find facts and present the evidence, and it is then up to the investigator, the defense, or the prosecutor to explain how the evidence supports the investigation.

Comments and conclusions

The final section of the report will outline the key points of the examination. Here, the examiner can point out any observations, describing the results of the tests and examinations. The relevance of the data should be explained by correlating different sources. For example, merely stating in the report that a message was sent from the device is not enough; the artifacts from the messaging application should be correlated to the data regarding the device's date and time, time zone, pattern-of-life data, and application usage logs. It is good practice to describe how the examiner validated their findings and what measures were put in practice to guarantee the repeatability and reproducibility of the forensic process.

Appendices

At the end of the report, it may be useful to include any kind of reference material for the reader, such as a list of common forensics terms and acronyms and their descriptions. Copies of any automated, tool-generated reports should also be included.

While a report can be much longer depending on the complexity of the case, these points should be sufficient to give you a general feel of a typical forensic report.

In the next section, we'll learn how to automatically generate reports using forensic software.

Creating reports using Cellebrite Physical Analyzer

Many forensic tools can automatically generate reports from artifacts and notes that the examiner made when working on a case. Typically, the report can be exported in a variety of formats, such as a Microsoft Word document, PDF, or HTML page. Although these built-in features are huge time-savers, it's up to the examiner to explain the significance of that evidence and understand the limitations of automatically generated reports.

In this section, we'll learn how to create reports using one of the most popular forensic tools, **Cellebrite Physical Analyzer**.

There are two types of reports in Cellebrite Physical Analyzer:

- **Preliminary device reports**, which are brief documents that only include basic device information and user account information

- **Complete reports**, which can be customized to include or exclude any kind of artifact that was parsed by the tool

Let's start by generating a preliminary report.

Generating a preliminary device report

A preliminary device report can be used by the investigation team to quickly identify a device based on some basic data that is extracted once the acquisition has been loaded into Cellebrite Physical Analyzer.

There are two ways to choose from to generate this report:

- From the tool's main menu, choose **Reports | Generate preliminary device report**.
- From **Extraction Summary**, click on **Generate preliminary device report**.

The following screenshot shows where the button is located:

Extraction Summary

Figure 12.2 – A preliminary device report generated from Extraction Summary

The report will be created in PDF format and stored at the default reporting path location. The default path is `C:\Users\<user>\Documents\My Reports\`.

In the following screenshot, you can see an example of what this type of report looks like:

Preliminary Device Report - Apple iOS iTunes (Backup)

Device Information

Name	Value
Legacy	
iPhone XR	
MSISDN	
Backup password	
OS Version	15.3.1
Unique ID	00008020-000954DA3C79002E
Detected Phone Model Identifier	iPhone11,8
Serial	
Is encrypted	True
Owner Name	iPhone XR
ICCID	
IMEI	
Phone Settings	
Message Retention Duration	Forever
Location Services Enabled	True
Find my iPhone enabled	True
Apple ID	
iCloud account present	True
Model number	N841AP
Last user ICCID	
Last used MSISDN	
AirDrop ID	
Last Cloud Backup Date	
Time Zone	(UTC+01:00) Rome (Europe)
ICCID	
MSISDN	
Detected Phone Model	iPhone XR
Tethering	
Last Hotspot Activity	2/27/2022 3:04:50 PM(UTC+0)

User Accounts (22)

#	Source	Account Name	User name	Service Type	Creation time	Entries
1				6DE9BF4F-3851-426C-9A1B-EF52BBFE9881	11/6/2021 12:06:09 PM(UTC+0)	Unknown: Account Description IMAPMail
2				85BDDDF2-0CBC-4816-A8FB-641B96C0F253	11/6/2021 12:06:13 PM(UTC+0)	Unknown: Account Description Device Locator
3				D54A7D3C-C1D3-47B2-8654-54A56472136C	11/6/2021 12:06:14 PM(UTC+0)	Unknown: Account Description Find My Friends
4				A78F32F8-204B-488B-B08A-83E1D4CBB24D	11/6/2021 12:06:16 PM(UTC+0)	Unknown: Account Description iTunes Store
5				7482D0CF-21B1-4364-A123-59B088C5F3D9	11/6/2021 12:13:33 PM(UTC+0)	Unknown: Account Description iTunes Store (Sandbox)
6				A95E99D6-4D90-4B86-95F3-9AEF0AE27DE5	11/6/2021 12:22:03 PM(UTC+0)	Unknown: Account Description Gmail
7				91916FC8-758F-493E-8120-FB4C9C22944D	11/8/2021 1:04:22 PM(UTC+0)	Unknown: Account Description Gmail
8				03C2C429-2110-4BFA-B3C4-D77117447F29		Unknown: Account Description iTunes Store
9				F64E6AC0-E358-443B-B4E4-416C8E348B3C	11/6/2021 12:05:30 PM(UTC+0)	Unknown: Account Description IDMS
10				B16C129F-9256-4A70-B52D-DEEFC72B71E1	11/6/2021 12:05:30 PM(UTC+0)	Unknown: Account Description Apple ID
11				6E6A2B8C-F745-4E5F-B53D-24F813A35442	11/6/2021 12:05:38 PM(UTC+0)	Unknown: Account Description Game Center
12				CB10DC6C-45F7-401E-865C-5725791F5843	11/6/2021 12:05:38 PM(UTC+0)	Unknown: Account Description Messages
13				BBD32FAF-A172-4067-A05A-F54E728DE6B6	11/6/2021 12:05:38 PM(UTC+0)	Unknown: Account Description CloudKit

Figure 12.3 – An example of a preliminary device report

The report includes data that identifies the device, such as the model, iOS version, serial number, ICCID, IMEI, and phone number, and details that relate to the device's owner, such as the **Apple ID** that was signed into the device or the user accounts that were found in the extraction.

In the following section, we'll learn how to create a complete report.

Generating a complete report

The first step in the process of creating a report in Cellebrite Physical Analyzer is deciding which artifacts should be included in the report. An examiner will typically include all of the data but, on some occasions, especially if the investigation is focused only on a few artifacts, including every piece of data would make the report too long and the most important details may be missed.

For every single record of every artifact, the examiner can choose to include it or exclude it from the report by ticking the checkbox that is highlighted in the following screenshot:

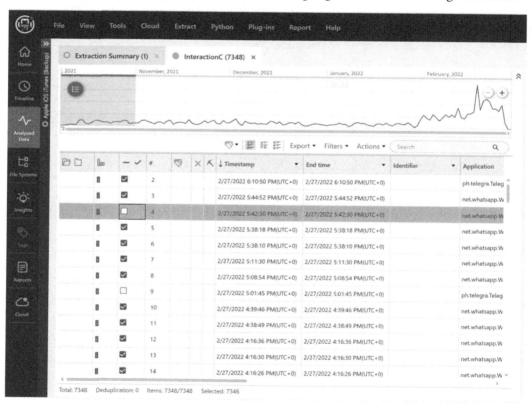

Figure 12.4 – An artifact will be included in the report if the checkbox is enabled

Keep in mind that, by default, all artifacts are included in the report when the tool loads an extraction. If you want to change this setting and exclude all artifacts by default, go to **Tools | Settings | General settings** and disable **Check all entities by default**.

Once the examiner has determined what artifacts should be included, follow these steps to create the report:

1. From the menu, choose **Report | Generate report**. The **Generate Report** window will appear, as you can see from the following screenshot:

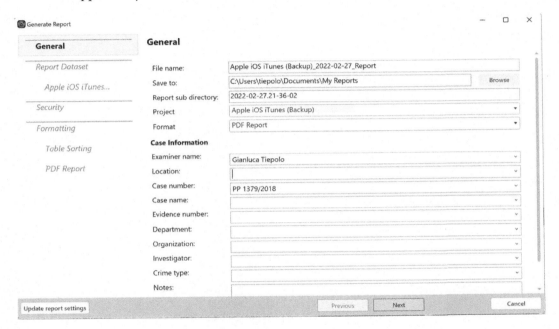

Figure 12.5 – The Generate Report window

2. Enter the relevant information, such as the output directory, format, and examiner name. Then, click **Next** to proceed. The **Report Dataset** window appears.

3. In this window, the examiner can choose to only include artifacts generated in between a specified timeframe. In the **Data types** section, individual categories can be included or excluded from the report. In this example, we're only interested in application usage logs and log entries, so we enable the relevant checkboxes:

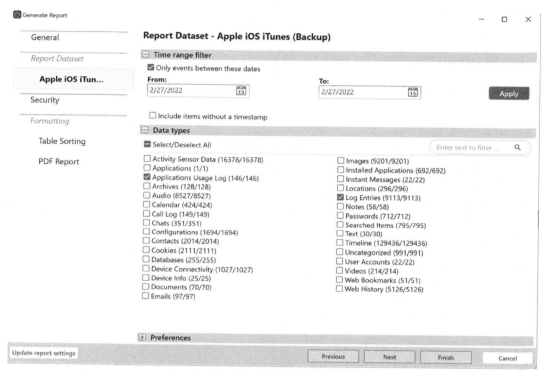

Figure 12.6 – The Report Dataset window

4. Additional settings can be fine-tuned in the **Preferences** panel, such as including hashes for each source, translating artifacts, and enriching the results with external data, for example. Click **Next** to continue.

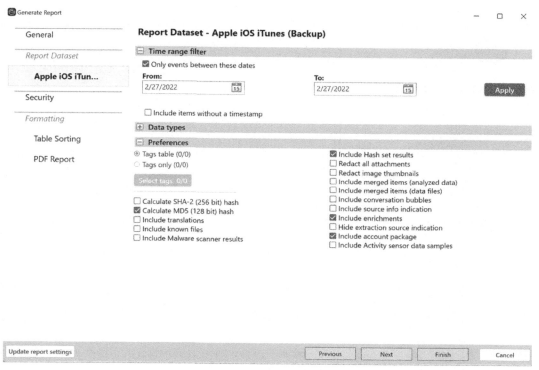

Figure 12.7 – The Preferences tab

5. The **Security Settings** window appears. From here, you can enable an additional layer of protection, such as setting a password for the report. Click **Next**.

6. From the **Report Format** window, the examiner can customize the report by setting a logo, choosing the font, and setting the general look and feel. Once everything is set, click **Finish** to generate the report.

7. When the report is successfully generated, it will be stored at the default reporting path location.

The following screenshots show what a complete report looks like. The first page of the report contains the **Summary** and **Source Extraction** sections, which describe what tool was used, the name of the examiner, and the name of the device:

Figure 12.8 – The Extraction Report Summary

The following pages describe the artifacts:

118		ph.telegra.Telegraph		outgoing message		2/26/2022 10:29:50 PM(UTC+0) End time: 2/26/2022 10:29:50 PM(UTC+0)	PID: 0 TID: 0 Effective UID: 0	Source: InteractionC	
119		ph.telegra.Telegraph		outgoing message		2/26/2022 10:29:37 PM(UTC+0) End time: 2/26/2022 10:29:37 PM(UTC+0)	PID: 0 TID: 0 Effective UID: 0	Source: InteractionC	
120		ph.telegra.Telegraph		incoming message		2/26/2022 10:29:34 PM(UTC+0) End time: 2/26/2022 10:29:34 PM(UTC+0)	PID: 0 TID: 0 Effective UID: 0	Source: InteractionC	
121		ph.telegra.Telegraph		incoming message		2/26/2022 10:29:32 PM(UTC+0) End time: 2/26/2022 10:29:32 PM(UTC+0)	PID: 0 TID: 0 Effective UID: 0	Source: InteractionC	
122		ph.telegra.Telegraph		incoming message		2/26/2022 10:29:29 PM(UTC+0) End time: 2/26/2022 10:29:29 PM(UTC+0)	PID: 0 TID: 0 Effective UID: 0	Source: InteractionC	
123		ph.telegra.Telegraph		outgoing message		2/26/2022 10:28:57 PM(UTC+0) End time: 2/26/2022 10:28:57 PM(UTC+0)	PID: 0 TID: 0 Effective UID: 0	Source: InteractionC	
124		ph.telegra.Telegraph		outgoing message		2/26/2022 10:28:53 PM(UTC+0) End time: 2/26/2022 10:28:53 PM(UTC+0)	PID: 0 TID: 0 Effective UID: 0	Source: InteractionC	
125		ph.telegra.Telegraph		outgoing message		2/26/2022 10:28:45 PM(UTC+0) End time: 2/26/2022 10:28:45 PM(UTC+0)	PID: 0 TID: 0 Effective UID: 0	Source: InteractionC	
126		ph.telegra.Telegraph		outgoing message		2/26/2022 10:28:39 PM(UTC+0) End time: 2/26/2022 10:28:39 PM(UTC+0)	PID: 0 TID: 0 Effective UID: 0	Source: InteractionC	
127		ph.telegra.Telegraph		incoming message		2/26/2022 10:28:27 PM(UTC+0) End time: 2/26/2022 10:28:27 PM(UTC+0)	PID: 0 TID: 0 Effective UID: 0	Source: InteractionC	
128		ph.telegra.Telegraph		incoming message		2/26/2022 10:28:23 PM(UTC+0) End time: 2/26/2022 10:28:23 PM(UTC+0)	PID: 0 TID: 0 Effective UID: 0	Source: InteractionC	
129		ph.telegra.Telegraph		incoming message		2/26/2022 10:28:20 PM(UTC+0) End time: 2/26/2022 10:28:20 PM(UTC+0)	PID: 0 TID: 0 Effective UID: 0	Source: InteractionC	
130		ph.telegra.Telegraph		outgoing message		2/26/2022 10:27:56 PM(UTC+0) End time: 2/26/2022 10:27:56 PM(UTC+0)	PID: 0 TID: 0 Effective UID: 0	Source: InteractionC	

22

Figure 12.9 – The Extraction Report Evidence list

As you can see from the previous screenshot, for each artifact, Cellebrite Physical Analyzer will output the **name** of the artifact, the **description**, the **timestamp**, and the **source file**. Having the source file for each record is particularly useful, as it allows the reader to easily understand where a particular artifact was located.

In the final part of this chapter, we'll learn all about timelines and why they're useful.

Introducing timelines

Timeline analysis is used extensively in forensic investigations that mainly involve collecting and analyzing large volumes of data within a particular timeframe. This is a great technique to determine what activity occurred on a system at a certain time and allows examiners to make inferences easily.

A **timeline** is essentially a list of events displayed in a particular order, usually chronologically. Timelines can be displayed as lists, tables, charts, or graphs.

By analyzing the timeline, a forensic analyst can easily find out when a particular event or incident happened. Timelining also helps figure out any other event that took place during the same time interval, and how these events are interconnected to one another.

Most forensic tools provide the examiner with the option of automatically generating a timeline of events that occurred during a specific timeframe. The timeline's data can then be exported as a CSV document and used to generate charts and graphs.

In the following section, we will learn how to generate and export a timeline using **Magnet AXIOM**.

Building a timeline with Magnet AXIOM

The **Timeline Explorer** within Magnet AXIOM gives the examiner a clear view of what's happening on a device at a certain point in time.

At the top of the view, an interactive graph visually displays time, allowing the examiner to identify spikes in device activity, focus on a specific time frame, and establish behavioral patterns. At the bottom of the screen, a table will list all the timestamped artifacts in chronological order.

The following screenshot shows what a timeline looks like:

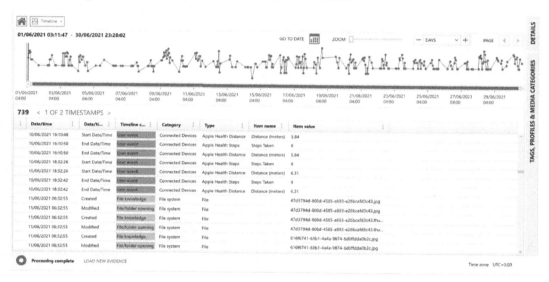

Figure 12.10 – A timeline displayed in Magnet AXIOM

Before a timeline can be viewed, the tool will need to complete an indexing process that, in turn, generates the timeline. If default options are enabled, Magnet AXIOM will not automatically build the timeline, so the examiner will need to manually start the process by following these steps:

1. From the **AXIOM Examine** main menu, choose **Tools | Build timeline**.

Figure 12.11 – Building a timeline in Magnet AXIOM

2. Wait for the analysis and indexing process to complete. This could take some time, depending on the size of the extraction.

3. Once the timeline has been built, the tool will automatically update the **Timeline Explorer** view if new data is added to the case. To zoom in on the timeline, from the top area of the screen, select a date or date range of evidence that you'd like to view and click **OK**.

4. You can interact with the timeline by going back or forward in time. To do so, click on the graph and drag your mouse left or right. To help decrease the scope of evidence to be searched, the examiner can apply filters to the data, including timeline categories, dates, and time ranges.

Once the timeline has been built, the examiner can share the data by exporting it to a CSV file. To do so, follow these steps:

1. In **Timeline Explorer**, select the artifacts that should be exported and right-click on them. Click on **Create export / report**.

2. Click **Browse**, and select the location in which you want to save the exported data:

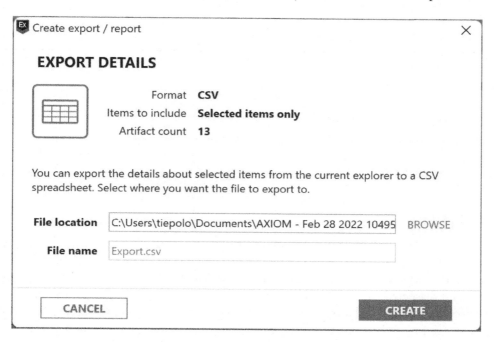

Figure 12.12 – Exporting the timeline to a CSV file

3. Click **Create** to generate the CSV file.

4. Once the CSV file has been generated, the data can be imported into a tool, such as **Apple Numbers** or **Microsoft Excel**, to generate charts and graphs.

The following figure shows an example of a timeline created with Microsoft Excel based on the data from the CSV file:

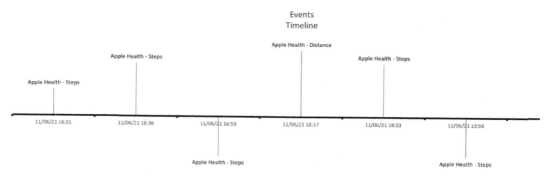

Figure 12.13 – A timeline created in Microsoft Excel

Visualizing the data through a timeline during the examination process provides the investigator with an opportunity to discover patterns or links that were missed when the evidence was looked at previously, in a somewhat isolated manner.

Summary

In this chapter, we introduced the topic of reporting and learned about the best practices for creating a mobile forensic report. First, we discussed how a report should be structured and what questions should be answered. We divided the report into different sections and dissected each of them separately. Then, we learned how an examiner can benefit from using forensic tools to automatically generate reports based on the data being examined. We focused on one tool, Cellebrite Physical Analyzer, and learned how to generate a preliminary report and a complete report with this tool.

In the final part of the chapter, we introduced timeline analysis and learned how an examiner can spot connections between different events by visualizing them in a timeline. We learned how to generate a timeline with Magnet AXIOM, how to interact with it, and how to export the data into a CSV file.

I hope that by reading this book, you have gained the knowledge that will help you acquire and analyze any kind of artifact from iOS devices. Congratulations on getting this far! Remember that practice and training will make you better at your job and will help you to perfect the art of mobile forensics. Digital forensics is constantly evolving; becoming an expert in this field requires an individual to constantly adapt to the changing environment to seek new ways to solve problems.

Index

Packt.com

Subscribe to our online digital library for full access to over 7,000 books and videos, as well as industry leading tools to help you plan your personal development and advance your career. For more information, please visit our website.

Why subscribe?

- Spend less time learning and more time coding with practical eBooks and Videos from over 4,000 industry professionals

- Improve your learning with Skill Plans built especially for you

- Get a free eBook or video every month

- Fully searchable for easy access to vital information

- Copy and paste, print, and bookmark content

Did you know that Packt offers eBook versions of every book published, with PDF and ePub files available? You can upgrade to the eBook version at packt.com and as a print book customer, you are entitled to a discount on the eBook copy. Get in touch with us at customercare@packtpub.com for more details.

At www.packt.com, you can also read a collection of free technical articles, sign up for a range of free newsletters, and receive exclusive discounts and offers on Packt books and eBooks.

Other Books You May Enjoy

If you enjoyed this book, you may be interested in these other books by Packt:

Practical Memory Forensics

Svetlana Ostrovskaya, Oleg Skulkin

ISBN: 9781801070331

- Understand the fundamental concepts of memory organization
- Discover how to perform a forensic investigation of random access memory
- Create full memory dumps as well as dumps of individual processes in Windows, Linux, and macOS
- Analyze hibernation files, swap files, and crash dumps
- Apply various methods to analyze user activities
- Use multiple approaches to search for traces of malicious activity
- Reconstruct threat actor tactics and techniques using random access memory analysis

Learn Computer Forensics

William Oettinger

ISBN: 9781838648176

- Understand investigative processes, the rules of evidence, and ethical guidelines
- Recognize and document different types of computer hardware
- Understand the boot process covering BIOS, UEFI, and the boot sequence
- Validate forensic hardware and software
- Discover the locations of common Windows artifacts
- Document your findings using technically correct terminology

Packt is searching for authors like you

If you're interested in becoming an author for Packt, please visit `authors.packtpub.com` and apply today. We have worked with thousands of developers and tech professionals, just like you, to help them share their insight with the global tech community. You can make a general application, apply for a specific hot topic that we are recruiting an author for, or submit your own idea.

Share Your Thoughts

Now you've finished *iOS Forensics for Investigators*, we'd love to hear your thoughts! Scan the QR code below to go straight to the Amazon review page for this book and share your feedback or leave a review on the site that you purchased it from.

https://packt.link/r/1803234083

Your review is important to us and the tech community and will help us make sure we're delivering excellent quality content.